"With kindness, erudition, and humor, the authors of *Get Out of Your Mind and Into Your Life* educate readers into a new way of thinking about psychological issues in general and life satisfaction in particular. Their combination of cutting-edge research and resonance with ancient, tried-and-true practices makes this one of the most fascinating and illuminating self-help books available. If you're tired of standard psychological parlance and still frustrated with your quality of life, this book can be a godsend."

—Martha Beck, columnist for *O Magazine* and author of
Finding Your Own North Star and *Expecting Adam*

"This manual, firmly based on cutting edge psychological science and theory, details an innovative and rapidly growing approach that can provide you with the power to transform your very experience of life. Highly recommended for all of us."

—David H. Barlow, professor of psychology, research
professor of psychiatry, and director of the Center for
Anxiety and Related Disorders at Boston University

"This is the quintessential workbook on acceptance and commitment therapy. Written with wit, clinical wisdom, and compassionate skepticism, it succeeds in showing us that, paradoxically, there is great therapeutic value in *going out of our minds*. Once released from the struggle with thought, we are free to discover that a life of meaning and value is closer at hand than thought allowed. This book will serve patients, therapists, researchers, and educators looking for an elegant exposition of the nuts and bolts of this exciting approach."

—Zindel V. Segal, Ph.D., the Morgan Firestone Chair
in Psychotherapy and professor of psychiatry and
psychology at the University of Toronto and author
of *Mindfulness-Based Cognitive Therapy for Depression*

Get Out of Your Mind & Into Your Life

The New Acceptance & Commitment Therapy

STEVEN C. HAYES, PH.D.
with SPENCER SMITH

New Harbinger Publications, Inc.

Publisher's Note

This publication is designed to provide accurate and authoritative information in regard to the subject matter covered. It is sold with the understanding that the publisher is not engaged in rendering psychological, financial, legal, or other professional services. If expert assistance or counseling is needed, the services of a competent professional should be sought.

Distributed in Canada by Raincoast Books

Copyright © 2005 by Steven C. Hayes and Spencer Smith
New Harbinger Publications, Inc.
5674 Shattuck Avenue
Oakland, CA 94609

Cover design by Amy Shoup
Author photo by Emily Neilan
Text design by Michele Waters-Kermes
Acquired by Catharine Sutker

New Harbinger Publications' website address: www.newharbinger.com

Library of Congress Cataloging-in-Publication Data

Hayes, Steven C.
  Get out of your mind and into your life : the new acceptance and commitment therapy / Steven Hayes & Spencer Smith.
     p. cm.
  Includes bibliographical references.
  ISBN-10 1-57224-425-9
  ISBN-13 978-1-57224-425-2
  1. Cognitive-experiential psychotherapy. 2. Behavior therapy. 3. Self-acceptance. 4. Commitment (Psychology) I. Smith, Spencer Xavier. II. Title.
  RC489.C62H395 2005
  616.89'142—dc22
                                        2005022640

To my mom
Ruth D. H. Sundgren
My first model of love and commitment
—SCH

To my wife and son
Together may we accept life's trials and commit to our mutual path
—SS

Contents

Acknowledgments

I would like to thank a number of people who have contributed to this volume. My wife, Jacque Pistorello, was constantly supportive and inspirational during the writing of the book. My children, Camille, Charlie, and Esther, were understanding when I had to focus on the book and not them for a few critical weeks. Like Jacque, Spencer Smith's wife, Marie, also supported us during our "writing binges."

Many of the ideas in this book have been influenced by members of the ACT Listserv. One, David Chantry, is listed as a chapter coauthor because he contributed so many different ideas, some of which went beyond that chapter (e.g., a variant of the Coping Strategies Diary; the railroad bridge exercise; the empty head exercise; the valued living recording sheet). I thank him for his permission to use these ideas in the book. My students (several of whom provided materials that found their way into specific chapters and are listed as chapter coauthors) were a source of ideas and support throughout. The idea for a book that could be used directly by the public was first proposed to me by Don Kuhl of The Change Companies. The project did not reach fruition, but I would nevertheless like to acknowledge his role in getting me to think about such a project. Kirk Strosahl has prodded me periodically for years to do a popular book, which also had a role in my willingness to do this work. New Harbinger, particularly Matt McKay and Catharine Sutker, allowed me the freedom to approach the book in my own way.

ACT and RFT are collective, not personal, works that have been influenced by the hands of many: students, colleagues, and clients. I cannot thank them all in this forum, but I surely do in my head and heart. You know who you are. Thank you.

—Steven C. Hayes
Reno, NV
May 2005

First and foremost I would like to thank Steve Hayes for inviting me on board to help him create a trade version of this work. It has been a pleasure working with him. I believe the work on this book has affected my life in some very direct ways, and I am thankful for that opportunity.

I would also like to thank his various family members who showed me much hospitality on trips to Reno when we were writing the book.

My wife, Marie, has been patient and helpful in supporting me throughout this process. Aside from giving me the space to work on this project, she also took on the burden of staying up nights with our newborn son, Tristan, on her own so that I could get the extra sleep needed to keep working.

Thank you to the people at New Harbinger who made my involvement with this project possible. I would especially like to thank Catharine Sutker, who introduced me to the project, and Matthew McKay, our publisher, in this regard. It has been and continues to be a pleasure to work with you.

Finally I would like to thank you the reader. I hope our efforts in presenting this material will impact your life in some positive ways.

—Spencer Smith
Santa Rosa, CA
May 2005

Introduction

People suffer. It's not just that they have pain—suffering is much more than that. Human beings *struggle* with the forms of psychological pain they have: their difficult emotions and thoughts, their unpleasant memories, and their unwanted urges and sensations. They think about them, worry about them, resent them, anticipate and dread them.

At the same time, human beings demonstrate enormous courage, deep compassion, and a remarkable ability to move ahead even with the most difficult personal histories. Knowing they can be hurt, humans still love others. Knowing they will die, humans still care about the future. Facing the draw of meaninglessness, humans still embrace ideals. At times, humans are fully alive, present, and committed.

This book is about how to move from suffering to engagement with life. Rather than waiting to win the internal struggle with your own self so that your life can begin, this book is about living now and living fully—*with* (not in spite of) your past, *with* your memories, *with* your fears, and *with* your sadness.

ACT: WHAT IT IS AND HOW IT CAN HELP YOU

This book is based on Acceptance and Commitment Therapy, or ACT. ("ACT" is spoken as a single word, not as separate initials.) This is a new, scientifically based psychotherapeutic modality that is part of what is being called the "third wave" in behavioral and cognitive therapy (Hayes 2004). ACT is based on Relational Frame Theory (RFT): a basic research program on how the human mind works (Hayes, Barnes-Holmes, and Roche 2001). This research suggests that many of the tools we use to solve problems lead us into the traps that create suffering. To put it bluntly, human beings are playing a rigged game in which the human mind itself, a wonderful tool for mastering the environment, has been turned on its host.

Perhaps you've noticed that some of your most difficult problems have paradoxically become more entrenched and unmanageable, even as you've implemented ideas about how to solve them. This is not an illusion. This results from your own logical mind being asked to do what it was never designed to do. Suffering is one result.

This may seem like a very odd claim, particularly if you picked up this book to help yourself overcome some of your psychological issues. As a rule, people turn to self-help books for tools to solve specific problems: depression, anxiety, substance abuse, trauma, stress, burnout, chronic pain, smoking, to name just a few. For the average person, overcoming these problems implies not just an ultimate *end* but also an end reached by specific means.

For example, overcoming stress seemingly must first involve eliminating stressful feelings; overcoming smoking seemingly must first involve getting rid of urges to smoke; overcoming anxiety disorders seemingly must involve learning how to relax instead, or to dispute and change overblown and worrisome thoughts; and so on. In this book, ends and means are carefully distinguished, and you will learn that many of these common sense routes to a better life are now thought to be both risky and unnecessary in current psychological theory.

If you are suffering with a psychological problem, you should know that research suggests that ACT helps with many common psychological difficulties (Hayes, Masuda, et al. 2004), and its underlying model has received considerable support (Hayes et al. forthcoming). We will discuss these data throughout this book.

The fact that you are reading an empirically based account is all the more important because this book will take some seemingly strange twists and turns. At times, it may be confusing. To some degree that is unavoidable because ACT challenges some of the most culturally ingrained forms of conventional thinking about human problems. Research indicates that ACT's methods and ideas are generally sound, which provides reassurance that these concepts and procedures are effective. (See the appendix for a partial list of studies on ACT and its components.) That doesn't mean they are easy to grasp. Then again, if these ideas and methods were already well-known to you, this book would probably not be useful.

Here's a sample of some of the unconventional concepts you will be asked to consider:

■   Psychological pain is normal, it is important, and everyone has it.

■   You cannot deliberately get rid of your psychological pain, although you can take steps to avoid increasing it artificially.

■   Pain and suffering are two different states of being.

■   You don't have to identify with your suffering.

■   Accepting your pain is a step toward ridding yourself of your suffering.

■   You can live a life you value, beginning right now, but to do that you will have to learn how to get out of your mind and into your life.

Ultimately, what ACT asks of you is a fundamental change in perspective: a shift in the way you deal with your personal experience. We can't promise that this will quickly change what your depression, anger, anxiety, stress, or low self-esteem looks like, at least, not anytime soon. We can, however, say that our research has demonstrated that the role of these problems as barriers to living can be changed, and sometimes changed quite rapidly. ACT methods provide new ways to approach difficult psychological issues. These new approaches can change the actual substance of your psychological problems and the impact they have on your life.

Metaphorically, the distinction between the function of a psychological disorder and the form it takes in one's life can be likened to someone standing in a battlefield fighting a war. The war is not going well. The person fights harder and harder. Losing is a devastating option; but unless the war is won, the person fighting it thinks that living a worthwhile life will be impossible. So the war goes on.

Unknown to that person, however, is the fact that, at any time, he or she can quit the battlefield and begin to live life *now*. The war may still go on, and the battlefield may still be visible. The terrain may look very much as it did while the fighting was happening. But the outcome of the war is no longer very important and the seemingly logical sequence of having to win the war before beginning to really live has been abandoned.

This metaphor is intended to illustrate the difference between the appearance of psychological problems and their true substance. In this metaphor, the war looks and sounds much the same whether you are fighting it or simply watching it. Its appearance stays the same. But its impact—its actual substance—is profoundly different. Fighting for your life is not the same as living your life.

Ironically, our research suggests that when the substance changes, the appearance may change as well. When fighters leave the battlefield and let the war take care of itself, it may even subside. As the old slogan from the 1960s put it: "What if they fought a war and nobody came?"

Compare this metaphor with your own emotional life. ACT focuses on the substance, not the appearance, of problems. Learning to approach your distress in a fundamentally different way can quickly change the impact it has on your life. Even if the appearance of distressing feelings or thoughts does not change (and who knows, it might), if you follow the methods described in this book, it is far likelier that the substance of your psychological distress, that is, its impact, *will* change.

In that sense, this is not a traditional self-help book. We aren't going to help you win the war with your own pain by using new theories. We are going to help you leave the battle that is raging inside your own mind, and to begin to live the kind of life you truly want. Now.

SUFFERING: PSYCHOLOGICAL QUICKSAND

This counterintuitive idea of abandoning the battlefield rather than winning the war may sound strange, and implementing it will require a lot of new learning, but it is not crazy. You know about other situations like this. They are unusual, but not unknown.

Suppose you came across someone standing in the middle of a pool of quicksand. No ropes or tree branches are available to reach the person. The only way you can help is by communicating with him or her. The person is shouting, "Help, get me out," and is beginning to do what people usually do when they are stuck in something they fear: struggle to get out. When people step into something they want to get out of, be it a briar patch or a mud puddle, 99.9 percent of the time the effective action to take is to walk, run, step, hop, or jump out of trouble.

This is not so with quicksand. To step out of something it is necessary to lift one foot and move the other foot forward. When dealing with quicksand, that's a very bad idea. Once one foot is lifted, all of the trapped person's weight rests on only half of the surface area it formerly occupied. This means the downward pressure instantly doubles. In addition, the suction of the quicksand around the foot being lifted provides more downward pressure on the other foot. Only one result can take place: the person will sink deeper into the quicksand.

As you watch the person stuck in the quicksand, you see this process begin to unfold. Is there anything you can shout out that will help? If you understood how quicksand works, you would yell at the person to stop struggling and to try to lie flat, spread-eagled, to maximize contact with the surface of the pool. In that position, the person probably wouldn't sink and might be able to logroll to safety.

Since the person is trying to get out of the quicksand, it is extremely counterintuitive to maximize body contact with it. Someone struggling to get *out* of the mud may never realize that the wiser and safer action to take would be to get *with* the mud.

Our own lives can be very much like this, except the quicksand we find ourselves in, often is, in one sense, endless. Exactly when will the quicksand of a traumatic memory completely vanish? At what moment will the painful quicksand of past criticism from parents or peers disappear? Right now think of a psychological aspect of yourself that you like the least. Take a moment to consider this question. Now ask yourself, "Was this an issue for me last month? Six months ago? A year ago? Five years ago? Exactly how old is this problem?"

Most people find that their deepest worries are not about recent events. Their deepest worries have been lurking in the background for years, often many years. That fact suggests that normal problem-solving methods are unlikely to be successful. If they could succeed, why haven't they worked after all these years of trying? Indeed, the very longevity of most psychological struggles suggests that normal problem-solving methods may themselves be part of the problem, just as trying to get free is a huge problem for someone stuck in quicksand.

You've picked up this book for a reason. Our guess is that you find yourself in some sort of psychological quicksand and you think you need help freeing yourself. You've tried various "solutions" without success. You've been struggling. You've been sinking. And you've been suffering.

Your pain will be an informative ally on the path that lies ahead. You have an opportunity that someone who hasn't experienced psychological pain doesn't have, because it is only when common sense solutions fail us, that we become open to the counterintuitive solutions to psychological pain that modern psychological science can provide. As you become more aware of how the human mind works (particularly your mind), perhaps you will be ready to take the path less traveled. Haven't you suffered enough?

We haven't written this book to help you free yourself from the quicksand you find yourself in, but to get with it. We wrote to relieve your suffering and empower you to lead a valued, meaningful, dignified human life. Psychological issues that you've previously struggled with may technically remain (or they may not), but what will it matter if they remain in a form that no longer interferes with you living your life to the fullest?

THE UBIQUITY OF HUMAN SUFFERING

This book starts from a different set of assumptions than most popular psychology books do. We indicated what that difference is in the first two words of this introduction: People suffer. We don't assume that left to their own devices, normal human beings are happy and that only an odd history or a broken biology disturbs the peace. We assume instead that suffering is normal and it is the unusual person who learns how to create peace of mind. Why this is so is a puzzle; this book is about that puzzle.

It's remarkable how many problems human beings have that nonhumans can literally not imagine. Consider the data on suicide. It occurs in every human population, and serious struggles with suicide are shockingly commonplace. Throughout your lifetime, you have about a fifty-fifty chance of struggling with suicidal thoughts at a moderate to severe level for at least two weeks (Chiles and Strosahl 2004). Almost 100 percent of all the people on the planet will at some point in their life contemplate killing themselves. Preverbal children do not make suicide attempts but even very young, newly verbal children occasionally do (Chiles and Strosahl 2004). Yet we have little reason to believe that *any* nonhuman animals deliberately kill themselves.

That basic pattern repeats itself in problem area after problem area: Most human beings struggle, even in the midst of what appear to be successful lives. Ask yourself this question: How many people do you know really well who don't experience periods in which they struggle with serious psychological or social problems, relationship issues, problems at work, anxiety, depression, anger, self-control issues, sexual problems, fear of death, and so on? For most people, a list of such contented acquaintances will be very short indeed, perhaps even empty.

The scientific data on human problems confirms this impression. Let's just mention a few random facts. About 30 percent of all adults have a major psychiatric disorder at any given point in time, about 50 percent will have such a disorder at some point in their lives, and nearly 80 percent of these will have more than one serious psychological problem (Kessler et al. 1994). Americans spend huge sums of money in their efforts to alleviate their psychological pain.

For example, antidepressants are a ten-billion-dollar industry, even though their average impact on depression is only 20 percent better than a placebo, too small to be clinically significant (Kirsch et al. 2002). Indeed, our consumption of antidepressants is so high that our rivers and streams have become polluted with them, contaminating the fish we eat (Streater 2003). But these statistics, sad though they are, grossly underestimate the extent of the problem. When people are given open access to mental-health care, only about half of those who seek help are diagnosed with a serious mental-health disorder (Strosahl 1994). The other half are having problems at work, or in their marriages, or with their children, or they suffer from the lack of purpose in their lives, what the philosophers call "existential dread," or from "angst," which is a strong ever-present feeling of apprehension and anxiety.

Marriages, for example, are probably the most important voluntary adult relationship most humans enter into, yet about 50 percent of all marriages end in divorce and remarriages are no better (Kreider and Fields 2001). The dismal statistics on fidelity, abuse, and marital happiness show that many intact marriages are based on unhealthy relationships (Previti and Amato 2004).

This litany could go on and on easily. By the time all of the major behavioral problems human beings face are added together, in effect, it is "abnormal" not to experience significant psychological struggles.

How can this be? We could understand it if we were discussing people without resources in ravaged societies. If a Sudanese child must hide from the violence of a rebel militia, we can easily appreciate her misery. If a grieving mother in Indonesia loses everything to a tsunami, her suffering is horrible but, given her horrific circumstances, it is to be expected. This is mostly not true for the people who read this book, as most of us realize when we compare our lives to the lives of those suffering from war or horrendous natural disasters. Yet in many problem areas, people who are intelligent and successful are not necessarily happier than their less fortunate counterparts in other parts of the world. People who live in countries with spectacularly successful economies do not have fewer social or interpersonal problems (e.g., suicide) than their counterparts in more difficult economic circumstances (Chiles and Strosahl 2004). How can this be?

Apply this question to your own life. Isn't it true that the things you are struggling with and trying to change tend to persist, even though you are competent and able in so many other areas of your life? Isn't it true that you've tried to solve these problems, but so far have failed to find a real solution?

Indeed, you may have already tried *many* solutions . . . and yet here you are buying another book designed to help you. How can *this* be?

We ask you to keep these questions in mind as you read this book: Why is human suffering so pervasive, why is yours so difficult to change, and what can you do about it? The rest of this book will explore these questions in detail. We think we can supply at least part of the answers.

We don't ask these questions from an arrogant or critical perspective. This book won't blame you for your troubles, conveying the not-so-subtle message that your life would be fine if only you tried harder. This book comes from a stance of compassion and identification; it has emerged from our own struggles and those of our patients. The questions above are those we've asked ourselves, sometimes from the depth of despair. We believe that science has begun to provide an unexpected answer however; and it is one that can be directly helpful to you.

MINDFULNESS, ACCEPTANCE, AND VALUES

ACT is not a set of idiomatic phrases or wise sayings that will lead you toward a personal revelation. Although some of the principles in ACT are as old as history, there is one major component of the therapy that is new. ACT is based on a new model of human cognition. This model underlies specific techniques presented in this book, which are designed to help you change your approach to your problems, and the direction in which your life has been going. These techniques fall into three broad categories: mindfulness, acceptance, and values-based living.

Mindfulness

Mindfulness is a way of observing your experience that has been practiced in the East through various forms of meditation for centuries. Recent research in Western psychology has proven that practicing mindfulness can have notable psychological benefits (Hayes, Follette, and Linehan 2004). In fact, mindfulness is currently being adopted as a means of enhancing treatment in a number of different psychological traditions in the West (Teasdale et al. 2002).

A large part of our approach has to do with mindfulness. What ACT brings to this ancient set of practices is a model of the key components of mindfulness and a set of new methods to change these components. Weeks, months, or years of meditation, helpful as they can be, are not the only practices that can increase mindfulness, and in today's busy world, new means are needed to augment those that evolved in another, slower millennium.

In this book we will help you learn to see your thoughts in a new way. Thoughts are like lenses through which we look at our world. We all have a tendency to cling to our particular lens and allow it to dictate how we interpret our experiences, even to the point of dictating who we think we are. If you are now stuck in the lens of your psychological pain, you may say things to yourself like, "I'm depressed." In this book we will help you see the dangers of holding on to thoughts of that kind, and we will provide concrete methods to help you avoid those dangers.

As you free yourself from the illusions of language, you will learn to become more aware of the many verbal lenses that emerge every day, and yet not be defined by any one of them. You will learn how to undermine your attachment to a particular cognitive lens in favor of a more holistic model of self-awareness. Using specific techniques, you will learn to look at your pain, rather than seeing the world from the vantage point of your pain. When you do that, you will find there are many other things to do with the present moment besides trying to regulate its psychological content.

Acceptance

ACT draws a clear distinction between pain and suffering. Because of the nature of human language, when we encounter a problem, our general tendency is to figure out how to fix it. We try to get out of the quicksand. In the outside world this is very effective 99.9 percent of the time. Being able to figure out how to rid ourselves of undesirable events, such as predation, cold, pests, or flooding, was essential in establishing the human race as the dominant species on our planet.

It is an unfortunate consequence of the way our minds work, however, that we try to use this same "fix-it" mentality when it comes to understanding our internal experiences. When we encounter painful content within ourselves, we want to do what we always do: fix it up and sort it out so that we can get rid of it. The truth of the matter (as you have likely experienced) is that our internal lives are not at all like external events. For one thing, humans live in history, and time moves in only one direction, not two. Psychological pain has a history and, at least in that aspect, it is not a matter of getting rid of it. It is more a matter of how we deal with it and move forward.

The "acceptance" in Acceptance and Commitment Therapy is based on the notion that, as a rule, trying to get rid of your pain only amplifies it, entangles you further in it, and transforms it into something traumatic. Meanwhile, living your life is pushed to the side. The alternative we will teach in this book is a bit dangerous to say out loud because right now it is likely to be misunderstood, but the alternative is to accept it. Acceptance, in the sense it is used here, is not nihilistic self-defeat; neither is it tolerating and putting up with your pain. It is very, very different than that. Those heavy, sad, dark forms of "acceptance" are almost the exact opposite of the active, vital embrace of the moment that we mean.

Most of us have had little or no training in active forms of acceptance so we suggest that you thank your mind for whatever it says this term might mean, but don't try to do anything with it right now. This is hard to describe, and learning to be willing to have and live your own experience is something we will focus on quite a bit later in the book. In the meantime, we ask for your patience and openness—and a bit of skepticism about what your mind might right now be guessing we mean.

Commitment and Values-based Living

Are you living the life you want to live right now? Is your life focused on what is most meaningful to you? Is the way you live your life characterized by vitality and engagement, or by the weight of your problems?

When we are caught in a struggle with psychological problems we often put life on hold, believing that our pain needs to lessen before we can really begin to live again. But what if you could have your life be about what you want it to be about right now, starting this moment? We don't ask you to believe that this is so, but merely to be open to the possibility it is so, open enough that you are willing to work with this book.

Getting in touch with the life you want to live and learning how to bring your dreams to life in the present isn't easy because your mind, like all human minds, will spring trap after trap, throw up barrier after barrier. In chapters 1 to 10, you will learn how to free yourself from those traps and how to dissolve those barriers. In chapters 11 to 13 we will discuss what you really want your life to be about, and we will show you how to complete the process of shifting from useless mental management to life engagement.

At this point we aren't asking you to agree with any of the claims being made or for you to say you understand any of the methods we have just begun to describe. We ask only for your engagement with a journey fundamentally focused on the puzzle of your suffering and that of others. This journey seeks a fundamental change in the very game being played, not just a new strategy for winning it. ACT is not a panacea, but the scientific results are both broad and positive (see appendix). We believe that we can help you take advantage of this new knowledge.

By all means, bring your skepticism, even your cynicism, along for the ride. They will not be harmful, provided you are willing to apply the methods you will learn even to that skepticism and cynicism. And bring your hopes and ability to believe along, as well, although they will not necessarily be helpful until they too are considered from the point of view of the methods to be described. You are a whole person, and all of your experiences, thoughts, feelings, bodily sensations, and behavioral predispositions are welcome to come along on this journey of discovery.

What do you have to lose? Wouldn't it be a good thing if you could get out of your mind, and into your life?

CHAPTER I

Human Suffering

You've probably opened this book for this reason: You are hurting and you're not sure what to do about it. Perhaps you've been suffering from a chronic depression or an anxiety disorder. Perhaps a struggle with drug abuse or alcohol has been costing you your life in your futile attempt to numb your pain. Perhaps a relationship is stumbling, or you are wondering whether life itself matters. It may be that you've been in and out of therapy trying to cope with your inner turmoil. Or perhaps, you're one of the millions who just feels stuck—not vital and engaged in life, but distant, deadened, numbed, or overwhelmed.

If you've been struggling for some time, you've probably plagued yourself with different forms of the "why?" question: "Why can't I just get over it?" "Why can't I feel better?" "Why is life so hard?" "Why hasn't therapy worked?" "Why can't I be a normal person?" "Why can't I be happy?" You may feel victimized somehow by questions that seem not to have any ready answers. Cornered by your own emotional pain and your struggle with it, you may feel as if your life is narrowing in around you.

If you've been fighting a war inside your head, what would it be like if instead of trying to win that war, you knew a way to step out of it? This doesn't mean that the war would stop; it may continue. Rather, it means that you would no longer try to live inside a war zone, with your psychological survival seemingly dependent on the outcome of the war. What if that were possible?

This book invites you to examine your perspective not only on what psychological pain is and how it operates, but on the very nature of your consciousness, even your identity, that is, who you take yourself to be. No issue is too "basic" if it seems necessary to address it. The concepts and methods you will find here may shake you up a bit. Initially, some may be hard to swallow and may even fly in the face of what you've been taught are the "solutions" to your problems.

We have three requests to ask of you. The first is for you to agree to persistent, active engagement with the text. At times, it may be a bumpy ride. We ask only that you stick with it and really try the methods we will put on the table. There may be something here for you, but you will not know if that is so unless you learn and use the concepts and methods before you try to evaluate their actual impact on your life.

The second request is to ask for unrelenting honesty from you. We don't ask you to believe what we've written here; we do ask you to look directly at your experience without blinking. Use this book as an opportunity to explore what is really true for you. For the moment put aside what others expect, what the world around you demands, what you've long been told is true, or even what your own mind tells you—if it contradicts what your direct experience suggests.

Since we can't actually be there as you try out these methods, you will need to rely on your own experience to know whether the approach described here is helpful to you in the long run. There is a growing base of empirical support for the basic concepts discussed here, and some of the methods have been evaluated in laboratory studies (see appendix) presented outside of a therapeutic relationship, using written or oral presentations of these ideas and exercises, much as you might encounter them in this book. Today, there is enough scientific evidence that we believe this is the time to introduce these ideas and methods to the public. But your experience is the actual bottom line.

Our third request concerns your intention: we ask that you intend this book to make a difference in your life. You don't have to believe that it will. Rather, we ask you to remain open to that possibility by answering yes to this next question: While you are learning and trying out these methods, if you see in your actual experience the possibility of using them to transform your life for the better, will you be willing to move forward in that direction? If your answer is yes, we are ready to begin. If it is not (remember: be honest), it would be worthwhile to know how deep your resistance to change may be, and it would be worth considering whether such resistance is in your best interest.

Before we begin, we think that a bit of consumer education may be in order. ACT is part of a school of clinical psychology that is committed to delivering treatment methods based in science. If you have a significant area of difficulty, and you haven't undergone a well-planned course of therapy with a behavioral therapist, cognitive behavioral therapist, or other professional who used methods supported by scientific research, you should seek that out. In that instance, this book can be used as an adjunct to a course of therapy with a therapist who understands this approach. (See the appendix for suggestions about finding such a therapist.) A growing base of scientific evidence supports the use of these methods in a psychotherapy context.

HUMAN SUFFERING IS UNIVERSAL

Often many people we meet in our daily lives seem to have it all. They seem happy. They look satisfied with their lives. You've probably had the experience of walking down the street when you're having a particularly bad day, and you've looked around and thought, "Why can't I just be happy like everyone around me? They don't suffer from chronic panic (or depression, or a substance abuse problem). They don't feel as if a dark cloud is always looming over their heads. They don't suffer the way I suffer. Why can't I be like them?"

Here's the secret: They do and you are. We all have pain. All human beings, if they live long enough, have felt or will feel the devastation of losing someone they love. Every single person has felt or will feel physical pain. Everybody has felt sadness, shame, anxiety, fear, and loss. We all have memories that are embarrassing, humiliating, or shameful. We all carry painful hidden secrets. We tend to put on shiny, happy faces, pretending that everything is okay, and that life is "all good." But it isn't and it can't be. To be human is to feel pain in ways that are orders of magnitude more pervasive than what the other creatures on planet Earth feel.

If you kick a dog, it will yelp and run away. If you kick it regularly, any sign of your arrival eventually will produce fear and avoidance behavior in the dog by means of the process called "conditioning." But so long as you are out of the picture and are not likely to arrive, the dog is unlikely to feel or show significant anxiety. People are quite different. As young as sixteen months or even earlier, human infants learn that if an object has a name, the name refers to the object (Lipkens, Hayes, and Hayes 1993). Relations that verbal humans learn in one direction, they derive in two directions. Over the past twenty-five years, researchers have tried to demonstrate the same behavior in other animal species, with very limited and questionable success so far (Hayes, Barnes-Holmes, and Roche 2001). This makes a huge difference in the lives people live as compared to animals.

The capacity for language puts human beings in a special position. Simply saying a word invokes the object that is named. Try it out: "Umbrella." What did you think of when you read that word? Alright, that one's pretty harmless. But consider what this means if the named object was fearful: anything that reminded the person of its name would evoke fear. It would be as if all the dog needs to feel fear is not an actual kick, but the *thought* of being kicked.

That is exactly the situation you are in. That is exactly the situation *all* humans are in with language.

Here is an example: Take a moment now to think of the most shameful thing you have ever done. Take a moment to actually do this.

What did you just feel? It's very likely that as soon as you read the sentence, you felt some sense of either fear or resistance. You may have tried to dismiss the request and quickly read on. However, if you paused and actually tried to do what we asked, you probably began to feel a sense of shame while you remembered a scene from your past and your actions in it. Yet all that happened here was that you were looking at patterns of ink on paper. Nothing else is in front of you but that. Because relations that verbal humans learn in one direction, they derive in two, they have the capacity to treat anything as a symbol for something else. The etymology of "symbol" means "to throw back as the same," and because you are reacting to the ink on this paper symbolically, the words you just read evoked a reaction from you; perhaps they even reminded you of a shameful event from your past.

Where could you go so that this kind of relation could not take place? The dog knows how to avoid pain: avoid you and your foot. But how can a person avoid pain if anytime, anywhere, pain can be brought to mind by anything related to that pain?

The situation is actually worse than that. Not only can we not avoid pain by avoiding painful situations (the dog's method), pleasurable situations also might evoke pain. Suppose someone very dear to you recently died, and today you see one of the most beautiful sunsets you have ever seen. What will you think?

For human beings, avoiding situational cues for psychological pain is unlikely to succeed in eliminating difficult feelings because all that is needed to bring them to mind is an arbitrary cue that evokes the right verbal relations. This example of a sunset demonstrates the process. A sunset can evoke a verbal history. It is "beautiful" and beautiful things are things you want to share with others. You cannot share this sunset with your dear friend, and there you are, feeling sad at the very moment you see something beautiful.

The problem is that the cues that evoke verbal relations can be almost anything: the ink on paper that made up the word "shame," or a sunset that reminded you of your recent loss. In desperation, humans try to take a very logical action: they start trying to avoid pain itself.

Unfortunately, as we will discuss in some detail throughout the rest of this book, some methods of avoiding pain are pathological in and of themselves. For example, dissociation or illegal drug use may temporarily reduce pain, but it will come back stronger than ever and further damage will be caused. Denial and learned numbness will reduce pain, but they will soon cause far more pain than they take away.

The constant possibility of psychological pain is a challenging burden that we all need to face. It is like the elephant in the living room that no one ever mentions.

This doesn't mean that you must resign yourself to trudging through your life suffering. Pain and suffering are very different. We believe that there is a way to change your relationship to pain and to then live a good life, perhaps a great life, even though you are a human being whose memory and verbal skills keep the possibility of pain just an instant away.

The approach we will explore in this book is suggested by the word "suffering." The primary root of suffer is the Latin *ferre,* which means "to bear or carry" (the English word "ferry" comes from the same root). The prefix "suf" is a version of "sub" and, in this usage, means "from below, up (hence) away." In other words, suffering doesn't just involve having something to carry; it also involves moving away. The word "suffer" connotes the idea that there is a burden you are unwilling or unable to carry, perhaps because it seems "too heavy," "too unfair," or it just seems "beyond you." That connotation refers to more than pain alone; in fact, it provides a different way to address the problem of pain.

EXERCISE: Your Suffering Inventory

We would like you to write down a list of all of the issues that are currently psychologically difficult for you. Use the left-hand side of the space provided below. Do not write about purely external or situational events, independent of your reactions to them. In this book we will focus on how you react. Some of your psychological issues will be clearly related to specific situations; others may not be. For example, "my boss" would not be a good example of a difficult issue you experience; but "getting frustrated with my boss" or "feeling put down by my boss" might be. The left-hand column can include any of your thoughts, feelings, memories, urges, bodily sensations, habits, or behavioral predispositions that may distress you, either alone or in combination with external events. Don't overthink it. Just write down what plagues you and causes you pain. Be honest and thorough and create your "suffering inventory" in the space below.

After you've completed your list, go back and think about how long these issues have been a problem for you. Write that down as well.

Painful and difficult issues I experience　　　　　　　　　**How long this has been the case**

_____

_____

_____

_____

_____

_____

_____

Now we would like to ask you to organize this list. First, go back and rank these items in terms of the impact that they have on your life. Then, in the space provided below, write down the same items, but rank them in order. The order should range from those items that cause you the most pain and difficulty in your life to those that cause you the least trouble. You will use this list as a guide throughout the remainder of this book. We'll ask you to refer back to this list as your touchstone for the events and issues that cause you pain.

_____

_____

_____

_____

_____

_____

Finally, in the area to the right of this list, draw arrows between every item on the list that is related to another item. You will know that two items are related if changes in one might alter another. For example, suppose one of your items is "self-criticism" and another is "depression." If you think the two are related (that is, the more self-critical you are, the more likely you are to feel depressed, or vice versa), draw a two-headed arrow between self-criticism and depression. You may find that this area becomes cluttered with arrows. That's fine. There is no right or wrong way to do this. If everything is related, it's important to know that. If some items relate to only a few others, that is useful information too. The higher on your list the items are and the more other items they connect to, the more important they become. This may suggest a reranking of your problems and you may find that you now want to combine some items or to divide them into smaller units. If that is so, you can create your final working list below, ranked from highest to lowest in order of impact on your life.

_____

_____

_____

_____

_____

_____

_____

This is your personal suffering list. For you, it is what this book is about.

THE PROBLEM WITH PAIN

Psychological pain hurts, by definition. But it does more than that. Often pain holds you back from living the kind of life you want to live. There is no question that a person with a panic disorder would rather not experience the feeling of extreme fear, because it is so unpleasant. But that discomfort is compounded by the fact that the panic seemingly gets in the way of living itself.

If you have a panic disorder, you may have begun feeling too afraid to engage in the activities you normally would because of your fear that you might panic. It may be that you no longer go to the supermarket because you are afraid you might have a panic attack there. Perhaps you are uncomfortable in social situations, because you don't want anyone to see you panic. You cultivate friends with whom you feel safe, but then you are dependent on their schedules and availability. You start to live your life in ways to accommodate your problem, and, as a result, your life becomes narrower and narrower, less and less flexible.

It is worth noting how much of the pain we feel is a focus of attention because it seems to interfere with other activities. One way to get at this core issue is to imagine how your life would be different if your pain went away. Imagine that someone has waved a magic wand over you, and your pain has vanished. Imagine that you wake up one morning and suddenly, for no reason at all, the chronic depression you've suffered from all these years (or the anxiety, or worry, or whatever your core struggles may be) is gone. The cloud has lifted and the pain is over. What would you do? This question isn't a rhetorical one, we mean it literally: What would you do? What would you want your life to be about? How has your current psychological struggle interfered with your goals and aspirations? Let's explore that in the exercise below.

EXERCISE: The Pain is Gone, Now What?

If _____ weren't such a problem for me, I would

_____

_____.

If I didn't have _____, I would

_____

_____.

We would like you to fill in the blank lines above in the sentences you've just read, but first let us describe how to do that. Take an item from your suffering inventory. It could be any item, but it might be best to start with an item high on your list and connected to other items. This is probably an issue that greatly inhibits your life. Go ahead and fill in your problem, but don't fill in what you would do if it were gone.

Now, think about what you would do if that pain were suddenly lifted. The point of this exercise is not to think about what you might like to do on a given day if your problems weren't plaguing you. The idea isn't to celebrate by saying, "My depression is gone, I'm going to Disneyland!" The point is to think more broadly about how your life course would change if your constant struggle with emotional pain was no longer an issue. Don't worry if you think that you don't have a good grip on this yet. We will do a whole lot more work on these issues later in the book. Just go with your gut instinct. Somewhere within yourself you have some idea about the things that really matter to you. Concentrate on those.

Here are three examples to give you an idea of what we mean:

If *anger* weren't such a problem for me, I would *have more intimate relationships.*

If I didn't have *so much stress,* I would *work harder at my career, and I would try to find the job I always dreamed of having.*

If *I wasn't so anxious,* I would *travel and participate more fully in life.*

Now, go back and fill in the blank lines about what you would do if your pain disappeared. Be honest with yourself and think about what you really want. Think about what has value to you. Think about what gives your life meaning.

Now, let's do that again but this time, let's use a different area of suffering (although it certainly wouldn't hurt to do this exercise with all of the items on your Suffering Inventory). This time, choose an item that appears to affect a different area of your life than the first one you chose. (Although after thinking about them you may find that they are not as different as they seem to be.)

If _____ weren't such a problem for me, I would

_____

_____.

If I didn't have _____, I would

_____

_____.

THE PROBLEM WITH PAIN: REVISITED

You've just discovered that all of your problems provide you with two sources of pain. It is not just your anxiety or depression or worry that creates pain. Your pain is also holding you back from living the life you want to lead. There are activities you would be engaged in if it weren't for your pain and the role it has played in your life.

The problem you wrote down in the exercises above refers to the *pain of presence* (issues that are present that you would prefer to go away). Social anxiety might be an example of the pain of presence. The anxiety you feel on social occasions is real and present in the moment you feel it. You may wish it would go away. Nonetheless, it persists in the face of your best efforts to defeat it. This is the pain of presence.

Those activities you would engage in if matters changed, represent a different kind of pain: they are called the *pain of absence.* As an example, consider the same socially phobic person above. Perhaps this person truly values engaging with other people but their fear keeps them from doing so in ways that are meaningful. The connection with others that is so yearned for is not there. This is the pain of absence. You have pain on top of pain, suffering on top of suffering. Not only must you deal with the immediate pain of your thoughts, feelings, and physical ailments, you also must deal with the pain caused by the fact that your pain prevents you from living the kind of life you want to live.

Now see if this next sentence is true for you: Generally, the more you live your life trying to ward off the pain of presence, the more pain you get, particularly in the form of the pain of absence.

Remember, we asked for honesty and openness about your own experience. Even if it doesn't seem logical that this should be so, look and see if it isn't true. While you've focused more on getting rid of the pain of presence, you've been feeling more of the pain of absence. If that's what's been happening for you, it may feel as though life is closing in around you. It may feel as though you're in some kind of trap. If you've been experiencing those kinds of feelings, then this book is about finding a way out. There's an alternative to living as though you've been trapped.

LIVING A VALUED LIFE: AN ALTERNATIVE

Often, we attach ourselves to our pain, and we start to judge our lives based on how we feel and not on what we do. In a way, we become our pain. The answers you've filled in as your responses to the four sentences in the two exercises above contain the seeds of another kind of life: a life in which what you do is connected not to your pain, or to the avoidance of your pain, but to the kind of life you truly want to live.

This book is not about solving your problems in a traditional way so much as it is about changing the direction of your life, so that your life is more about what you value. Moreover, the unnecessary amplification of pain stops. When that happens, the issues you've been struggling with will begin to diminish. Your life will begin to open up and become more wide-ranging, more flexible, and more meaningful.

We ask you to allow the possibility of living a life you value to be your guide as you read these pages and work with the exercises. We aren't asking you to go out and lead a different life right this minute. There is a lot of work to do first. None of this will be easy because the traps our minds set for us will continue to be laid.

In our work on Acceptance and Commitment Therapy (ACT) we've developed a set of processes that appear to empower the people who work with these processes to improve their lives and to dismantle troublesome traps and dead ends. Gradually, step by step, we will walk you through those processes in the service of living a vital, valued, meaningful life.

If you are willing, let's begin.

CHAPTER 2

Why Language Leads to Suffering

What is the human mind? Why are we different than the birds flying outside our windows? And why do we suffer so? These kinds of questions have puzzled humankind for eons. We think we have some answers, and we think those answers may inform the process you will go through while you work with this book.

THE NATURE OF HUMAN LANGUAGE

As we noted in the introduction, ACT is based on Relational Frame Theory (RFT; Hayes, Barnes-Holmes, and Roche 2001). The basic premise of RFT is that human behavior is governed largely through networks of mutual relations called relational frames. These relations form the core of human language and cognition, and allow us to learn without requiring direct experience. For example, a cat won't touch a hot stove twice, but it needs to touch it at least once to get the hint. A human child need never touch a hot stove to be taught verbally that it can burn. In the outside world, this ability is a tool beyond compare. But in terms of our inner lives, verbal rules can restrict our lives in fundamental ways.

We set out twenty years ago to try to discover the core features of human thinking. Today, we think that we've isolated some of the key components. Perhaps it's risky to say it so boldly, but we think we've found what is at the core of the human mind itself. Humans think relationally; nonhumans apparently do not. Exactly what this means will become evident in this chapter but, in broad terms, humans are able to arbitrarily relate objects in our environment, thoughts, feelings, behavioral predispositions, actions (basically anything) to other objects in our environment, thoughts, feelings (basically anything else) in virtually any possible way (e.g., same as, similar to, better than, opposite of, part of, cause of, and so on).

This characteristic is essential to the way the human mind functions because it is our key evolutionary asset and has permitted the human species a dominant role in the animal kingdom. The ability to think relationally allows us to consciously analyze our environment, develop tools, build fires, create art, make computers, and even do our taxes. This same ability creates suffering.

The Idea Isn't Entirely New

Often, the words about language were once metaphors, and their etymology focuses on that relational core. One word mentioned in the last chapter, the word "symbol," comes from an ancient Greek root, "bol," which means "to throw." Combined with "sym" (which means "the same"), a symbol literally means "thrown as the same." When our minds throw words at us, those words appear to be much the same as the things to which they "refer." The etymology of "refer" completes the picture. Do you remember we discussed the root of "fer" in chapter 1, when we explored the word "suffering"? "Fer" means "to carry" (hence the word "ferry"), and "re" means "again." So, "to refer" to something involves carrying something again.

This early common sense understanding corresponds to our research findings about the nature of human thinking. When we think, we arbitrarily *relate* events. Symbols "carry back" objects and events because they are related to these events as being "the same." These symbols enter into a vast relational network that our mind generates and expands on over the course of our lives. What follows is a brief list of relational frames. This is not at all comprehensive. Such a list could fill pages and isn't important to understand the parts of RFT that are necessary for the work we are about to do.

Relational Frames

■   Frames of Coordination (such as "same as," "similar," or "like")

■   Temporal and Causal frames (these include "before and after," "if/then," "cause of," "parent of," and so on)

■   Comparative and Evaluative frames (a whole family of relations such as "better than," "bigger than," "faster than," "prettier than," and so on)

■   Deictic frames (these are frames with reference to the perspective of a speaker, such as "I/you" or "here/there")

■   Spatial frames (such as "near/far")

It is this repertoire—this set of learned relations that can be applied at your whim to anything at all—that we mean when we refer to the human "mind."

EXERCISE: Relate Anything to Anything Else

You can test the idea that you develop arbitrary relationships all the time quite easily. To do so, try the following:

Write down a concrete noun here (any type of object or animal will do): _____

Now write another concrete noun here: _____

Now answer this question: How is the first noun like the second one? When you have a good answer, go on to this next question: How is the first noun better than the second one? When you have a good answer, go on to this question: How is the first one the parent of the second one? Finding an answer to this final question may not be straightforward. Stick with it. It will come.

That last question may have been the hardest, but if you do stick with it, you will always find an answer. And note that the good answers somehow seem to be "real" in the sense that the relation you see seems to be actually in or justified by the related objects (that is, they often seem to be not arbitrary at all).

This exercise demonstrates that the mind can relate anything to anything in any possible way. In technical terms it suggests that relational responding is "arbitrarily applicable." This fact is hidden from view because the mind justifies these relations by features it abstracts from the related facts. As you can see from this silly exercise, that cannot be wholly true. It cannot be that, in fact, everything actually can be "the parent of" everything else. Yet your mind can always find a justification for that relation or any other (we will apply this insight to the "story of your life" in chapter 7).

Even Human Babies Can Do It

Even very young human babies use these relational sets quite naturally, but nonhumans arguably do not. In this area, even the so-called "language-trained" chimpanzees fail the tests a human infant would easily pass (Dugdale and Lowe 2000). For example, suppose a baby learned that a particular imaginary animal had a name, and that this animal made a sound. We might show the baby a drawing of our imaginary creature and say, "This is a gub-gub. Can you say 'gub-gub'?" After the baby learns this, we might show the same picture to her and say, "This goes 'wooo.' Can you go 'wooo'?"

In this example, we have three pieces of a relational network: the picture, the name of the animal the picture represents (gub-gub), and the sound that animal makes ("wooo"). The relationships between the fictional creature, its sound, and the picture could be mapped inside a triangle (see figure 2.1). At this point in the lesson, we have only trained two relationships: the one

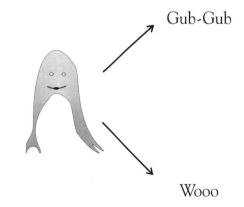

Figure 2.1: The gub-gub and its directly trained name and sound.

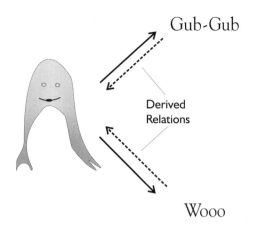

Figure 2.2: The relational network expands.

between the picture and the name of the creature and the one between the picture and the sound the creature makes.

Any complex organism—including human babies and chimpanzees alike—can learn this. But this is the point where humans start to differ from other animals. At age fourteen to sixteen months (perhaps even earlier; scientists are still trying to pinpoint exactly when this ability is activated), humans will reverse the direction of what they learned. When presented with an assortment of pictures of imaginary creatures and asked, "Which one is the gub-gub?" they will point to the picture they were trained to call a gub-gub and not to another imaginary creature they also learned to name. Human children do this without training. They realize not only that the picture refers to the word "gub-gub," but that the word "gub-gub" also refers to the picture.

This seems so obvious that it may seem unimportant. But research suggests this process is at the very core not only of how humans think, but why they suffer. (We will expand on this shortly.) This ability to reverse relationships holds true for the references between the picture and the sound the creature makes as well. If you ask a child of this age, "Which one goes 'wooo'?" the child will again point to the picture of the gub-gub and not to a drawing of another creature.

At this point, we have developed four relationships from two trained relations. Following the example above, these are as follows: the picture to the word "gub-gub," the word "gub-gub" to the picture, the picture to the sound "wooo," and the sound "wooo" to the picture (see figure 2.2).

Then, from around twenty-two to twenty-seven months (Lipkens, Hayes, and Hayes 1993), human children will combine all these reversible relations. When asked, "What does the gub-gub say?" the child will say "wooo." When asked, "Who says 'wooo'?" the response will be "gub-gub." Note that the child not only retains the previous four relationships we've explored, she creates two new relationships in our triangle that she had no prior training in whatsoever. She has seen a picture that we have taught her is a gub-gub, and she has been taught that the picture this fictional creature represents makes the sound "wooo." She has never been distinctly trained in any relationship between the word "gub-gub" and the sound "wooo." Nonetheless, she can derive the connections between these various parts of this relational network. Now the triangle is completely filled in. Out of two trained relationships we have developed six (see figure 2.3).

Furthermore, if one of these events becomes associated either with something frightening, or pleasing, all other related events are likely to be scary or pleasant. For example, if the baby is accidentally stuck with a diaper pin while you say "wooo," the baby might cry whenever you mention a gub-gub or the gub-gub's picture is seen. On the other hand, if the baby is given a sweet when you first say "wooo," the baby might expect a goodie whenever the sound of "wooo" is heard.

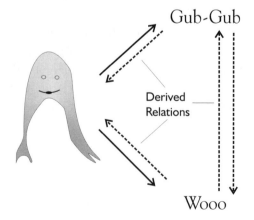

Figure 2.3: Gub-gubs go "wooo": the relational network is completed.

So far, we've been considering relations of sameness and, after twenty-five years of research, there is still disagreement about whether, with enough training, nonhumans may be able to develop relations of sameness that can be applied to anything (Hayes and Barnes-Holmes 2004). As humans mature, they learn other relations that show the many other kinds of relational frames mentioned earlier in the chapter, such as comparison, causality, and so forth. How humans create these relational frameworks has been the focus of a great deal of RFT research, and we now know enough to be able to teach these sets of relations to children who have not yet acquired them (Barnes-Holmes, Barnes-Holmes, and Smeets 2004). However, for our present purposes, the fact that human beings do this kind of relational thinking naturally is our main point. It fundamentally changes the world that human beings live in.

Each learned relation is like the triangle shown in figure 2.2, but the specific relation and thus the specific network is different. For example, a child who can recognize opposites and has learned that "frio" is the opposite of "hot," and "frio" is also the opposite of "caliente," will know the reverse relations without needing further training (e.g., caliente is the opposite of cold) and the combined terms (caliente and hot are the same, not opposites). If this child burned himself with "hot" water, he might begin to avoid "caliente" water and not avoid "cold" water.

This is one reason that even beautiful sunsets may not be safe for human beings in pain, as mentioned in chapter 1. If "happy" is the opposite of "sad," then happiness can remind human beings of being sad. The two are related. This is probably part of the reason that relaxation can induce panic (Schwartz and Schwartz 1995). Dogs do not know how to do this. People do.

The Advantage of Our Abilities with Language

As best we can tell, the ability to derive relations like this is probably only about 75,000 to 100,000 years old, and in highly elaborated forms it is much younger than that. Written language marks a real transition in the ability to relate events in this way and it is only five- to ten-thousand-years old, depending on what you count as written symbols. By animal standards, humans are frail, slow-moving creatures. We do not have the strength of gorillas, the teeth of tigers, the speed of cheetahs, or the venom of snakes. Nevertheless, over the last 10,000 years we have taken over the planet. Why is that? We believe that the answer lies in these relational frames.

Now, let's try an interesting exercise that will help to illustrate this point.

EXERCISE: A Screw, a Toothbrush, and a Lighter

Consider this simple problem. Watch carefully what your mind does with it.

Suppose you have a slotted screw in a board and you want to get it out. You can use only a normal toothbrush and a cigarette lighter to do so. What will you do? Take a moment to think about it and write down your thoughts, even if they are fragmentary:

_____

_____

_____

If nothing comes to mind yet, remember that the toothbrush is plastic (watch carefully what your mind does now, and write down your thoughts, even if fragmentary):

_____

_____

_____

If nothing comes to mind yet, remember that plastic is made from oil. Now write down any thoughts, even if fragmentary:

_____

_____

_____

If nothing comes to mind that would work yet, remember that plastic can melt (watch carefully what your mind does now):

_____

_____

_____

If nothing comes to mind yet, remember that when melted, plastic is pliable. Now write down any thoughts this fact evokes:

_____

_____

_____

If nothing comes to mind yet, remember that pliable plastic can form a shape (watch carefully what your mind does now):

_____

_____

_____

If nothing comes to mind yet, remember that melted plastic hardens when cooled. Write down your ideas for removing the screw using only a toothbrush and lighter:

_____

_____

_____

How Helpful Skills Cause You to Suffer

Hopefully, by now, you should be able to remove the screw, if it's not screwed in too tightly and the melted plastic holds. (Presumably the plastic was melted by heating the end of the toothbrush with the lighter and inserting it into the screw while it was still pliable. Then waiting for the plastic to cool.) Now look at what you thought and wrote down.

Notice whether your thoughts had these qualities: you named objects and noted their properties; you described temporal (time-oriented) and contingent relations (if I did this, then. . . .); and you evaluated or compared anticipated outcomes. See if it's true that sometimes you literally "pictured" your ideas. That is, you saw the toothbrush, or pictured melting its handle at the end.

By doing this exercise, you've just demonstrated the main reason why humans, for good or for ill, have become the dominant species on the planet. These following relations are necessary for any verbal problem solving:

- events and their attributes;

- time and/or contingency;

- and evaluation.

With these three sets of simple verbal relations we can think about the future, make plans, and evaluate and compare outcomes.

Unfortunately, with just these three sets (and not the scores of additional relations that language contains) you also have the capability to cause mental distress. Simply by having names for events and their attributes you can do a better job of remembering and thinking about them. You can, for example, remember and describe a past trauma and start sobbing as a result. You can be afraid of knives because you know they can cut and injure you (even if you've never seen that happen or had it happen to you).

With an *if . . . then,* or a temporal relation, you can predict bad events that may not happen, you can be afraid that pain or depression will return in the future, or you can know that you will die and you can worry about that imagined future. As a result of these symbolic temporal relations, most people tend to live more in the verbally remembered past and the verbally imagined future than in the present moment.

With comparative and evaluative relations we can compare ourselves to an ideal and find ourselves wanting, even though we are actually doing quite well. We can think we are much worse than others, or (perhaps just as bad) that we are much better than others. We can be afraid of negative evaluations from others, even if we haven't ever experienced them, and we can become socially inhibited as a result.

These processes are quite primitive. Consider what a six-year-old child is like and then read this sad news story:

Dania, Fla. June 16 (AP)—A six-year-old girl was killed today when she stepped in front of a train, [after] telling siblings that she "wanted to be with her mother." The authorities said that her mother had a terminal illness. (*New York Times* 1993)

Suicide is unknown among two-year-olds, but just a few years later, when we are able to think about the future and evaluate what we imagine, we have the tools to imagine we would be better off dead. If a six-year-old can step in front of a train to be with her mommy in heaven, a person as complex as you are has all of the cognitive tools needed to be tormented.

This is our point: humans suffer, in part, because they are verbal creatures. If this is so, then here is the problem: the verbal skills that create misery are too useful and central to human functioning to ever stop operating. That means suffering is an unavoidable part of the human condition, at least until we know how to better manage the skills language itself has given us.

WHY LANGUAGE CREATES SUFFERING

In normal problem-solving situations, when there is something we don't like, we figure out how to get rid of it and we take actions to do that. If we don't like dirt on the floor, we get out the vacuum cleaner. If we don't like a leaky roof, we fix it. The human approach to solving problems can be stated as, "If you don't like something, figure out how get rid of it, and then get rid of it." That's exactly why the linguistic and cognitive processes we've just described are useful. But when we apply this strategy to our own inner suffering, it often backfires.

Suppressing Your Thoughts

Suppose you have a thought you don't like. You'll apply your verbal problem-solving strategies to it. For example, when the thought comes up, you may try to stop thinking it. There is extensive literature on what is likely to happen as a result. Harvard psychologist Dan Wegner (1994) has shown that the frequency of the thought that you try not to think may go down for a short while, but it soon appears more often than ever. The thought becomes even more central to your thinking, and it is even more likely to evoke a response. Thought suppression only makes the situation worse.

EXERCISE: A Yellow Jeep

Let's try an experiment and see whether suppressing a thought can work.

1. Get a clear picture in your mind of a bright yellow Jeep. How many times during the last few days have you thought of a bright yellow Jeep? Write down your answer in the space provided: _____

2. Now get your watch out and spend a few minutes (five would be ideal) trying as hard as you can not to think even one single thought of a bright yellow Jeep. Really try hard. Return to this page when you are finished.

3. Write down how many times you had a thought about a bright yellow Jeep, however fleetingly, during the last few minutes while you were trying so hard not to think of it.

   _____

4. Now get your watch out and spend a few minutes (five would be ideal) allowing yourself to think whatever thoughts come to your mind. Return here when you are finished.

5. Write down how many times you had a thought about a bright yellow Jeep, however fleetingly, during the last few minutes while you were allowing yourself to think of anything.

_____

If you are like most people, the number of times you thought about a bright yellow Jeep went up over time. You might have been able to keep the thought of a yellow Jeep out of your mind while directly suppressing it, but sometimes even that breaks down, and the number of times such thoughts occur soars. Even if you were able to suppress the thought for a short period of time, at some point, you will no longer be able to do so. When this happens, the occurrence of the thought tends to go up dramatically. That is not simply because you were reminded of a yellow Jeep. In controlled research studies, when participants are told about the Jeep but are not instructed to suppress thinking about it, the number of thoughts does not increase.

When you try not to think of something, you do that by creating this verbal rule: "Don't think of x." That rule contains x, so it will tend to evoke x, just as the sounds "gub-gub" can evoke a picture of an imaginary animal. Thus, when we suppress our thoughts, we not only must think of something else, we have to hold ourselves back from thinking about why we are doing that. If we check to see whether our efforts are working, we will remember what we are trying not to think and we will think it. The worrisome thought thus tends to grow.

If you have obsessive thoughts or worries, this pattern is probably familiar to you. Research has shown that the vast majority of people without obsessions have odd intrusive thoughts from time to time, just as people with obsessions do (Purdon and Clark 1993). What is the difference? Part of the answer to that question may be that those with severe obsessive thinking problems spend more effort on trying not to think these thoughts (Marcks and Woods 2005). If normal people are asked to not think certain thoughts, they too will begin to feel more distressed about their negative thoughts (Marcks and Woods 2005).

Now, let's try this exercise again using one of the thoughts that contributes to your suffering.

EXERCISE: Don't Think About Your Thoughts

Psychological problems of any kind become entangled with our thoughts, and as a result, if you are struggling psychologically, you probably also have recurring thoughts that cause you pain. For example, if you are depressed, you may have the thought, "I'm worthless and no one loves me" or even just "When will this depression go away?" If you are suffering from generalized anxiety disorder, you may have the thought, "Vigilance is the only way to be safe." Now, try to isolate a single thought that contributes to your current suffering. You can use the examples above as models. If you can, deconstruct your thought until you have it in the form of a short sentence or simple phrase. When you have this sentence or phrase in mind, complete the exercise.

1. Write down a thought that contributes to your suffering in the space below.

_____

2. How many times have you had this thought in the last week? (If you don't know exactly how many times, make an approximation.)

    _____

3. Now, get out your watch again, and try as hard as you can not to think that thought for the next few minutes (again, five minutes would be ideal). Return here when you are finished.

4. Write down the number of times you had your thought, however fleetingly, while you were trying not to think about it. _____

5. Now, take another five minutes, and again allow yourself to think anything you want. Come back here when you are finished.

6. How many times did you think your thought when you allowed yourself to think about anything at all?

    Go ahead and write down your answer here: _____

As you began to try to suppress your thought, what was your experience? Did it become less heavy, less central, and less evocative? Or did it become more entangling, more important, and even more frequent? If your experience was more like the second description than the first, this exercise illustrated an important point. That is, it can be useless or even actively unhelpful to try to get rid of those thoughts you don't like. In controlled research, this doesn't always work the way it does with arbitrary thoughts like those about bright yellow Jeeps. That may be because personally relevant negative thoughts are often already the target of chronic thought-suppression and those thoughts are already quite high in frequency.

What Is True for Thoughts Is Also True for Emotions

This same process applies to emotions. If you try not to feel a bad feeling, such as pain, not only do you tend to feel it more intensely, but previously neutral events also become irritating (Cioffi and Holloway 1993). Any parent knows this. If the kids are irritating you by making too much noise and you are trying to ignore it, the noise just becomes more and more irritating and, eventually, even little annoyances can cause you to explode.

Emotions link to thoughts in the same way. Research has shown that when you suppress thoughts in the presence of an emotion, eventually the emotion evokes the thought, and the suppression strategies evoke both the thought and the emotion (Wenzlaff and Wegner 2000).

For example, suppose you are feeling sad and you are trying not to think of a recent loss, such as the death of a friend. Perhaps you'll listen to your favorite music to try to keep your mind off the friend who will no longer be in your life. What would be the result? Eventually, when you feel sad, you'll be more likely to think of your loss, and your favorite music will tend to sadden you and remind you of your dead friend. In a sense you will have amplified your pain in your attempt to avoid feeling it.

Behavioral Predispositions and the Thought Trap

Finally, the same results apply to *behavioral predispositions*, behaviors that are programmed to the degree that the mere thought of them sets off a chain of bodily and psychological events that predispose us to behave in the programmed way.

In an almost nightmarish effect known to every weekend golfer trying to make a pressure putt, researchers have asked subjects to hold a plumber's pendulum (a weight on a string) over a spot on the floor and not to let it move at all, but especially not forward and back. The effect? It tends to move forward and back, not side to side, simply because thinking about not having it move forward and back activates the very muscles that move it that way (Wegner, Ansfield, and Pilloff 1998). The effect is especially strong under pressure situations, precisely when you would most wish it were not there.

If you have a fear of heights, this effect may be quite familiar to you. When you look over a ledge from a great height, you almost feel a pull as if some invisible force were causing you to be unsteady precisely when you wish that would not happen. If we can generalize from the literature on suppression, this effect is probably not just in your mind: your fear activates some of the muscles that move you toward the ledge, as well as those that move you away from it. As a result, you feel unsteady.

WHAT YOU'VE BEEN DOING

It's likely you've been using a verbally guided "fix-it" mentality to find a solution for the causes of your suffering. If you've opened this book, it's also likely that your attempts haven't been entirely successful. (Otherwise, why did you open it?) The coping techniques you've developed to fix or counteract the pain you struggle with belong to the same class of language-based, problem-solving behaviors described in the exercises above.

Let's look at this a little more carefully. What kinds of actions do you take to suppress or otherwise reduce, diminish, control, or counteract your painful thoughts, feelings, and bodily sensations? Consider all the rituals you engage in as a means to keep yourself from feeling pain. These might be as extreme as incessant hand washing if you are suffering with OCD, or as simple as turning on the tube at night to numb yourself from the aftereffects of the irritation you felt on your way home from work. Your coping behaviors might include purely psychological behaviors like thought-suppression or rationalization. Or perhaps you engage in physical activities like obsessive exercise, habitual smoking, or even intentional self-harm, like cutting, to ameliorate your pain. Whatever you do (and we all do some of these things to a greater or lesser degree), you can explore them in the exercise below.

EXERCISE: The Coping Strategies Worksheet

Please glance at the Coping Strategies Worksheet below, and then return here for directions on how to work with it. In the column on the left, first write down a painful thought or feeling. (This can be taken from the Suffering Inventory you generated in chapter 1 if you wish. It can also be something entirely different if you have a more pressing thought or feeling that you would like to address right now.)

Then, in the second column, write down one strategy you've used to cope with this painful thought or feeling. Once you've done this, please rank your coping strategy for two sets of outcomes. The first asks you to rate how effective your coping strategy has been in the short-term. That is, how much immediate relief do you get from the behavior? For the second ranking, rate your strategy for how effective it's been in the long-term.

Think about how much of your total pain is caused by your painful thought or feeling. Has your coping behavior reduced your pain over time? Rate each short- and long-term strategy on a scale from 1 to 5 where 1 is not effective at all and 5 is incredibly effective. For the time being, simply note your rankings. We will look at what they mean in greater detail later in this chapter.

For example, suppose someone writes a thought like this: "I'm not sure life is worth living" in the "Painful thought or feeling" column. The coping technique the person uses may be to have a beer, watch sports, and try not to think about it. While watching TV, the short-term effectiveness of the strategy may be ranked a 4; but later, the thoughts may be stronger than ever and the long-term effectiveness may be ranked a 1.

Coping Strategies Worksheet			
Painful thought or feeling	Coping technique	Short-term effectiveness	Long-term effectiveness

Coping Strategies Diary

If you find that you aren't sure what you've been doing to cope, it may be best to collect this information first in diary form. You can copy the form below and use it to record what happens in your life when you experience something psychologically painful. Note the situation (what happened that evoked a difficult private experience); what your specific internal reactions were (particular thoughts, feelings, memories, or physical sensations); and the specific coping strategy you used then (e.g., distracting yourself, trying to argue your way out of your reactions, leaving the situation). After making entries like these in diary form for a period of one week, you should have a better understanding of what coping strategies you have been using and how effective they are.

Coping Strategies Diary Entries		
Date	**Situation**	
Difficult private reactions: (e.g., thoughts, feelings, sensations)		
Distress/disturbance level: (when it first happened)		Not distressing/ disturbing Extremely distressing/ disturbing 1 2 3 4 5
Coping strategy: (my response to my private reactions)		
Short-term effects:		Not at all effective Incredibly effective 1 2 3 4 5
Long-term effects:		Not at all effective Incredibly effective 1 2 3 4 5

THE PROBLEM WITH GETTING RID OF THINGS—SQUARED

There is another important reason that figuring out how to get rid of troublesome thoughts or feelings often backfires when your verbal skills are applied to your internal processes: it reminds you of bad consequences. Suppose you are feeling anxious while doing something challenging (say, giving a speech), and you think, "I'd better not feel anxious or I will completely fail at this." Thoughts of failure can elicit anxiety for the same reason that a baby might be afraid of a gub-gub if it had been pricked with a diaper pin while hearing the word "wooo": the negative consequence and current event are arbitrarily related.

Anxiety is a normal response to poor performance, or humiliation. The problem is that we can bring these consequences into the current situation at any moment through verbal relations. People with panic disorder, for example, tend to think about losing their minds, losing control, humiliating themselves, or dying of a heart attack in association with the anxiety they feel. These thoughts create more anxiety partly because they relate the present to an imagined future in which there is the possibility of these dire results happening. If you have an anxiety condition, then you know that this can become a vicious circle.

The Shark Tank Polygraph

Suppose you were sitting over a dunk tank full of sharks while you were wired up to the world's best tuned polygraph. You have a very simple task: don't get anxious at all. If you do, the seat will flip you over, and into the tank you'll go.

What do you think would happen? It seems extremely likely you would be anxious. This is exactly what happens during a panic attack: First you feel a twinge of anxiety, then you imagine the horrors that can arrive, you react to those, and, in a matter of seconds, boom. You're in the shark tank.

EXPERIENTIAL AVOIDANCE

Language creates suffering in part because it leads to experiential avoidance. *Experiential avoidance* is the process of trying to avoid your own experiences (thoughts, feelings, memories, bodily sensations, behavioral predispositions) even when doing so causes long-term behavioral difficulties (like not going to a party because you're a social phobic, or not exercising because you feel too depressed to get out of bed). Of all the psychological processes known to science, experiential avoidance is one of the worst (Hayes, Masuda, et al. 2004).

Experiential avoidance tends to artificially amplify the "pain of presence" discussed in chapter 1, and it is the single biggest source of the "pain of absence," since it is avoidance that most undermines positive actions. Unfortunately, this strategy is built into human language for two reasons: language naturally targets our reactions, not just our situations (a point we will explain later in chapter 5), and it makes it impossible to control pain by controlling situations, since any situation can be arbitrarily related to pain and thus evoke it (see the sunset example in the last chapter).

Outside the body, the rule may indeed be, "If you don't like it, figure out how to get rid of it, and then get rid of it." Inside the body, the rule appears to be very different. It's more like, "If you aren't willing to have it, you will." In practical terms, this means for example, that if you aren't willing to feel anxiety as a feeling, you will feel far more anxiety, plus you will begin to live a narrower and more constricted life.

Go back now and review your Coping Strategies Worksheet. If you are like most people, the majority of your coping strategies are focused on your internal processes. Usually, these coping strategies help to regulate your internal processes a little in the short run, but in the long run, they often fail or even make matters worse.

Now, consider the possibility that this is so because each of the coping strategies you've developed is a way to avoid your experiences. You develop specific means by which you try to stop feeling the feelings you are feeling or thinking the thoughts you are thinking. You try to avoid the experience of painful thoughts or feelings by burying yourself in distracting activities, combating your thoughts with rationalizations, or trying to quash your feelings through the use of controlled substances. If you are suffering, you may spend a lot of time performing these distracting coping techniques. Meanwhile, your life is not being lived.

Rankings for the Coping Strategies Worksheet

In your review of your worksheet, you may have found that your scores in the "Short-term effectiveness" column are relatively high, while your scores in the "Long-term effectiveness" column are relatively low. This is a dangerous trap because short-term effects are far more reinforcing than long-term effects, and these problem-solving strategies do work in most areas of life for a short time. The coping techniques you've developed to combat your anger, anxiety, or depression probably do cause these feelings to go away for a short while; otherwise, you wouldn't engage in them. But how powerful is the long-term effect? How much do your coping strategies really change your condition in the long run?

If you're reading this book, we're guessing that the long-term impact your strategies have had on your suffering is fairly minimal or even negative. What you are left with are behaviors that have become deeply embedded in your day-to-day life due to their short-term effectiveness; but for long-term relief they are sadly lacking.

It's like the diagram shown in figure 2.4. Human beings have a core of pain because life inherently contains difficulties, such as disease, want, and loss, but language keeps us amplifying these difficulties into larger patterns of human suffering. Like the rings around the black center in figure 2.4, we build out that core of pain by our patterns of cognitive entanglement and avoidance.

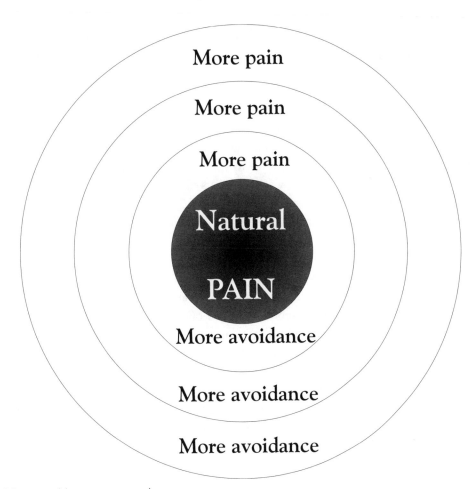

Figure 2.4: More avoidance, more pain.

When we try to run away from a painful thought, feeling, or bodily sensation, it becomes more important and tends to occur more intensely or frequently. Because running away also means that we are taking our fearful thoughts literally, they become more believable and entangling. As a result, the "pain of presence" grows. Meanwhile life is put on hold while we struggle with our internal processes. As a result, the "pain of absence" grows as well. The black spot in the middle grows bigger and bigger.

THE MIND-TRAIN

Unfortunately, these processes are not easy to control because they are so tightly linked to our normal use of language. People tend to "live in their minds," that is, to engage with the world on the basis of these verbal processes. Living in your mind can be likened to riding a train. A train has its own tracks and it goes where they lead. That's fine when the tracks are going where you want to go. But if you were traveling in the direction you want to be going, you probably would never have stopped to read this book. If the life you want to live is "off the tracks," then you have only one option: you must learn how to get off the train … at least sometimes.

Riding your mind-train has become an automatic process. You believe the thoughts that your mind presents to you. Getting the train going in the first place happened innocently enough: you learned language; you learned how to speak, reason, and solve problems. Once you did that, your mind-train became a permanent presence in your life. Now, there is no way that you will stop thinking and generating thoughts—your mind-train will keep on running, in part, because language is so useful in so many areas. But just because the train keeps running all the time doesn't mean you have to stay on it every moment.

On a real train, you're allowed to ride as long as you follow the rules. You play an active part on the trip. You've got to cooperate with the rules by showing your ticket when you're asked for it, sitting in your assigned seat and staying seated, and not raising a ruckus when you miss your stop or you find out the train's taking you in a direction you don't want to go.

The rules and conditions our minds lay down for us are simple but powerful: act on the basis of belief and disbelief. They say that you must react to your mind either by agreeing with it or arguing with it. Unfortunately, both reactions are based on taking your thoughts literally. Rather than seeing your thoughts merely as an ongoing process of relating, they are reacted to based on what they relate to. They are "factually" correct or incorrect.

When you take your thoughts literally, you are "riding the mind-train." That is, you are responding to the thoughts your mind presents to you purely in terms of the facts they are about. Agreeing and disagreeing are both within the rules, so neither response gets you off the train. However, if you break the rules, you will find yourself off the mind-train—and isn't this one train you'd like to get off of now and then?

To know what an experience is really like, you've got to experience it for yourself, not just think about it. To see what it's like to jump off the mind-train, you have to actually do it. You do that by breaking some of the rules and conditions your mind sets for you. And how do you jump off that train? Well, that is precisely what this book is about. At this point, all we can say is that once you are off of the train with your feet on the ground, you will see whether you are in a better position to choose a direction and live according to your values rather than simply riding the rails of your verbal conditioning.

It will take a while to learn how to do this. But that's the direction in which we are headed.

CHAPTER 3

The Pull of Avoidance

The situation you are in now may feel like being in a tug-of-war with a big, ugly monster (whether you are dealing with depression, anxiety, physical pain, sorrowful memories, or some other negative situation). It seems as though you can't win. The harder you pull, the harder the monster pulls back. Sometimes it even may feel as if there's a bottomless pit between you and the monster and, if you lose, you'll be pulled into the pit and be completely destroyed. So, you pull and pull. You try harder and harder. You look for different ways to pull, better ways to pull, stronger ways to pull. You try digging in your heels for more leverage or you try strengthening your muscles. You keep hoping that something will work. Suppose, however, that you have a completely different job to do. Perhaps it's not your job to win this tug-of-war. Perhaps it's your job to find a way to drop the rope.

WHY WE DO WHAT CAN'T WORK

When unhappy people really look at their behavior, it's usually easy to see that that their experiential avoidance isn't working. Think about what you discovered when you completed your Coping Strategies Worksheet in chapter 2. By now, it should be clear to you that the behaviors you've developed to avoid your pain have not been particularly effective in the long run. If they had worked, you wouldn't be where you are now. The problem is that it's devilishly difficult to see that experiential avoidance behaviors can't be effective. There are at least five reasons why it is so difficult to see this truth.

1. Controlling works so well in other areas of your life (the world outside your body) that you assume it will work for your thoughts and feelings as well.

   This point is easy to understand. For example, in the space provided below, list some examples of successful occasions when controlling by conscious problem-solving worked for you in the external world: _____

   _____

   _____

   It's very likely you were able to generate some relatively noncontroversial examples of times when being able to control events in the external world worked for you.

2. You were taught that you should be able to control your thoughts and feelings. For example, when you were little, you may have been told, "Stop crying, or I will give you something to cry about," or, "Big boys don't cry," or, "Don't be afraid, only sissies are afraid."

   Now, think of yourself when you were a child. See whether you can remember any messages given to you by others that suggested you should easily be able to control your emotions or thoughts. If you remember any, list them here: _____

   _____

   _____

3. When you were very young, the giants around you called "grown-ups" seemed able to control their thoughts and feelings. For example, you might have felt scared a lot, but it seemed as though Daddy wasn't ever scared; you might have cried a lot, but the grown-ups around you hardly ever cried. This fact, when combined with point 2 above, may have caused you to internalize this message: You should be able to control your scary or sad feelings because others are successful at exercising that kind of control. This doesn't mean you actually learned to control your feelings, but it might mean that you learned to keep quiet about how you really felt so others wouldn't be disturbed by your emotions.

   If your experience was something like this description, in the space below, try to list examples of how other people seemed more confident, calmer, or happier, and more able to control their internal emotional states than you were: _____

   _____

   _____

   Sometime later in life, we learn that the idea that other "grown-ups" can control their feelings is an illusion. For example, when we grow up, we might learn that Daddy wasn't really so "calm." He may have had an alcohol problem you didn't fully appreciate as a child, or perhaps he was taking tranquilizers to cope. Or, when you're an adult, you might learn that the kids at school who looked so together on the outside were struggling on the inside in some of the same ways that you were struggling.

Now, see if you can remember when you first realized that the people who looked so together to you when you were very young were actually struggling. List those occasions here: _____

_____

_____

4. While you were growing up, you received a constant stream of messages that good health and great happiness depended on the absence of difficult private experiences. For example, think of all the commercials you've seen in your lifetime for products like beer, cigarettes, psychiatric drugs, vacations, sexy cars, fashionable clothes, and so on. Isn't it true that many of these commercials convey this message: "Happiness equals the ultimate absence of painful thoughts or feelings—and, if you buy this product, you will feel better and be that much closer to happiness"?

See if you can remember some media messages like that, and write down the message or commercial. Then answer this question: What do you think the underlying experiential avoidance message was? _____

_____

_____

5. Sometimes, it appears that controlling our unwanted thoughts and feelings actually does work in the short-term. For example, you might have had a recurring thought that you are worthless, and to compensate for this thought you became a workaholic. This may seem to have solved the problem of feeling worthless, but, generally, working so much just pushes the feeling deeper. This process is explored, in part, in chapter 2 where we discussed thought-suppression. If you have dark feelings and deliberately cover them up, whatever you do to compensate for feeling bad about yourself may begin to remind you that "Deep down there is something wrong with me."

If you've tried to use your accomplishments to cover up your difficult feelings, you probably know what happens when you act like a workaholic. When you are applauded for your accomplishments, you may feel as though you are fooling others because you know what is really going on for you beneath your calm appearance. You might be thinking, "If they only knew." Even positive feedback (although it feels good for a while) can have a hollow ring. This is sometimes called the "imposter syndrome." Fooling others doesn't work partly because who can be buoyed up by the opinions of fools?

If this is your experience, list examples of those times when you did things just to get the approval of others that in the long run felt false to you: _____

_____

_____

_____

_____

ACCEPTING THE POSSIBILITY THAT EXPERIENTIAL AVOIDANCE CAN'T WORK

Two main factors keep people stuck in the system of experiential avoidance. The first factor is that the rule "If you don't like something, get rid of it" works very well in the outside world. The second factor is that the short-term effects of experiential avoidance, that is, the application of that rule to our private experience, often can be positive. The linchpin that holds together the system of experiential avoidance is that the utility of human language in dealing with the world outside is based on the rule "If you don't like something, get rid of it," and the short-term effects of experiential avoidance, the application of that rule to our private experience, often can be positive.

For example, think of someone who has a snake phobia. His friends are all planning to visit the zoo, and this person is afraid to go with them. He is terrified they'll want to go to the snake exhibit and that he won't be able to handle being there. Although he wants to spend time with his friends and he would love to see the other animals at the zoo, ultimately, he finds an excuse not to go. Now, try to imagine what it's like to be this person and answer the following questions by circling one of the answers on the right.

- What does he probably feel immediately after finding an excuse not to go with his friends?   Relieved or Anxious

- Will avoiding the zoo (experiential avoidance) be more or less likely the next time?   More or Less

- Will his phobia become stronger or weaker?   Stronger or Weaker

Isn't it clear what the answers are? How could they be otherwise?

Your own situation is analogous to this person's experience. Every time you engage in a behavior specifically designed to avoid some negative personal pain, you start the same set of reactions outlined in the questions above. You are likely to feel an immediate sense of relief from not having to deal with the painful thought, feeling, or bodily sensation. The sense of relief you gain reinforces your desire to use the same strategy the next time you are faced with the possibility of having to cope with your pain. Yet, each time you do this, you actually give the painful content, that is, your painful thought, feeling, or bodily sensation, more power.

The Metaphor of the Hungry Tiger

Imagine you wake up one morning and just outside your front door you find an adorable tiger kitten mewing. Of course you bring the cuddly little guy inside to keep as a pet. After playing with him for a while, you notice he is still mewing, nonstop, and you realize he must be hungry. You feed him a bit of bloody, red ground beef knowing that's what tigers like to eat. You do this every day, and every day your pet tiger grows a little bigger. Over the course of two years, your tiger's daily meals change from hamburger scraps, to prime rib, to entire sides of beef. Soon your little pet no longer mews when hungry. Instead, he growls ferociously at you whenever he thinks it's mealtime. Your cute little pet has turned into an uncontrollable, savage beast that will tear you apart if he doesn't get what he wants.

Your struggle with your pain can be compared to this imaginary pet tiger. Every time you empower your pain by feeding it the red meat of experiential avoidance, you help your pain-tiger grow a little bit larger and a little bit stronger. Feeding it in this manner seems like the prudent thing to do. The pain-tiger growls ferociously telling you to feed it whatever it wants or it will eat you. Yet, every time you feed it, you help the pain to become stronger, more intimidating, and more controlling of your life.

Consider the possibility, as unlikely as it may seem, that it's not just that these avoidance strategies haven't worked—it's that they can't work. Avoidance only strengthens the importance and the role of whatever you are avoiding—in other words, when you avoid dealing with your problem, it only grows.

The Chinese Finger Trap

The situation is something like the Chinese finger traps you might have played with as a kid (see figure 3.1). The trap is a tube of woven straw about as big as your index finger. You push both index fingers in, one at each end, and as you pull them back out, the straw catches and tightens. The harder you pull, the smaller the tube becomes, and the stronger it holds your fingers. If the trap is built strongly enough, you'd have to pull your fingers out of their sockets to get them out of the tube by pulling, once they've

been caught. Conversely, if you *push* into it, your finger will still be in the tube, but at least you'll have enough room to move around and live your life.

Now, suppose that life itself is like a Chinese finger trap. So, it's not a question of getting free of the tube, it's a question of how much "wiggle room" you want to have in your life. The more you struggle, the more constricted your movements will be. If you let go of the struggle, the more freedom you have to make new choices.

Figure 3.1: The Chinese finger trap.

SO, WHAT ARE YOU SUPPOSED TO DO?

First, give yourself a break. Given all of the reasons discussed earlier, it's no surprise that you've been focusing on experiential avoidance strategies. You're doing exactly what logical, reasonable people are taught to do: to take care of themselves. It's a rigged game but you didn't know it was rigged, and it's certainly not your fault that it isn't working. If you were gambling at a rigged roulette wheel, you'd be sure to lose your money. You're in a similar situation with your pain. So now, put a check mark next to the ways that you would be willing to try to give yourself a break.

❑   I could face the possibility that my avoidance strategies will never work.

❑   I could have compassion for myself for how hard I've tried to deal with my pain.

❑   I could stop blaming myself for not being able to make my avoidance strategies work.

Now, list any other ideas you might have for how to give yourself a break:

_____

_____

_____

Responsibility and Response-ability

Second, accept response-ability. There is a slight but important difference between accepting "responsibility" and accepting "response-ability." Accepting "responsibility" often carries the implication of blame. Blame is what we do when we try to motivate people to change a behavior or do the right thing. But does accepting the thought "I'm at fault" really motivate anyone to change?

EXERCISE: The Blame Game

In the space provided below, write down some examples of blaming yourself or others for any negative events that you've experienced. Then, on a scale of 1 to 10, rate how well your examples worked to motivate and empower you to live your life in a more vital, fulfilling, and liberated way. (In this scale, 1 means not empowered at all and 10 means empowered to the max.)

Blaming Examples	Vitality Empowerment Ratings 1–10

How many times did you score high in terms of feeling vital and empowered when you were blaming yourself or someone else for negative events in your life? We are betting you didn't feel particularly empowered when playing the blame game. If you scored low consistently, it could mean blaming isn't working for you. If blame isn't working, clearly, you need something else.

As an alternative, accepting response-ability means to acknowledge the possibility that you are able to respond. This ability has nothing to do with blame. For the most part, your pain isn't anyone's fault; pain automatically accompanies the verbal system all normal humans acquire. Even in extreme situations (like rape or incest) when another person is actually at fault for perpetrating an evil act on you in a purposeful and deliberate manner, you still have the ability to respond to the pain it causes you.

It is as if there are two radio dials that control your suffering. One is labeled Pain. You've been trying very hard to turn that dial down to a lower level, but it doesn't seem to be working. The other dial is in the back of the radio and you didn't know it was there. Its settings control how much you struggle with pain and how much effort you expend trying to control your pain. We are guessing that you thought you needed to learn to control the Discomfort dial when you began reading this book. But what does your actual experience tell you about who sets that dial? Do you set the dial? Can you just "dial down" the level of pain you experience to a level you would prefer?

If your answer is no, perhaps you are not response-able for that dial. But now ask yourself this: Who sets the dial in the back of the radio? Who determines what you do with pain when it shows up? Being response-able means acknowledging that there is, in fact, some response you can make—you are able to respond. Later in this book, we will explore those areas where you can always respond.

Third, begin to consider the possibility that there is a real alternative to your struggle. Up until now, it's likely that you've rarely experienced thoughts or feelings you didn't want without trying to control them in some way. One of our goals is to show you what happens when you let go of your efforts to control your unwanted thoughts or feelings.

This is not easy, because controlling is what the human mind is programmed to do. At this point, we ask only that you begin to really examine what your experience is telling you. To do this, for the next two weeks fill out the following form. You may want to make a photocopy of this form so that you'll have a clean copy to fill out each day, or you can date each line and enter each day's observations on this copy. At the end of each day, rate the following three items:

1. How much psychological pain you experienced this day. (If your pain is due to a specific problem, such as anxiety or depression, use that more precise label instead of the word "pain.") When you do your rating for the day, use a scale where 1 means no pain and 100 means extreme pain.

2. After you have rated your pain for the day, then rate how much effort and struggle you needed to exert to control the pain you felt this day. Use the same scale, where 1 means no effort and 100 means an extreme level of effort and struggle.

3. The final step is to rate how workable the day was. That is, if every day were like today, how much overall vitality and aliveness would characterize your life? Again, use the same 1 to 100 scale.

EXERCISE: Judging Your Own Experience: Examining What Works

Day	Pain	Struggle	Overall Success
_____	_____	_____	_____

Any notes about painful events felt today? _____

Day	Pain	Struggle	Overall Success
_____	_____	_____	_____

Any notes about painful events felt today? _____

Day	Pain	Struggle	Overall Success
_____	_____	_____	_____

Any notes about painful events felt today? _____

Day	Pain	Struggle	Overall Success
_____	_____	_____	_____

Any notes about painful events felt today? _____

Day	Pain	Struggle	Overall Success
_____	_____	_____	_____

Any notes about painful events felt today? _____

Day	Pain	Struggle	Overall Success
_____	_____	_____	_____

Any notes about painful events felt today? _____

Day	Pain	Struggle	Overall Success
_____	_____	_____	_____

Any notes about painful events felt today? _____

Fourth, make room for the possibility that the alternative to control is frustratingly subtle. If you found in the last exercise that you are spending a lot of energy struggling with your pain, but not getting much out of the struggle in terms of empowerment (creating a sense that your life is expanding), then this is another clue that your attempts to control your pain may not be working as well as they logically should. Yet, years of conditioning have convinced you that this is the only correct option open to you.

Letting go of control does not require a lot of effort. But letting go of control (where control does not belong) is tricky. It is confusing. It can be frustrating. This is not something the "word machine" that is your mind is accustomed to doing.

That's why it's necessary for you to go through each of the exercises in this book slowly and carefully. The alternative to useless efforts aimed at exerting control over your thoughts and feelings offered here will require diligence, honesty, skepticism, confusion, and compassion from you. It isn't an easy path to follow. Your most important ally in taking this new path is your own pain. Only when you consider all the time and energy you've already spent fruitlessly trying to control your pain and avoid negative experiences, and then weighing the painful results, will you discover that the effort to do something radically different is worth it.

MOVING ON

Before you can move on with your life, you need to look directly at where you presently are. The exercises in the previous chapters were designed to help you begin doing just that. You need to be aware of the types of thoughts, feelings, and bodily sensations that have been plaguing you. And, just as important, you need to be aware of the habitual coping strategies you've been using to manage those thoughts, feelings, and bodily sensations.

At this point it wouldn't be wise to do anything differently. In fact, we suggest that you shouldn't try to change anything yet. Just try to become more mindful of what it is you've been doing, and more mindful of how this has really been working.

EXERCISE: What Are You Feeling and Thinking Now?

We've found that when people start looking more carefully at their own experiences, without running away or covering up, that, occasionally, experiences that were below their threshold of awareness percolate up to their conscious mind. So, to end this chapter, in the space provided below, list any thoughts and feelings you're having right now about the difficulties that motivated you to pick up this book. If you begin to see some issues that have been buried below the surface, take this opportunity to describe them; put them out on the table where they can be seen in the light of day.

_____

_____

_____

_____

In the chapters that follow, we will begin to explore how to take different approaches of relating to the pain with which you've been struggling. Don't expect yourself to master these new skills overnight. It will take time. The measure of success is one thing and one thing only: Your own experience. We aren't asking you to "buy a pig in a poke." We aren't asking you to believe in our alternative approach. We ask only that you be willing to try the new suggestions that we will put on the table, and that you allow your own direct experience to be the judge.

CHAPTER 4

Letting Go

Before you start reading this chapter, get a watch and sit somewhere where you won't be disturbed for a minute. When you are seated, take a deep breath and hold it as long as you can. When you're finished, write down how long you held your breath:

I held my breath for _____ seconds.

We will tell you why we've asked you to do this later in the chapter.

In the first two chapters we looked at your current suffering and your efforts to cope with it. We described an innate trap, a pitfall, inherent to human thought because of the way that language works, especially when thought and language are applied to private experiences. We called that trap experiential avoidance. We tried to see whether experiential avoidance is a part of the purpose of your existing coping strategies, and we examined the possibility that experiential avoidance is generally unhelpful. In chapter 3, we discussed five of the reasons why this unhelpful strategy is the normal, logical response most people have to their psychological pain.

Throughout, we've hinted at an alternative to experiential avoidance. It has been variously described as willingness, acceptance, or letting go. In this chapter, we want to start discussing this alternative more thoroughly. We will explain why acceptance is so important and give you a taste of what it means to be accepting by offering you the opportunity to experience it in some very simple ways. We aren't presenting this information now so that you can immediately apply it to the problems that have been troubling you the most. Rather, you should look at this chapter as a primer.

This is a brief introduction that will set the stage for the road ahead. Before you can actively apply acceptance in your daily life successfully, you will need to acquire a greater understanding of the way your mind works, how your mind is affecting your behaviors, and how you can interrupt that chain of events. There will be many opportunities for you to explore these things in the chapters that follow.

Acceptance (which we will also refer to as willingness) is a skill you may have heard about or experimented with in the past. It is certainly something that *you* can learn to do. Unfortunately, it is not something *your mind* can do, and that's why learning more skills will be required before you can implement it in your daily life. After all, your mind is aware of what you are reading right now. And, in this area, your mind is not your ally.

IF YOU'RE NOT WILLING TO HAVE IT, YOU WILL

In chapter 2 we said that perhaps the rule that applies to private experience goes something like this: "If you aren't willing to have it, you will." We implied that this rule is important for dealing with your suffering, although we didn't say exactly where its importance lies. So, let's take a look at what the human mind does with such an idea.

Suppose that the rule is true (if you aren't willing to have it, you will). Given that you've already suffered a great deal, what can you logically do that would apply that rule to your suffering? Take a moment now to write down any ideas about this that come to your mind.

_____

_____

_____

_____

_____

If you're like most people, you began by thinking about how you might be willing to have negative private experiences, if that meant those negative experiences would begin to diminish or even disappear. For example, suppose that anxiety is your issue. You hate how anxious you are. You've just read a sentence that purports to be a rule to help you deal with your problem. It states, "If you aren't willing to have it, you will." What can that mean for your anxiety? What follows is the kind of speculation that the word machine we call our mind does best.

"Hmmm. So, if I'm not willing to be anxious, I will be anxious. I suppose that means if I were more willing to be anxious, I might not be so anxious. I hate being anxious, so I guess I could give it a try. I'll try to be more willing to feel my anxiety so I won't be so anxious." With that, the thought trap slams down around you, because if you are willing to be anxious only in order to become less anxious, then you are not really willing to be anxious, and you will become even more anxious!

This is not psychobabble. Read the sentences again. Yes, they are paradoxical, but the paradox seems to be true. Those sentences demonstrate the merry-go-round ride that can result from trying to force the mind to do something it can't do. If the only reason you're willing to allow yourself to feel anxiety today is the hope that feeling it today will free you from the necessity of feeling it in the future, then it can't work. Because what your "willingness" here really means is you don't want to feel anxiety, and you'll try to jump through all kinds of mental hoops not to feel it. That's not the same as being willing to feel your anxiety.

This is why we've said that the approaches that might help with the causes of your pain are difficult to learn; not in the sense that they are effortful, but because they are tricky. For that reason, we are putting the concept of willingness on the table here, but we will deal with quite a bit of other material before returning to this topic to try to apply it to the core areas of your struggle.

ACCEPTANCE AND WILLINGNESS

"Accept" comes from the Latin root "*capere*" meaning "take." Acceptance is the act of receiving or "taking what is offered." Sometimes, in English, "accept" means "to tolerate or resign yourself" (as in, "Aw, gee, I guess I have to accept that"), and that is precisely *not* what is meant here. By "accept," we mean something more like "taking completely, in the moment, without defense."

We use the word "willing" as a synonym for "accepting" to stay true to that meaning of accept. "Willing" is one of the older words in the English language. It comes from an ancient root meaning "to choose." Thus "acceptance" and "willingness" can be understood as an answer to this question: "Will you take me in as I am?" Acceptance and willingness are the opposite of effortful control. Remember the dial at the back of the radio in chapter 3? Now you know its name: the Willingness dial.

What follows is a description of what "to take me in as I am" really means.

In our context, the words willingness and acceptance mean to respond actively to your feelings by feeling them, literally, much as you might reach out and literally feel the texture of a cashmere sweater. They mean to respond actively to your thoughts by thinking them, much as you might read poetry just to get the flow of the words, or an actor might rehearse lines to get a feel for the playwright's intent.

To be willing and accepting means to respond actively to memories by remembering them, much as you might take a friend to see a movie you've already seen. They mean to respond actively to bodily sensations by sensing them, much as you might take an all-over stretch in the morning just to feel your body all over. Willingness and acceptance mean adopting a gentle, loving posture toward yourself, your history, and your programming so that it becomes more likely for you simply to be aware of your own experience, much as you would hold a fragile object in your hand and contemplate it closely and dispassionately.

The goal of willingness is not to feel better. The goal is to open up yourself to the vitality of the moment, and to move more effectively toward what you value. Said another way, the goal of willingness is to feel all of the feelings that come up for you more completely, even—or especially—the bad feelings, so that you can live your life more completely. In essence, instead of trying to feel *better*, willingness involves learning how to *feel* better.

To be willing and accepting is to gently push your fingers into the Chinese finger trap in order to make more room for yourself to live in, rather than vainly struggling against your experience by trying to pull your fingers out of the trap (see figure 3.1). To be willing and accepting means to give yourself enough room to breathe.

By assuming the stance of willingness and acceptance you can open all the blinds and the windows in your house and allow life to flow through; you let fresh air and light enter into what was previously closed and dark. To be willing and accepting means to be able to walk through the swamps of your difficult history when the swamps are directly on the path that goes in a direction you care about.

To be willing and accepting means noticing that you are the sky, not the clouds; the ocean, not the waves. It means noticing that you are large enough to contain all of your experiences, just as the sky can contain any cloud and the ocean any wave.

We don't expect this foray into poetic metaphors to make any difference yet. But the sense conveyed by them may give you an idea of what we are aiming for in pursuing acceptance in this book.

If you find your mind agreeing or resisting, just thank your mind for the thought. Your mind is welcome to come along for the ride. But willingness and acceptance are states of being that minds can never learn how to achieve. Fortunately, there is more to you than just your repertoire of relating and symbolizing (see chapter 2). Even if your mind can't learn how to be willing and accepting, *you* can learn.

Why Willingness?

One reason willingness is worth trying is that it is remarkable how consistently the scientific literature reveals its value and the danger of its flip side—experiential avoidance. One reason this book is not about anger, depression, anxiety, substance abuse, chronic pain (or any of the other disturbances and disorders that thrive in modern life) is that we are trying to teach a set of skills that has extremely broad applicability, and that should empower your therapy work or self-directed efforts to change your life.

We first reviewed the literature on experiential avoidance about a decade ago (Hayes et al. 1996) and since then it has exploded. We'll discuss just a few areas to show how broadly applicable this process can be for psychological suffering.

Physical pain. In virtually every area of chronic pain, physical pathology (the objectively assessed physical damage) bears almost no relation to the amount of pain, reduced functioning, and disability (Dahl et al. 2005). The relationship between the amount of pain and degree of functioning is also weak. What predicts functioning is (a) your willingness to experience pain, and (b) your ability to act in a valued direction while experiencing it (McCracken, Vowles, and Eccleston 2004). These are precisely the processes targeted in this book. Training people how to accept their pain and how to watch it or "defuse from" their thoughts about it (see chapter 6) greatly increases their tolerance of pain (Hayes et al. 1999) and decreases the amount of disability and sick leave downtime caused by their pain (Dahl, Wilson, and Nilsson 2004).

Physical trauma, disease, and disability. In head injury, spinal injury, heart attack, and other areas of physical illness or injury, the degree of physical pathology is a very poor predictor of rehabilitation success and long-term disability. What is predictive is the patient's acceptance of the condition and the willingness to take responsibility for her or his predicament (Krause 1992; Melamed, Grosswasser, and Stern 1992; Riegal 1993).

In chronic diseases like diabetes, your acceptance of the difficult thoughts and feelings the disease gives rise to, and your willingness to act in the presence of these thoughts and feelings predict good self-management of the disease (Gregg 2004). Other health-care problems, such as smoking, show the same results (Gifford et al. 2004). ACT promotes better health management as a result of changes in your willingness to accept discomfort, unhook from your thoughts, and move toward what is most personally meaningful to you (Gifford et al. 2004; Gregg 2004).

Anxiety. Unwillingness to have anxiety predicts having anxiety in many different forms (Hayes, Strosahl, et al. 2004). For example, when exposed to the same levels of physiological arousal, experiential avoiders are more likely to feel panic than those who willingly accept their anxiety (Karekla, Forsyth, and Kelly 2004). This is particularly true if experiential avoiders are actively trying to control their anxiety sensations (Feldner et al. 2003).

Among people who habitually pull out their own hair, experiential avoidance predicts more frequent and intense urges to pull, less ability to control urges, and more hair pulling–related distress than among people who are not experientially avoidant (Begotka, Woods, and Wetterneck 2004).

People with generalized anxiety disorder are more likely to have high levels of emotional avoidance (Mennin et al. 2002), and both the amount of worry and degree of impairment they suffer correlates with experiential avoidance (Roemer et al. 2005). Even a very small amount of training in acceptance can be helpful, however. For example, just ten minutes of acceptance training made panic-disordered persons more able to face anxiety; training in distraction and suppression was not helpful (Levitt et al. 2004). Similarly, for anxious people, teaching them a simple ACT acceptance metaphor, the Chinese finger trap (see chapter 3), reduced avoidance, anxiety symptoms, and anxious thoughts more successfully than did breathing retraining (Eifert and Heffner 2003).

Childhood abuse and trauma. Childhood abuse predicts current distress to some degree, but the practice of willingness mediates that relationship (Marx and Sloan, forthcoming [b]). In other words, if you are unwilling to experience the memories, thoughts, and feelings that childhood abuse produces, you get stuck with chronic distress as an adult. However, if you are willing to experience those thoughts, memories, and feelings again, the same abuse history is significantly less destructive to your life. When people with initially equal levels of post-traumatic stress have been compared over time, research has shown that those who are willing to have these private experiences have less post-traumatic stress over time (Marx and Sloan, forthcoming [a]).

Job performance. People who are more emotionally willing to experience negative emotional experiences enjoy better mental health and do better at work over time. The effect is significantly greater than the effects of job satisfaction or emotional intelligence (Bond and Bunce 2003; Donaldson and Bond 2004).

Substance abuse. Substance abuse is typically motivated by an attempt to avoid negative private experiences (Shoal and Giancola 2001). The more substance abusers believe that drugs or alcohol reduce their negative emotions, the more likely they are to relapse (Litman et al. 1984).

Depression. Up to half of the variations in the symptoms of depression can be accounted for by a lack of acceptance and willingness (Hayes, Strosahl, et al. 2004).

This review could go on for many more pages, and deal with many more areas, but perhaps these examples are enough to make the point. The scientific literature is filled with evidence that the person's willingness to experience whatever emotion is present is of central importance to many areas of human psychological functioning.

So, why is willingness so important? Perhaps some first person accounts of the importance of willingness will be more convincing than our capsule review of the literature. Read the following statements and see if they hold true for you, too.

- Why willingness? Because when I am struggling against my painful experiences, the struggle seems to make them all the more painful.

- Why willingness? Because when I move away from the pain that I meet when I'm pursuing what I value most, I also move away from the richness of life that those valued actions bring to me.

- Why willingness? Because when I try to close myself off from the painful parts of my past, I also close myself off from the helpful things I've learned from my past.

- Why willingness? Because I experience a loss of vitality when I am not willing.

- Why willingness? Because my experience tells me that being unwilling just doesn't work.

- Why willingness? Because it is a normal human process to feel pain, and it is inhumane and unloving to try to hold myself to a different standard.

- Why willingness? Because "living in my experience," that is, living in the moment, seems potentially more rewarding than "living in my mind."

- Why willingness? Because I absolutely know how my pain works when I am unwilling, and I'm sick and tired of it. It's time to change my whole agenda, not just the moves I make inside a control and avoidance agenda.

- Why willingness? Because I have suffered enough.

EXERCISE: Why Willingness?

Now it's your turn. Write down three or four of your own responses that come to mind. If you feel resistance, just notice that, and in a kind, compassionate way allow yourself to feel resistant, and then return to the question, bringing your sense of resistance with you.

- Why willingness? Because _____

  _____

- Why willingness? Because _____

  _____

- Why willingness? Because _____

  _____

- Why willingness? Because _____

  _____

WILLINGNESS AND DISTRESS

Brown University psychologist Rick Brown and his colleagues (forthcoming) have recently demonstrated that people who cannot make room for their distressing feelings have a very hard time with self-control.

For example, they worked with a group of chronic smokers trying to end their addiction to nicotine by using a self-help book.

Before the subjects began seriously trying to quit, however, Brown set three preliminary tasks for them. He had them hold their breath for as long as they were able; solve simple but confusing math problems faster and faster until they gave up; and breathe carbon dioxide (CO_2) (which creates anxiety symptoms), until they indicated they wanted to stop breathing the CO_2. The great majority of those who were good at all three tasks were able to stop smoking. Very few of those who did poorly on the three tasks were able to break their addiction (Brown et al., forthcoming). In other words, if you cannot feel your distressing feelings, you cannot take proper care of your own health. No wonder experiential avoidance predicts a gradual worsening quality of life over time (Hayes, Strosahl, et al. 2004).

EXERCISE: Being Willingly Out of Breath

Now, you are about to find out whether you can use acceptance to increase your ability to sit with your uncomfortable emotions. Get a watch and sit in a place where you won't be disturbed for a few minutes. You are going to see how long you can hold your breath again, but this time, as you hold it, follow the instructions listed below. Read them over several times until you are confident you will be able to remember to do them, even when feeling painful feelings start up for you. Do not start yet. Don't start until you see the word "start." Just read over the following bulleted list:

- When you do the exercise and the urge to breathe becomes stronger, we want you to do the following: Notice exactly where the urge to breathe begins and ends in your body. Locate exactly where you feel the urge to breathe.

- See if you can allow that feeling to be precisely there and, at the same time, keep on holding your breath. Turn your willingness dial all the way up! Just feel the feeling and do not breathe … think of this as a cool opportunity to feel something you rarely feel.

- Notice any thoughts that come up, and gently thank your mind for the thought, without being controlled by that thought. Watch out for sneaky thoughts that can quickly lead to breathing before you decide to breathe. After all, who is in charge of your life? You or your word machine?

- Notice other emotions that may emerge other than the urge to breathe. See if you can make room for those emotions, as well.

- Survey your entire body and notice that, in addition to the urge to breathe, your body contains other sensations and continues to function.

- Stay with the commitment to hold your breath as long as you can. As the urge to breathe becomes stronger, imagine that you are continuously creating that urge deliberately. Close your eyes and see if you can replicate this urge in your imagination, divorced from your body. With every pang in your chest, every worry you have about passing out, every instinct to breath, shift it from something unwelcome that is being visited upon you to something you are creating deliberately, just for the sake of feeling what that feels like.

This new urge is formally the same, but it is of your creation. Do you need to be threatened by your own creation?

- Before beginning to hold your breath, list one or two other actions you might do during this exercise that might help you to be aware of all of your feelings, thoughts, sensations, and urges while you are holding fast to the goal of holding your breath. Write down only acceptance strategies, not experiential control or suppression strategies.

_____

_____

Read the bulleted list several times, until you feel you completely understand the instructions. You can leave the book open as you do the exercise, so you can glance at pages 49 and 50 and remind yourself of things to do while really feeling what it feels like to want to breathe while not breathing.

You are ready to see if it is possible to better control your behavior (holding your breath) by learning to accept and make room for your thoughts and feelings.

Now, **start:**

Take a deep breath and hold it as long as you can. When you are finished, write down how long you held it: _____ seconds.

Describe your experience during this exercise.

_____

_____

_____

Did the aversiveness of not breathing tend to come and go? When did it go up or down?

_____

_____

_____

How did your mind try to persuade you to breathe before you really had to?

_____

_____

_____

What was the sneakiest thing your mind did?

_____

_____

_____

Do you see any possible implications this simple exercise might have for how your life has been going, especially in the area you've been struggling with? If so, what do you see?

_____

_____

_____

Now look back at the amount of time you were able to hold you breath before you started reading this chapter. If you weren't able to see any possible applications for this exercise in the areas you've been struggling with, does this comparison open up any new doors for you?

_____

_____

_____

The types of strategies we asked you to employ to help you hold your breath longer are the very kinds of techniques we will introduce you to in the remainder of this book. If you were able to hold your breath longer the second time around, that provides some evidence that the information in this book may be worthwhile to you. Of course, we will be applying this idea to more complex problems than the simple urge to breath. However, the principle is the same. If you commit to a particular act, use mindfulness and defusion strategies when your mind starts giving you problems with pursuing that path, and move forward accepting what your mind offers you; you will be in a better position to live a full and meaningful life—with or without unpleasant thoughts, emotions, and sensations.

THE "WILLINGNESS TO CHANGE" QUESTION

Remember the two dials on the experiential radio we discussed in chapter 3? Suppose it was the case that to live the life you really want, the way you want to live it, it is first necessary to turn your Willingness dial all the way up. That means you would be willing to feel whatever feelings, memories, thoughts, or bodily sensations take place in your life. You would feel these fully and not erect any psychological defenses against them.

Said another way, suppose that in order to live a healthy, vital, meaningful, and satisfying life you needed to give up trying to control your internal thoughts and feelings before you could move in the direction you want to go. If that was what was required, to what degree would you be willing to do that? (We are not assuming that you know how to do that yet, we are only asking about your openness to that path.) If 1 means totally unwilling and 100 means totally willing, how willing would you be to begin to experience what your history gives you, focusing your control strategies on your actions rather than your insides? Write that number here: _____

If you find yourself writing a low number, are you holding on to the idea that a low number means that you will experience much less pain. But if that is what your experience has taught you, you wouldn't have had a reason to pick up this book. A lower number doesn't mean less pain, it mean less room to live. We aren't asking if you believe that willingness will work. We are asking if willingness is needed in order to live a healthy, vital, meaningful, and satisfying life, would you move in that direction? If you still find yourself writing down a low number, reconsider your answer and see if you want to stick to it.

What shows up for you when you think about this? In the space provided below, write your thoughts on this matter:

_____

_____

_____

If you had been willing to experience fully what your personal history gave you while you were engaged in actions that were important to you, how would your life have been different than it has been?

_____

_____

_____

_____

We don't expect this to make a difference yet. Your mind may be telling you that kind of willingness is impossible or that it would condemn you to constant misery. If so, just thank your mind for its input and don't argue back. It could be that pain is not really synonymous with suffering. It could be that pain plus unwillingness to feel that pain equals suffering. We won't argue it either way; your own experience is the final judge. But if you are ready to begin learning new strategies that eventually will make that kind of willingness possible, turn the page.

CHAPTER 5

The Trouble with Thoughts

In this chapter you will start to explore the ways that your mind produces thoughts. Have you ever considered how pervasive thinking itself is? Sometimes you may not even be aware of this process. Like the rhythmic hum of a heater circulating air through a room, the mind chugs along, doing what it was designed by evolution to do: categorize, predict, explain, compare, worry, judge. And just like the hum of a heater, you can go for long periods of time without even noticing it's there.

If we are going to do something different with thinking, first we need to catch the process in flight. Otherwise, we are constantly dealing with the unfortunate behavioral results of buying into our thoughts; that is, we tend to take our own thoughts as gospel truth, missing the pivotal point that can create their destructive effects.

You may have had the experience of driving your car and suddenly noticing that you've driven for miles without any awareness of the world outside the car. Your driving habits may be so automatic that it is quite possible for you to drive mindlessly.

The situation you are in with thought-directed behavior can be compared to finding that you've driven off the road and down an embankment while you were in that blank state of mind. It wouldn't be wise to try to "solve" the repeated problem of driving into in a ditch by changing the wheels on your car. It's too late in the process for that to help at all, and such changes are largely beside the point anyway.

Better to back up to the moment you turned the steering wheel. It is that moment and that action that caused you to leave the road and drive down the embankment. What you first need to look for are the hand-scribbled signs on the side of the road that pointed to the right saying, "This Way." Though you may not consciously be aware of them right now, such road signs are your thoughts. They are part (but only part!) of what leads you to drive over that embankment in the first place.

Aaron Beck, the father of cognitive therapy, used the term *distancing* to refer to the process of objectively noticing what you are thinking (this is why ACT was originally called "comprehensive distancing" when it was first developed [Hayes 1987]). In Beck's approach and in most forms of scientifically based therapy, however, distancing is only a first step in evaluating and disputing thought. Therapists use this method to teach clients to detect logical errors, search for new evidence, and change emotionally disturbing thoughts. It's something like seeing the sign on the side of the road, and trying stop the car in order to get out and destroy or rewrite what the sign says; that way when you see it in the future, you won't be tempted to drive over the embankment again.

We take a different approach, one that is simpler and, as current evidence suggests, more closely linked to positive outcomes. What we need to learn to do is to look *at* thought, rather than *from* thought. We need to notice the hand-scribbled sign in the same way we would notice graffiti. We don't have to follow or resist the sign, but we do need to notice it. We can notice it in the way we might notice the temperature of the room, the sounds from a CD player, or the smell of the air. The sign itself doesn't necessarily mean that you have to do anything, and it doesn't mean anything about you, the way it doesn't matter whether the graffiti is written in block letters or script, the air is hot or cold, the sound melodic or monotonous, or the smell sweet or sour. What matters is noticing the sign.

Because thought refers to something and "means" something it creates an illusion. When we think about something, it seems to us that we are really dealing with that thing, much as the child in chapter 2 thought about the gub-gub. When we evaluate something, it appears as though that thing is either enhanced or minimized depending on the content of the evaluation.

The signs on the side of the road that our minds construct are not just simple directions. They can be quite elaborate; they can even be what we call reasonable. "Get out of that relationship! You're getting too attached, and he is too nice. You will be badly hurt," says one sign. And even if you really want love in your life (if that is the road you've chosen), you may find yourself down in the ditch with yet another relationship smoldering from the impact of the crash, saying it was because he was "too into his work" or because he was "smothering me" and so on. To change a pattern like this you need to get back to the pivotal point when you first saw the sign. That is the focus of this chapter.

The foregoing doesn't mean you need to watch your thoughts obsessively, or that the only way to avoid driving over the embankment is to be ever-vigilant. As you learn to catch more of those moments when the signs first pop up, you will work out new ways to relate to them. (That work will begin in earnest in chapter 6.) As you build these new habits of mind, eventually you will be able to drive mindlessly for longer periods of time without driving off the road. Not that mindlessness is a goal, but no one is always mindful, and it's nice to know that, eventually, habits can work for you rather than against you, if you lay down the right habits. Laying down those new ways of relating to thoughts, however, requires you to catch more of these thoughts as they happen.

THOUGHT PRODUCTION

Your mind's job is to protect you from danger; to help you survive. It does so by constantly categorizing present events, relating them to analyses of the past and predictions of the future, and evaluating what has been or might be obtained by action. After building up a head of steam over the last 100,000 years it is unlikely that the human mind will stop doing these things anytime soon. Like it or not, inside your skull, you have a "word-generating machine" relating one event to another from morning to night.

It is impossible to stop thinking, especially deliberately. When we do things deliberately, we create a verbal path (a rule) and try to follow it. So, when we deliberately try to stop thinking, we create the thought that goes, "we shouldn't be thinking a thought," and we try to follow it. Unfortunately, since this verbal path is itself a thought, the process merely mocks us. The exercises in chapter 2 that demonstrated the internal inconsistency in thought-suppression explore this point in greater detail.

Your next step is to begin to notice your thoughts, in flight, in real-time. Although we are thinking constantly, we consciously notice that we are thinking only occasionally. Anything that comes so naturally and occurs so commonly recedes into the background. How often do you notice that you blink your eyes, or breathe?

We Are Fish Swimming in Our Thoughts

Fish swim in water naturally. They don't "know" they are under water, they just swim. Thinking is like this for human beings. Thoughts are our water. We are so immersed in them that we are hardly aware they are there. Swimming in our thoughts is our natural state. You can't take a fish out of the water and expect it to live as a fish. But what would happen if the fish became aware of the water?

EXERCISE: What Are You Thinking Right Now?

Try writing down your thoughts as they run through your mind right now. Take a few minutes and write down as many thoughts as you can, while they are occurring, in the space provided below:

_____

_____

_____

_____

_____

_____

_____

_____

_____

_____

What did you find? How many thoughts were you able to describe? As you wrote, wasn't it the case that other thoughts about the thoughts you were thinking popped up? If you stumbled for a moment and you thought something like, "I'm not thinking anything," did you understand that this too was a thought?

It is very likely that the small space above wasn't nearly enough to contain all of the thoughts you were thinking in those few moments. Consider what this means. If there was a constant stream of thought in the last few moments, aren't other moments much the same? If so, hundreds or (more likely) thousands of these events are occurring every day. It's no wonder we regularly drive off the road. Often the road itself is poorly lit (that's why we'll do some work with values in chapters 11 and 12), the signs at the side of the road are frequent and confusing (much of that seems built-into the human mind), and we give these signs power through our habits of mind.

One primary habit of mind we will work on dismantling is the habit of taking your thoughts literally. If thoughts are what they say they are, any experience that can program a thought is an experience that can control your behavior. When we take thoughts literally, we are at the mercy of every random experience life throws at us. Harvard psychologist Ellen Langer (1989) described an interesting example of how literal thought works when she considered the virtues of saliva.

The Virtues of Saliva

You've probably not thought much about the virtues of saliva but they are many. Feel how warm and moist the inside of your mouth is. Feel the slipperiness of your tongue inside your mouth. If your mouth were entirely dry, your tongue would rub against your mouth's interior in a very irritating way. If you've ever had "cottonmouth," you know how unpleasant that can be. Now, try swallowing and feel how your saliva makes the action of swallowing slick and smooth, comfortable and easy.

Imagine how it would feel if you didn't have any saliva. Have you ever tried to swallow when your throat was so dry that you felt as if there were sand in it? Saliva has antiseptic qualities that naturally wash away germs and protect your teeth and gums. That's why conditions that restrict saliva flow quickly lead to tooth decay and gum disease. For example, methamphetamine (also known as "speed") produces severe dry mouth, and after just a few years of use, meth addicts' teeth literally crumble and fall out (so-called "meth mouth") because chronic loss of saliva removes the protection that saliva provides.

Saliva also helps us to predigest our food. When we take the time to chew and swallow, food easily slides down the throat, and the stomach has a much easier time breaking it down. If you've ever wolfed down large quantities of food without chewing it, you know how it can create a heavy lump in your stomach, as your body struggles to compensate for your lack of chewing. Saliva is a truly wonderful substance.

Now imagine a clean, spotless, beautiful crystal wineglass and imagine that each time you feel you have a little extra saliva in your mouth, you release it into the glass. You keep doing this until the clean glass is full.

Next imagine this. Really imagine it. Try to picture it and bring the feelings that would come up for you to your mind. Imagine that you take hold of the wineglass full of your own spit, you tilt the glass into your mouth, and then you slurp down all the saliva you have collected in big gulps, until the glass is empty.

What was that like for you to imagine? For most of us, the idea of gulping down a wineglass full of our own saliva is disgusting. It's gross. It turns the stomach just to imagine it.

Isn't this strange? It's *your* saliva! You produce gallons of the stuff every day and you do indeed drink it down—all day long. Without it, you couldn't eat. As stated above, saliva has many virtues. However, the idea of drinking a glass of it is among the more disgusting acts we can imagine. The actual day-to-day experience of saliva is one thing. Thinking about saliva as a beverage is another. In this case, a wonderful substance becomes a disgusting substance. Why is that so?

WHY THINKING HAS SUCH AN IMPACT

Thoughts have meaning because they are symbolic; they are symbolic because they are arbitrarily and mutually related to something else. When we think, there is a mutual relationship established between the thought and the event we are thinking about. Each influences the other.

It is this process that makes thinking useful. Consider this scenario: "Suppose all of the doors and windows in the room you are in right now were locked. How would you get out?" Watch what your mind does. As you arrive at some options, you are dealing with real events in a symbolic manner. You are relating thoughts as if you were manipulating the actual objects to which they refer. This is part of the utility of language. We don't have to try out the various options for escape in reality; we can try them out in imagination. Remember the example of the slotted screw, the toothbrush, and the lighter in chapter 2?

Problems arrive, however, when this process is (a) taken to extremes, and (b) applied to all thought. *Cognitive fusion* refers to the tendency to allow thought to dominate other sources of behavioral regulation because of the failure to pay attention to the process of relating over and above the products of relating. To put it into less abstract terms, cognitive fusion involves treating our thoughts as if they are what they say they are.

When you're imagining how to escape from a locked room, this process is unlikely to be harmful. Suppose you think, "I'll call my friend for help on my cell phone." The symbolic event of "calling your friend" on the "cell phone" in your imagination, and an actual event of calling your friend are two different things, but, in this case, it doesn't matter much if the two are treated as if they were the same. You can picture your cell phone, and picture punching in your friend's phone number, just as you might, in actual fact, reach for your cell phone and push the keys to call your friend's number. For most forms of problem solving, thoughts are useful for that reason.

But in other situations cognitive fusion can be quite harmful. For example, think of all the "I am" statements you produce in relation to your pain: "I am so depressed." "I am so anxious." "God, I'm so stressed out." "I went to the therapist and she told me I am obsessive-compulsive." "I am so tired of being in constant pain." This kind of language puts you in a place where you actually identify yourself with your pain. Cognitive fusion means you are taking these statements as literal truths and, eventually, you begin to believe that you, in fact, are your pain. It becomes very difficult to see that your pain does not define you, in part because it is very difficult to see that these are thoughts that your mind has produced.

Similarly, since much of the content of thought is evaluative, cognitive fusion also means that evaluations can become attached to events as if they were in the event, not just in our thoughts about the event. This transforms not only the thought but also the functions of the actual event. For example, although the physiological functions of saliva are not aversive, the functions of language can make them so. Drinking saliva is "disgusting" because of cognitive fusion. We swallow saliva all day long quite happily; and thirsty, nonverbal animals presented with a bowl of saliva might lap it up, as we say, "without a thought." For us, however, the very idea makes us want to retch (notice we just said the very "idea" makes us want to retch).

There are few situations in which drinking a wineglass full of spit would be useful, so, for the most part, our distaste for the idea is harmless. Often, cognitive fusion is not a problem. If the process is allowed to spread, however, any evaluated event can become a target without awareness of what has actually taken place, and that can be very harmful indeed.

For example, any emotional reaction to an aversive event will itself usually be evaluated negatively. What we call "anxiety" tends to appear following an aversive event (e.g., the hypothetical dog you supposedly kicked in chapter 1 could be said to be "anxious" when you come home for that reason). We notice that emotional reaction, and we label both the aversive event and the emotional results as "bad."

It is only a small step from applying a negative label to emotional responses, to targeting those same responses for direct change efforts—even if such efforts aren't healthy or needed. Sadness, anxiety, boredom, pain, insecurity, and so forth will be avoided or escaped, even if the process of escaping them is harmful, simply because they are "bad" emotions. That's probably one reason why the simple belief "anxiety is bad" is correlated with many forms of psychological problems, from anxiety disorders to depression (Hayes, Strosahl, et al. 2004).

Experiential Avoidance and Cognitive Fusion

Throughout the earlier chapters of this book we have discussed experiential avoidance and why it poses such a problem. You've read about studies that suggest experiential avoidance is harmful and have tracked your own avoidance strategies to see how well they have worked (or haven't worked). Now it's time to link those ideas up to what we are exploring in this chapter. Put simply, the root cause of experiential avoidance is cognitive fusion.

Suppose you have a thought that you must avoid some difficult private experience (an emotion, thought, memory, or bodily sensation) because "it is too much to bear." Something that is "too much to bear" must not be borne or harm may be caused. Your mind, as we've discussed throughout this book, evolved over the millennia to help keep you from harm. If you become fused with the idea that this private experience is "too much to bear," then the experience manifests itself as though it were "too much to bear." That is, you identify the initial experience with this second thought so completely that they fuse themselves together. Once they are fused, you will naturally attempt to avoid this experience. That is why fusion underlies experiential avoidance. Let's look at an example to draw this point out a bit more clearly.

Suppose you are suffering from depression. Let's also suppose that you have tied yourself to the idea that such sad feelings "must not be borne." What will you do when these feelings come up? It's likely you'll do everything in your power to avoid them. You will avoid personal interactions that may occasion you feeling sad. You will stop going places that may occasion you feeling depressed. You will even try to stop feeling the feelings and thinking the thoughts that you believe drive the depression. Even if pursuing such a path means you drive off the road you really want to be on, you will still pursue it because the feelings you are having "must not be borne." This is what cognitive fusion leads to.

Assuming this is true, that means any road sign you encounter could lead off the road down into an embankment if it pushes your buttons sufficiently. The question is: What are those buttons?

Thinking Causes Pain

The two biggest buttons are the processes of evaluation and self-conceptualization. Thoughts, even those you use to soothe your mind, create pain in two ways: they bring painful events to mind, and they amplify the impact of pain through what cognitive fusion leads to, that is, avoidance. For example, think of a painful memory. It doesn't matter what it is. Just allow yourself to think of a painful memory, and spend a few moments observing it.

You just engaged in the first method by which minds create pain. The fact that we are able to bring to mind past events and to predict future ones is an integral part of being able to use language for verbal problem solving. This is an evaluative process. Language cannot work without these abilities or processes. The processes cannot be changed because you would have to become nonverbal to change them. The methods people use to try to eliminate them (like abusing alcohol or drugs, engaging in compulsive activities, or dissociating) themselves create horrific amounts of second-order pain.

The second process, self-conceptualization, is as important as evaluation (perhaps even more so). You can learn to change the process by which you perceive yourself. But to work on this process you must start with the pain you've been avoiding.

Keeping a Pain Diary

For the next week, using the exercise below, we would like you to track your pain to try to bring into the light of day some of the thoughts that co-occur when you are struggling. This will take some time and dedication, but it will pay off. Make seven copies of the exercise worksheet so that you'll have a new one to fill out every day. If you feel you need more space to write than what we provide here, you can set up your own worksheets in a journal or on your computer. However you do it, make sure that you carry your Daily Pain Diary with you at all times during the next week.

Whenever you find yourself struggling with emotional discomfort, difficult thoughts, painful memories, uncomfortable bodily sensations, or unwelcome urges, pull out your pain journal and record that information. You'll see that the journal page is divided into twenty-four-hour periods. It may be that you won't fill in something for every hour. (For example, it isn't likely that you're going to wake up in the middle of the night to fill out your pain diary, although you certainly could do that if you are up.) Just fill it in when you actually feel yourself struggling with some psychological or physical discomfort.

If you can't manage to get to your pain diary at the very moment you're having a problem (for example, when you're in a meeting), just go back and do the writing when you have the time. The main point here is that you should be diligent in completing this activity so that you'll have a catalog of what kind of pain is troubling you and what is going on for you when you feel that pain.

It would be especially worthwhile if you focused particularly on the core struggles you identified in chapter 1 when you did the exercise called "Your Suffering Inventory." You don't have to focus exclusively on this, but it would be a good idea to pay particular attention to the times when your reactions associated with those problems appear.

Most of the questions in this exercise are fairly straightforward. You should be able to answer them with relative ease. First look at the sample diary to get a feel for how to fill in your diary.

An Example of a Daily Pain Diary

Suppose someone who is stuck in a dead-end job and struggles with social anxiety filled out the Daily Pain Diary. It might look something like this:

Day: *Monday*

Time	What were you doing or what happened?	What did you start struggling with psychologically?	What thoughts (in addition to any in the third column) came up in association with that struggle?
12 am			
1 am			
2 am			
3 am			
4 am			
5 am			
6 am	*I woke up feeling pissed off*	*How much I hate my job*	*I'm wasting my life in this stupid job*
7 am			
8 am	*I was driving in for a meeting with my boss*	*I started to notice my heart beating faster and I thought "Oh God"*	*I can't stand this feeling of anxiety*
9 am			
10 am	*I had to make a "cold call" on a possible sale*	*I felt like I might be getting sick. I thought "not again"*	*If I get panicky, I might lose control of myself*

11 am		
12 pm	I was eating a cheap meal at a burrito place	My life doesn't seem to be going anywhere	I will always be like this
1 pm	I was feeling bored. I looked at my coworkers making calls in the "boiler room"	I started to sweat and I wanted to run out of the room	It's not fair I have to struggle when others are doing so well
2 pm			
3 pm	Someone hung up on me	Felt a strong and frightening urge to smash the phone	Everyone else is doing better than I am
4 pm			
5 pm			
6 pm	Relieved work was over	A feeling of loneliness and emptiness came up for me	I'm just a worthless person
7 pm			
8 pm			
9 pm			
10 pm	Lay down in my bed	Felt lonely. I thought "no one wants to be with me."	I'm not worthy of love
11 pm			

EXERCISE: Your Daily Pain Diary

Day: _____

Time	What were you doing or what happened?	What did you start struggling with psychologically?	What thoughts (in addition to any in the third column) came up in association with that struggle?
12 am			
1 am			
2 am			
3 am			
4 am			
5 am			
6 am			
7 am			
8 am			
9 am			
10 am			

11 am			
12 pm			
1 pm			
2 pm			
3 pm			
4 pm			
5 pm			
6 pm			
7 pm			
8 pm			
9 pm			
10 pm			
11 pm			

Looking at Your Daily Pain Diary

When you've kept your Daily Pain Diary for a week, you should have a better idea of the situations in which you struggle, the content of the struggle, and the thoughts that come up in association with your struggle.

Now, look back over your entries for the week and see whether there are particular thoughts, feelings, or events that tend to lead to you struggling (the items in the second column on the left). Write down any consistencies that you've observed on the six lines below. (Don't worry if you haven't observed six consistencies. One or two will do if that's all you see.)

1. _____

2. _____

3. _____

4. _____

5. _____

6. _____

Now look at what you tend to struggle with psychologically (items in the third column). Avoid externalizing. In other words, try to concentrate on what's happening for you internally. If external events came up for you, see if these items would fit better in the second column. As you write down consistencies, see if you can also categorize them into thoughts, feelings, bodily sensations, memories, or behavioral urges, and if you can do that, add that descriptive category in parentheses after you describe your struggle. Write down any consistencies that you see on the lines below:

1. _____

2. _____

3. _____

4. _____

5. _____

6. _____

Now look at the thoughts that came up in association with your psychological struggles (the items in the fourth and final column). Look at your consistent patterns. If you find that looking at your thoughts leads to more thoughts (that is, what do you think when you read your diary?), you can put these on the list as well. Write down the kinds of thoughts you tend to think on the lines below.

As you write down the consistencies, see whether you can classify them into evaluations (judgments you make about things); predictions (attempts to forecast the future); post-dictions (attempts to understand or sort through the past; this may occur if you are engaged in "what if-ing" past experiences);

or self-conceptualizations (judgments made about yourself; these often come in the form of "I am" statements); and if so, add that descriptive category in parentheses after you describe the thought.

For example, "I can't stand this anxiety" would take (evaluation); "I'm worthless" would take (evaluation and self-conceptualization). Write down any consistencies that you see on the lines below:

1. _____

2. _____

3. _____

4. _____

5. _____

6. _____

Finally, write down any consistencies you see in the relationships between columns two, three, and four. Are certain feelings and thoughts more likely in certain situations? If so, write them down (for example, "It seems that when I withdraw, then I struggle with loneliness or anxiety, and then I criticize myself.")

1. _____

2. _____

3. _____

4. _____

5. _____

6. _____

It's important that you don't grab hold of these formulations and try to solve them (for example, thinking, "I should stop criticizing myself"). We will work on what to do with them shortly. Right now, the job is more basic: let's see if you can look at what's been happening. Your job right now is simply to sit with the knowledge you collect.

LOOKING *AT* YOUR THOUGHTS RATHER THAN *FROM* YOUR THOUGHTS

If you are like most people on the planet, in reviewing your list, you probably discovered that when you are in the midst of struggle, you aren't able to look at your thoughts consistently. In that moment, you are probably looking from the thought; that is, you considered the content of your thought from the point of view of the thoughts you had already recorded. That's what we mean when we say that we look from our thoughts.

Does this bulleted list summarize some of what's been going on for you?

- You've been struggling at times to control what you think or feel.

- You've come to define yourself and the content of your experience in accordance with your thoughts.

- You tend to take your thoughts literally, so you see life from the vantage point of your thoughts.

- These thoughts you are fused with argue or advocate for more struggle.

- Struggle isn't working.

When put together, these factors create a dangerous set of circumstances that contribute to your suffering. If these five things hold true, then you are guaranteed to suffer. However, rather than trying to control what you think or feel, what if you could learn to see that you are merely having thoughts and experiencing emotions? The act of thinking is not dangerous in and of itself, rather the danger lies in the point at which you "buy into your thoughts"; that is, the point at which you take your thoughts literally, even if your experience tells you that this is a context in which cognitive fusion is not only unhelpful, it is also dangerous.

THE MIND-TRAIN

Sometimes it doesn't hurt to take your thoughts literally. When dealing purely with external problem solving, cognitive fusion is relatively harmless. That's not so for the internal world of the self. For that world, there are other skills to be learned: how to watch your thoughts without belief or disbelief, without entanglement, without struggle. This is the focus of the chapter 6, but you can prepare for that work with this simple exercise.

EXERCISE: Watching the Mind-Train

Imagine that you are standing at a railway bridge gazing down at three sets of train tracks. A slow mining train is on each set of tracks moving away from you. Each train is composed of a string of little cars carrying ore. Seemingly endless, all three chug slowly along underneath the bridge.

Now, as you look down, imagine that the train to the left carries only the "ore" of things you notice in the present moment. That ore is composed of sensations, perceptions, and emotions. It carries things like the sounds you hear; sweaty palms you feel; skipped heartbeats you sense; sadness you notice; and so forth. The middle train carries only your thoughts: your evaluations, your predictions, your self-conceptualizations, and so on. The train on your right carries your urges to act; your pull to avoid and look away; and your efforts to change the subject. Looking down on these three tracks can be seen as a metaphor for looking at your mind.

Now, find a comfortable chair to sit in for a while in a spot where you won't be disturbed and you can be quiet. Begin the exercise by thinking of something you've been struggling with lately, then close your eyes and picture the three tracks. Your job will be to stay on the bridge, looking. If you find your mind has gone somewhere else, or if you discover that you are in one of the cars chugging down the railroad track, struggling with its content, such as your judgment that you will never amount to anything or your belief that nothing good can ever happen to you in the future, this can be a very important moment (in fact, it is a major purpose of this exercise). Notice what just hooked you. File that away, and then mentally return to the bridge over the tracks and look down once again. If you are able to stay on the bridge, your experience might look like figure 5.1. If you disappear into the content, your experience might look like figure 5.2.

Figure 5.1: The mind-train.

Figure 5.2: Getting stuck on the mind-train.

Remember, present sensations, perceptions, and emotions are in the railroad car to your left. Your thoughts are in the middle car. Coping strategies and urges to do something are in the car on the right. See if you can stay on the bridge, but if you leave it, just notice what happened and then return to the bridge. Take at least three minutes just to watch what comes up for you.

Now, in the following chart, write down some of what you noticed when you were standing on the bridge observing the three sets of railroad cars:

The Ore on the Mind-Train		
Present sensations, perceptions, and emotions	Thoughts	Urges, actions, and coping strategies

If you psychologically disappeared, didn't get the exercise started, or rode off with something in a car, what happened just before that? What sort of content came up that took you off the bridge? (Some especially common ones are memories with strong emotions attached, thoughts about the exercise itself, and thoughts about your future.) Take a few minutes to note these things in the space below:

_____

_____

_____

_____

_____

These are things that "hooked" you, very likely because of cognitive fusion. Your job is to learn how to stay on the bridge longer and, when you leave the bridge, to get back there more quickly. This is the task we will turn to in chapter 6.

CHAPTER 6

Having a Thought Versus Buying a Thought

Of course, there's nothing wrong with thinking. Language and cognition have allowed humans to be enormously successful in an evolutionary sense, and people who are good at them generally do well in many areas, especially in their professions. Our problem-solving skills have allowed us to reshape the world we live in.

The problem arises when we can look only "from our thoughts" rather than "at our thoughts." That narrowness and rigidity can be costly because in some areas of life taking literally what your mind tells you is not the best approach. This is particularly true in regard to our own internal, emotional pain.

Consider what happens when we apply, say, temporal and evaluative relations to an object in our external environment. We can imagine what we might be able to do with it; we can picture what might happen; we can evaluate the image that our mind created. The ability to do this in an infinite number of ways can be helpful. We can easily test the workability of any concrete action implied by our thoughts. If, for example, you suppose that a hammer can break a nutshell, you can strike a nut with a hammer and test your supposition.

When applied to internal feelings and sensations however, thoughts are more entangling, harder to test, and thus more arbitrary. Look at how evaluations take place. Suppose you have a repetitious thought that goes, "I'm scum." It is not obvious what criteria of "workability" could test that thought. (Metaphorically, what nut can you hit with the "I'm scum" hammer?) The test is whether it is really true. But that is a fool's errand. Your mind can justify any relation. For example, pick out any inanimate object in your room right now. Now, find things to criticize about this object. If you stay with this task, you'll always be able to find things to criticize.

To directly challenge such internally focused evaluations just makes the mind busier and more evaluative. Try hard to think this thought and see if your mind doesn't get busier—and more evaluative: "I'm perfect." Give it a moment and try hard to think that thought.

What happened? Did the sky open up and peace begin to reign now that you know you are perfect? Unlikely. For most of us, a thought like that quickly dissolves into an argument (e.g., "No, I'm not" or "But I have a lot of faults"). In the external world, you can hit the nut and be done with it. Internally, you can climb inside your mind and take up permanent residence there.

There is an alternative: you can learn to look *at* your thoughts rather than *from* them. These *cognitive defusion techniques* are a core component of ACT. They help you to make the distinction between the world as structured by your thoughts, and thinking as an ongoing process. When your thoughts are about you yourself, defusion can help you to distinguish between the person doing the thinking and the verbal categories you apply to yourself through thinking. Defusion leads to peace of mind, not because the mental war necessarily stops but because you are not living inside the war zone anymore.

"Defusion" is a made-up word—you won't find it in the dictionary. We use it because in normal contexts words and the events they refer to can be treated almost as if they were the same thing: the two are "fused" (from the Latin root meaning "poured together"). Remember the triangle that described the relational frames established by a human infant around an imaginary creature called a gub-gub and the sound "wooo" this creature makes?" We pointed out that when these verbal relations form, and the child is stuck with a diaper pin while you are saying "wooo," then gub-gubs (not just the sound "wooo") could become fearful to the baby.

In Relational Frame Theory (RFT) we call this effect a *transformation of functions*. Normally, what therapists try to do with such matters is to change the fear associated with gub-gubs (e.g., through exposure to the feared event without anything bad happening such as being stuck by a diaper pin), or if we were dealing with an adult in psychotherapy, to rearrange the verbal relations (e.g., "wooo" is not the same as "gub-gub," so it is irrational to fear gub-gubs). RFT suggests that we can affect the transformation of functions themselves. This is precisely what defusion is designed to accomplish. Let us explain.

When you learn to view your thoughts as thoughts, occurring in the here and now, you still "know what they mean" (the verbal relations are still there; that is, you still know to what your thoughts refer). But the illusion dissolves that the thing being thought about is present merely when you think about it. This greatly reduces the impact of symbols. You may have noticed this yourself. You may have noticed that the thought, "I am having the feeling that I am anxious," is quite different from the thought, "God, I am so anxious!" The first statement is more defused than the second. For that reason, it is less anxiety-provoking. When you learn how to defuse language, it becomes easier to be willing, to be present, to be conscious, and to live the life you value, even with the normal chatter going on inside your head.

By the end of this chapter, you will not only learn some cognitive defusion techniques that ACT therapists use with their clients, you will learn how to create your own. You will also learn how to recognize the telltale signs that you are fused with your thoughts, so you will know when these techniques might be needed to restore you to better psychological balance.

COGNITIVE DEFUSION: SEPARATING YOUR THOUGHTS FROM THEIR REFERENTS

This part of the book will describe and explain a number of different cognitive defusion techniques. These techniques don't necessarily move in a specific predisposed order, in that they don't teach one skill that then leads to another skill in a particular sequence. Rather, they are a set of techniques that intertwine and overlap with one another. Some of the same concepts may be repeated in many different techniques. We've presented them here in an order that we think makes sense and will lead you to a better understanding of the principles of cognitive defusion.

Defusion techniques are not methods for eliminating or managing pain. They are methods for learning how to be present in the here and now in a broader and more flexible way. Suppose you put your hands over your face and someone asks you, "What do hands look like?" You might answer, "They are all dark." If you held your hands out a few inches away, you might add, "they have fingers and lines in them." In a similar way, getting some distance from your thoughts allows you to see them for what they are.

The point is to break through the illusion of language, so that you can notice the process of thinking (i.e., creating relations among events) as it happens rather than only noticing the products of that process—your thoughts. When you think a thought, it structures your world. When you see a thought you can still see how it structures your world (you understand what it means), but you also see that you are doing the structuring. That awareness gives you a little more room for flexibility. It would be as if you always wore yellow sunglasses and forgot you were wearing them. Defusion is like taking off your glasses and holding them out, several inches away from your face; then you can see how they make the world appear to be yellow, instead of seeing only the yellow world.

After you master defusion, you can make an informed judgment about whether it helps you to be more flexible in living the way you want to live. The best way to do this is practice, practice, practice. You won't be able to make these techniques a part of your behavioral response patterns without practicing them. You can't just read them passively and hope to "get it." Take these skills with you in your life and apply them. Let your experience be your guide. Practice doesn't make perfect, it makes permanent.

Having said that let's get moving with defusing.

Milk, Milk, Milk

To begin, we would like you to think about milk. What is milk like? What does it look like or feel like? Write down a few of the attributes of milk that come to your mind:

_____

_____

_____

Now, see if you can taste what milk tastes like. Can you do that? If so, write down what it tastes like as best you can. If not, you probably can do it this way: What does sour milk taste like? Can you get a little taste of that?

_____

_____

_____

It's unlikely that there is any milk in your mouth right now, but most of you can taste it. That is the transformation of function effect built into human language. Now, here is a simple exercise, almost one hundred years old, that has proven very effective for catching the word machine in action.

EXERCISE: Say the Word "Milk" as Fast as You Can

Now, go to a quiet place where no one will be disturbed when you do this next exercise, so you can really get into doing it. When you are comfortable, start saying the word "milk" out loud and as fast as you can for twenty to forty-five seconds. Just keep saying the word "milk" over and over for the whole time. Say it as fast as you can while still clearly pronouncing the word. Time yourself and watch what happens. Make sure that you don't do the exercise for less than twenty seconds, and that you don't do it for longer than forty-five seconds. Studies have shown this is the right time frame to establish the point we are making (Masuda et al. 2004). Start saying it now, "milk, milk, milk, milk …"

How did this feel to you? What was your experience with saying "milk" over and over again? Now, in the space below, jot down some notes on your response:

_____

_____

_____

After saying "milk" over and over again as rapidly as you could, what happened to the meaning of the word? What happened to the cold, creamy, white substance that you pour over your cereal in the morning? Did the word still invoke the image the same way that it might have before you did the exercise?

Finally, did you notice anything new that might have happened? For instance, it is common to notice how odd the word sounds, how the beginning and end of the word blend together, or how your muscles moved when saying it. If so, note these effects below:

_____

_____

_____

For most people, the meaning of the word begins to fall away temporarily during this exercise. Noticing that words may be, at their core, just sounds and sensations, is very hard to do when you are swimming in the stream of literal meaning. For example, a baby would see the paragraphs of print you are reading now as visual patterns. You don't see those patterns. You normally *can't* just see them; as your eyes move across this page notice that you keep seeing words, whether you like it or not. In the same way, adults normally cannot hear language as pure sound; they hear only words.

Now try something slightly different. Take a negative thought you often have about yourself and put it into one word, the shorter the word, the better. It could be something from your Suffering Inventory in chapter 1, or from your Daily Pain Diary and its associated exercises in chapter 5. Whatever it is, try to reduce your negative self-evaluation down to a single word. If you can come up with a short, one- or two-syllable word, that would be ideal. For example, if you think you are immature, you might distill the notion of immaturity all the way down to the word "baby." If you are afraid others think you are unintelligent, you might distill it down to the word "stupid." If you are disturbed about how mad you get at others, you might get down to the word "bully," or "abusive." Now, write down the negative word that best describes you when you are being really hard on yourself: _____

Next, you'll rate this word for two characteristics.

Right now, how distressing is it to think that this word applies to you? 1 means not at all distressing and 100 means maximally distressing: _____

Right now, how literally true or believable does this word seem as it applies to you? 1 means not at all believable and 100 means maximally believable: _____

Now take your word and do the exact same thing you did earlier with the word "milk." Say your word for yourself as fast as you can while still pronouncing it, and do this for twenty to forty-five seconds. Again, don't go under or over the time limit.

What was your experience? Did the word have the same emotional impact when you said it fast? How did it change? If the word didn't have the same emotional impact, how did it change?

Right now, how distressing is it to think that this word applies to you? 1 means not at all distressing and 100 means maximally distressing: _____

Right now, how literally true or believable does this word seem as it applies to you? 1 means not at all believable and 100 means maximally believable: _____

In our research (e.g., Masuda et al. 2004) we've seen that about 95 percent of those who do this exercise experience a reduction in the believability of the word. That effect kicks in by around twenty seconds (and reaches its maximum at forty-five seconds), which is why we asked you to do the repetitions for that long. Notice that you still know what the word means; but for most of you its emotional function has gone down. Said more technically, its derived functions wane while its direct functions (e.g., what it sounds like) become more prominent. The word is becoming (at least to some degree) just a word.

The Conditioned Nature of Thought

The point of the last exercise was to help you understand the nature of language. In addition to whatever they may be about, words are also just words. When you understand the idea that words are just words and you make use of that idea as a skill that you can develop, it becomes easier to understand and modify the words' relationship to your pain and to your life. Otherwise, you stand helpless as the target of whatever your verbal conditioning sets up in your head. After all, do you really know where all those words your mind throws at you come from?

Playing Word Games

Now, let's play a game. Complete the following phrases with whatever comes to mind.

Blondes have more _____

Eeny, Meeny, Miny, _____

There's no place like _____

Why do you think you wrote what you wrote? Isn't it because those phrases are a part of your history?

Now, let's see if we can eliminate the effects of this history easily. Suppose it was really important that the phrase "Blondes have more _____" didn't evoke "fun" or *anything having anything at all to do with "fun."* Suppose it is critical that you not even think "fun" for a second. Let's see if that's possible. We'll have you do it again. Write down a word, but make sure what comes up has nothing to do with "fun," not even for a second.

Blondes have more _____

Now, notice what your mind did and ask yourself:

Did you do the task (circle one):   Yes / No

If you circled no, you probably observed what actually happened. If you circled yes, pause for a minute and ask yourself how it was that you knew to circle yes? Remember we said, "It is critical that you not even think 'fun' for a second." If you circled yes wouldn't you have had to think, "I should circle yes because I wrote down _____ (whatever you just wrote) and not … ah … er … FUN"? But that is thinking of "fun!"

Our point is that once your history establishes a relational network, you can only elaborate on that network. You cannot make it go away. We are creatures of our histories, and our every moment adds to that history. Our nervous system works by addition, not subtraction. To some degree, things we learned once are still part of us. Words just rumble around within the verbal networks that comprise our minds. Typically, there they stay. When we try to get rid of them, they stick to us like sticky tape we've grabbed with the intention of throwing it away, but it won't let go.

Maybe that's fine, if the words rumbling around on their own are like "blondes have more fun" (as stupid and perhaps as sexist as that phrase may be). But language is not always so harmless.

For example, complete the following phrases:

I'm not a good person, I'm _____

I'm so sad I think I will just _____

The worst thing about me is that I'm _____

Some of those are words that can hurt you. But you know how to write them. You just did. They are in your history too somewhere and they come out from time to time.

And history is very easy to create. Suppose we were to say to you, "We plan to find you to ask you a question (and we know where you live). If you get the right answer, we will give you a million dollars on the spot. All you have to do is remember this: "Gub-gubs go 'wooo.'" Repeat. "Gub-gubs go 'wooo.'" Don't forget that sentence. It could be worth a million dollars to you. One day, we'll knock on your door and ask you to complete this line: "Gub-gubs go ____?" And if you say "wooo," you'll get a million dollars! Just like the magazine sweepstakes, the ACT prize patrol will show up and ask you a question, and, if you can answer it, you win. So let's say it again so you won't forget. "Gub-gubs go ____." Don't forget. "Gub-gubs go ____." Good.

Now, first to set matters straight, we lied. There is no million dollars and we don't know where you live. But even knowing that we lied, do you suppose that if we magically we knocked on your door tomorrow and said, "Gub-gubs go ____?" that you might remember what to say? That seems likely. (If you think not, your next assignment is to read the previous paragraph twenty more times.) How about next week? Might you remember that gub-gubs go "wooo"? Maybe even a year from now? Isn't it possible, just possible, that if we asked you on your deathbed about these stupid gub-gubs you might, just might, know they go "wooo"?

Isn't that silly? Here you are wasting precious brain space for the rest of your life for no other reason than you happen to read a silly example of the way language works in a weird little book written by odd-thinking people you don't even know? But that is how language works.

It's very easy to build a relational network that might last your lifetime. But if some of your history hurts, it's very easy to bring that to mind as well, and that too will last a lifetime. Some of the words in your head may be negative evaluations, like "Deep down I'm afraid I'm _____." Who knows where the rest of the sentence that you just thought of came from? Maybe it came from your parents, or TV, or a book, or just the logic of language itself. But it could make all the difference in the world to you if, when you struggle with your darkest thoughts, you were able to *also* see the words that hurt as *just words*. Milk, milk, milk …

The Say the Word "Milk" as Fast as You Can exercise punctures the illusion of language for just a moment. But with practice you can develop the skills you need to free yourself whenever you become entangled in your own conditioned network of words and they are leading you in a direction that will not work for you.

You don't need to do this all the time. Sometimes cognitive fusion is helpful. For example, when doing your taxes, there is no point in remembering that words are just words while you try to follow the complex rules involved in preparing a tax return. But when you are struggling with psychological pain, you need methods that will help you see the process of language, not just its products.

Labeling Private Experiences as What They Are

In the following exercise you will learn how to label each private experience as it arises. A good way to start this exercise is to allow your thoughts to flow for a few minutes as you did for the What Are You Thinking Right Now? exercise that was presented in chapter 5. Then pay attention to what your body is doing. Then, as your private experiences come up, watch them arise and do the next exercise.

EXERCISE: Labeling Your Thoughts

One approach that can help you catch your thoughts, feelings, memories, and bodily sensations' as they pass by, is to label them for what they are. Call out aloud exactly what it is you are doing, rather than just thinking the thought.

For example, if you are thinking that you have things to do later today, instead of saying, "I have things to do later today," add a label to the type of event that just took place: "I am having the thought that I have things to do later." If you feel sad, make note of it by saying to yourself, "I am having the feeling of sadness." When you apply your labels, they should take the following form:

- I am having the thought that … (describe your thought)

- I am having the feeling of … (describe your feeling)

- I am having the memory of … (describe your memory)

■   I am feeling the bodily sensation of ... (describe the nature and location of your bodily sensation)

■   I am noticing the tendency to ... (describe your behavioral urge or predisposition)

Now you are ready to try your hand at labeling. Let your experiences flow, and label them appropriately, as they arise.

_____

_____

_____

_____

_____

_____

_____

_____

_____

This process allows you to defuse yourself from the contents of your private experiences. For example, you may notice there is a big difference between the sentences "I am depressed" and "I am having the feeling that I am depressed." We encourage you to do this kind of labeling in your own self-talk, that is, the way you talk to yourself, and to be rigorous about applying labels for at least a week. After that, use labeling whenever you become entangled with your own thoughts and feelings and you need to establish some distance. You might not want to talk this way to others since it sounds so strange, but if your spouse or others are game, you can do this with them too.

Watch Your Thoughts Come and Go

In chapter 5 you practiced just noticing your thoughts as they came into your head (in the Watching the Mind-Train exercise). This time, we will do this in a more open way.

EXERCISE: Floating Leaves on a Moving Stream

This will be an eyes-closed exercise. First, read the instructions and then when you are sure you understand them, close your eyes and do the exercise.

Imagine a beautiful slow-moving stream. The water flows over rocks, around trees, descends downhill, and travels through a valley. Once in a while, a big leaf drops into the stream and floats away down the river. Imagine you are sitting beside that stream on a warm, sunny day, watching the leaves float by.

Now become conscious of your thoughts. Each time a thought pops into your head, imagine that it is written on one of those leaves. If you think in words, put them on the leaf as words. If you think in images, put them on the leaf as an image. The goal is to stay beside the stream and allow the leaves on the stream to keep flowing by. Don't try to make the stream go faster or slower; don't try to change what shows up on the leaves in any way. If the leaves disappear, or if you mentally go somewhere else, or if you find that you are in the stream or on a leaf, just stop and notice that this happened. File that knowledge away and then once again return to the stream, watch a thought come into your mind, write it on a leaf, and let the leaf float away down stream.

Continue doing this for at least five minutes. Keep a watch or clock close by and note when you start the exercise. This will be useful in answering some of the questions below. If the instructions are clear to you now, go ahead and close your eyes and do the exercise.

How long did you go until you got caught by one of your thoughts?

_____

If you got the stream flowing and then it stopped, or if you went somewhere else in your mind, write down what happened just before that occurred:

_____

_____

_____

If you never got the mental image of the stream started, write down what you were thinking while it wasn't starting:

_____

_____

_____

You can think of the moments when the stream wouldn't flow as moments of cognitive fusion, while the moments when the stream does flow are moments of cognitive defusion. Many times we become fused to a thought without even being aware of it. Thoughts about this exercise can be especially "sticky." If you thought "I'm not doing this right" or "this exercise doesn't work for me," these too are thoughts that you may become fused to quite easily. In many cases, you may not even notice them as thoughts. Other particularly sticky thoughts are emotional thoughts, comparative ones, and temporal or causal ones.

You may want to repeat this exercise regularly to see whether you can do better over time in allowing the stream just to flow.

Objectifying Your Thoughts and Feelings

When you look at an external object, it is quite evident that there is some distance between you and the object. When feelings and thoughts are right on top of you, they are hard to see and hard to make room for. It can help to bring your painful thoughts and feelings into the room, so that you can see them more clearly and see whether it is necessary to fight with them.

EXERCISE: Describing Thoughts and Feelings

Pick out one of the painful items you noted in your Suffering Inventory in chapter 1, or your Daily Pain Diary in chapter 5. Take a minute to get into experiential contact with it. Now in your mind's eye, put that painful item out on the floor in front of you, about four or five feet away. (Rest assured we will not leave it out there. Later in the exercise we will teach you how to take the painful experience back inside yourself.) When you get it out there, answer the following questions about it:

If it had a color, what color would it be? _____

If it had a size, how big would it be? _____

If it had a shape, what shape would it be? _____

If it had power, how much power would it have? _____

If it had speed, how fast would it go? _____

If it had a surface texture, what would it feel like? _____

Now, look at this object. This is a symbolic manifestation of your pain outside of your mind. See if you can let go of any struggle you have with it. Must this thing with that shape, color, texture, and so on be something you can't have? What, really, is in this experience that you have thought you can't have as it is? Must this creature be your enemy? After all, this poor thing has nowhere else to go.

Now, take a few minutes and write down some of the impressions that you have about your "pain creature" below. Note particularly any thoughts or emotions that you might have about it, and see if you can make progress in letting go of your struggle with it.

_____

_____

_____

_____

If you find you have a sense of resistance, fighting, loathing, judgment, and so on about this pain creature, leave it out there (several feet away from you) but move it off to the side. Now, find your sense of resistance and when you find it, place it in front of you, next to the pain creature. When you get it out there, answer the following questions about it:

If it had a color, what color would it be? _____

If it had a size, how big would it be? _____

If it had a shape, what shape would it be? _____

If it had power, how much power would it have? _____

If it had speed, how fast would it go? _____

If it had a surface texture, what would it feel like? _____

Now, look at this second object. This is a symbolic manifestation of your resistance. See if you can let go of any struggle with *it*. Letting go doesn't mean buying into the struggle. It means experiencing this symbolic object made up of this shape, color, texture, and so on. Is there anything in *this* experience that you have that you think you can't bear to have? Must this resistance creature be your enemy? Can you accept it as a private experience you sometimes have? After all, this poor thing also has nowhere else to go.

If you can drop the tug-of-war rope with this second object, take a peek now at the first one. Does it look any different in size, shape, color, and so on? If so, write down what you notice:

_____

_____

_____

When you are ready, take them both back inside you, one by one. Try to do this in a loving way, the way you might welcome your children into your home when they are dirty, smelly, and tired from a long day. You don't have to like how they look or smell to welcome them back in. These poor orphans have nowhere else to go.

A Variety of Vocalizations

Defusion exercises can be playful at times. When we say things to ourselves like "I'm so stressed out I feel I'm going to explode," or, "I'm a bad person," it can help to defuse from these thoughts by changing the normal context in which they occur. When these playful approaches are well-timed, they can be enormously liberating. Here are some examples.

Say It Very Slowly

Try saying your troubling thoughts or feelings very slowly. Imagine what a 45 rpm record played at 33 rpm sounds like. You may find that saying one syllable per breath is about the right speed. For example, if you're stuck on the thought, "I'm a bad person," stretch it out and say the word "I'm" to yourself on your in-breath, "a" on your out-breath, "bad" on your next in-breath, "per" on your next out-breath, and "—son" on your last in-breath.

Say It in a Different Voice

Another thing you can do is to say your thought aloud in a different voice. For example, if your thought is "I'm so worthless, I just can't seem to do anything right," try to say this either in a very low voice, or a very high voice. Or you could say it in Mickey Mouse's, or Howard Cosell's voice. You could try choosing the voice of your least favorite politician. Any voice you can think of will work. The point is not necessarily to change how you feel about your thought so much as it is to realize that these are *thoughts* and what you do with them then is up to you, not just up to your word machine.

Create a Song

Try making a song out of your difficult thoughts. You can take the lyrics of a popular song and adapt them or make up your own. Sing out in a full and powerful voice, *"My mind is alive with thoughts of my sadness."* Any song that you can think of will do. Don't do this to ridicule, satirize, or criticize your thoughts. Rather just notice as you sing the "lyrics" that these are thoughts.

Bad News Radio

Imagine your negative mind is a radio station, and then say in a station's announcer voice, "This is bad news radio! We're here 24/7. Remember. All bad news. All the time. That's bad news radio! Flash. [say your name] is a bad person! She thinks she's not as good as she needs to be! More news at 11." Continue in that way "reporting" whatever shows up. (If something "positive" shows up you can report that too, but the announcer might be pretty disturbed. After all, "This is bad news radio! All bad news! All the time!")

Later on, we'll give you ideas for many similar exercises and, at the end, you'll make up some of your own. They all have the same purpose. They are designed to help you catch the word machine in flight, rather than becoming entangled in the world seemingly structured by it.

Descriptions vs. Evaluations

Because our thoughts are so pervasive, we tend to position them as a part of the external world, forget that we've done that, and then feel oppressed by the external world we've unknowingly constructed. One good way to break this cycle is to learn to notice the difference between *descriptions* and *evaluations*.

Descriptions are verbalizations linked to the directly observable aspects or features of objects or events. These aspects or features are the *primary attributes* of an object or event. That is, they don't depend on your unique history; in common sense terms, they remain aspects of the event or object regardless your interaction with them.

Examples:

*This is a **wooden** table.* (Tables are hard, solid, have four or more legs, etc. This particular table is made of wood.)

*I am feeling anxiety and **my heart is beating fast.*** (Anxiety consists of certain feelings, sensations, and urges. This instance includes a rapidly beating heart.)

*My friend is yelling at me **loudly.*** (He/she is shouting and it is loud.)

Evaluations are your *reactions* to events or their aspects. We can compare events and assign an evaluative label (like good or bad, like or dislike, bearable or unbearable, rude or polite, prohibitive or permissive, and so forth). Evaluations are *secondary attributes*. Secondary attributes revolve around our interactions with objects, events, thoughts, feelings, and bodily sensations.

Examples:

*This is a **good** table.* (Good is in my interaction with the table … it is not in the table.)

*This anxiety is **unbearable.*** (Unbearable is in my interaction with anxiety, it is not in the anxiety.)

*My friend is **unfair** for yelling at me.* (Unfair is in my interaction with the yelling. It is not in the yelling.)

Much of our suffering comes from mistaking evaluations for descriptions. Very often we believe that our evaluative opinions are primary properties and thus that they are descriptions. Yet when we examine our evaluations more closely, they start to smell a little fishy.

EXERCISE: Exploring the Difference Between Descriptions and Evaluations

In this exercise we would like you to try to make some distinctions of your own between descriptions (primary attributes) and evaluations (secondary attributes). When we are dealing with external objects, it is relatively easy to notice the difference between these two kinds of properties because if you disappeared, these secondary properties would also disappear. Primary properties would not. If there were no living creatures anywhere in the universe, what would happen to the "good" part of the *good* table? It would be gone. What would happen to the "wooden" part of the *wooden* table? It is still wooden. It becomes a little harder when discussing your internal being because that rule of thumb doesn't work, but if we first practice a bit with external objects, we can do the same with our thoughts and feelings. So let's start with a few tangible objects.

Now, list some attributes of a tree:

Primary Attributes: (leaves, color, etc.) _____

_____

Secondary Attributes: (ugly, ominous, beautiful, etc.) _____

_____

List some attributes of a recent movie you've seen:

Primary Attributes: (ninety minutes long, Cameron Diaz was the lead actress, etc.) _____

_____

Secondary Attributes: (boring, exciting, too long, could've used more drama, Cameron Diaz is hot, etc.) _

_____

List some of the attributes of a close friend of yours:

Primary Attributes: (height, hair color, etc.) _____

_____

Secondary Attributes: (smart, dumb, beautiful, ugly, good, bad, etc.) _____

_____

Now try to distinguish the difference between the primary and secondary attributes of your emotional experience.

First jot down your painful emotion here: _____

Now list the attributes of this experience, just the way you did above. Remember that primary attributes are the direct qualities of the experience, while secondary attributes are the way you judge or evaluate the experience. For example, people who have had a panic attack may list increased heart rate and light-headedness as primary attributes of the experience, and they may list "This was the worst experience of my life" as a secondary attribute of the attack.

Primary attributes: _____

_____

Secondary Attributes: _____

_____

Being able to distinguish between descriptions and evaluations should allow you the freedom to recognize when your mind is recording or noticing your actual experience and when it is making its own judgment calls on that experience. You can amplify this distinction by adding it to your "labeling thoughts" list from the Labeling Your Thoughts exercise earlier in this chapter. For example, you could say, "I am having the evaluation that anxiety is bad."

A Few More Defusion Techniques

What follows is a further sampling of current cognitive defusion techniques employed by ACT therapists. As you can see, there are quite a few. In fact, this is a fairly small sampling because new ones are made up every day. When you get to understand the principles of cognitive defusion, you can generate these techniques readily.

In fact, that is just what we are getting ready to help you do. We provide the list here for two reasons. First, you may be able to apply some of these techniques to your own life and thus further your practice in cognitive defusion. The second reason is to show you that there are many, many of these techniques, and if you read through them all, that should help you create your own.

A Sampling of Cognitive Defusion Techniques	
The Mind	Treat "the mind" as an external event, almost as a separate person. (e.g., "Well, there goes my mind again" or "My mind is worrying again").
Mental appreciation	Thank your mind when you notice it butting in with worries and opinions; show aesthetic appreciation for its products (e.g., "You are doing a great job worrying today! Thanks for the input!") *This is not sarcasm ...* after all, the word machine is doing exactly what it was designed to do all of those thousands of years ago: "problem solve" and avoid danger.
Commitment to openness	If you notice you start to fight with your insides when negative content shows up, ask yourself if such negativity is acceptable, and try to get to yes.
Just noticing	Use the language of observation (e.g., noticing) when talking about private experiences. For example, "So, I'm just noticing that I'm judging myself right now."
"Buying" thoughts	Use active language to distinguish between thoughts that just occur and the thoughts that are believed, e.g., "I guess I'm buying the thought that I'm bad."
Pop-up mind	Imagine that your negative chatter is like Internet pop-up ads.
Cell phone from hell	Imagine that your negative chatter is like a cell phone you can't turn off (e.g., "Hello. This is your mind speaking. Do you realize you need to worry?")
Experiential seeking	Openly seek out more material, especially if it is difficult. If your mind tells you not to do something that is scary but worthwhile, thank your mind for the great hint and do the difficult thing with gusto.
Put it out there	Write down a negative evaluation you are ready to defuse from (e.g., mean, stupid, angry, unlovable, etc.) and put it on a name tag and wear it. Don't explain it to anyone for a while ... just feel how it feels to have it out there.
Mind T-shirt	Imagine that your negative evaluations you are ready to defuse from are written in bold letters on your T-shirt. If you feel especially bold, actually *do* that!

Think the opposite	If your mind is stopping action, practice deliberately engaging in a behavior while trying to command its opposite. For example, get up and walk around while saying, "I can't move while I'm reading this sentence!"
Thoughts are not causes	If a thought seems to be a barrier to an action, ask yourself, "Is it possible to think that thought, as a thought, AND do x?" Try it out by deliberately thinking the thought while doing what it has been stopping.
Monsters on the bus	Treat scary private events as monsters on a bus you are driving. See if it is okay just to keep on driving rather than doing what they say or trying to get them to leave.
Who is in charge here?	Treat thoughts as bullies; use colorful language. Who's life is this anyway? Your mind's or yours?
How old is this? Is this just like you?	When you are buying a thought, back up for a moment and ask yourself, "How old is this pattern?" or "Is this like me?"
And what is that in the service of?	When you are buying a thought, back up for a moment and ask yourself, "What is buying this thought in the service of?" If it is not in the service of your interests, stop buying the thought.
Okay, you are right. Now what?	If you are fighting to be "right," even if it doesn't help move you forward, assume the White Queen has decreed that you are "right." Now ask yourself, "So what? What can I actually *do* to create a more valued life from here?"
Get off your but	Replace virtually all self-referential uses of "but" with "and."
Why, why?	If you find that your "reasons why" are entangling, ask yourself repeatedly why the event exists and why it functions the way it does, until you have a very hard time answering. It may help to show how shallow the story really is and how experiential avoidance creates the pain of absence. For example, "I can't do it." Why? "I feel anxious." And why does that mean you can't do it? "Ahh … don't know."
Create a new story	If you find yourself entangled in a "logical" but sad story about your life, and why things have to be the way they are, write down the normal story, then take all the descriptive facts and write the same exact facts into a different story. Repeat until you feel more open to new possibilities *with* your history.
Which would you rather be?	If you are fighting to be "right," even if it doesn't help move you forward, ask yourself, "Which would I rather be? Right or alive and vital?"
Try not think x	Specify a thought not to think and then notice that you do think it.
Find something that can't be evaluated	If you find yourself entangled in negative evaluations, look around the room and notice that every single thing can be evaluated negatively if you choose to. So why should you be any different? This is just what the mind has evolved to do!

And how has that worked for me?	When you are buying a thought, back up for a moment and ask yourself, "How has that worked for me?" and if it hasn't worked ask, "Which should I be guided by, my mind or my experience?"
Carry cards	Write difficult thoughts on 3 x 5 cards and carry them with you. Use this practice as a metaphor for the ability to carry your history without losing your ability to control your life.
Carry your keys	Assign difficult thoughts and experiences to your keys. Then think the thought as a thought each time you handle your keys. Keep on carrying the keys and your thoughts.

CREATING YOUR OWN COGNITIVE DEFUSION TECHNIQUES

If you've done the work and practiced the techniques in this chapter to the degree that you understand cognitive defusion, you should be able to create your own techniques. Being able to do this will empower you to use cognitive defusion as you wish.

Start with a thought you are struggling with. Write it down here:

_____

_____

Now imagine a context in which those same words would not be something you had to believe or disbelieve, but would be only something you would notice. For example, when are you more likely to read, hear, or listen to words without struggling over their content? When are you more likely to read, hear, or listen to words with amusement or when their literal truth is not a big issue? Write down some examples here (for example, when I read stories in the *National Enquirer,* when I listen to a comedian, etc.):

_____

_____

_____

Now construct a defusion technique that links the thought you are struggling with and your answers to the last question. Describe how you might think _____ [write down the problem thought] in this way (e.g., the way the *National Enquirer* would handle this thought, or the way a comedian would treat this thought): _____

_____

Now, let's use this technique. Bring the problem to mind and give it a good try. Don't stop until you are sure you have done it long enough to assess its impact.

Write down what happened when you did that here:

_____

_____

_____

_____

_____

After you used the technique:

■   Were you better able to see the thought as a thought?

■   Did the believability of the thought go down?

■   Did the distress caused by the thought go down?

If you have two or more no answers, try it one more time. If you still have two or more no answers, this is not an effective defusion technique for you. Try again and develop something else. If you have mostly or all yes answers (especially to the first two questions), you are practicing defusion.

When to Use Defusion

Because fusion is everywhere, all the time, applied to everything, and unstoppable, we don't notice it. Here are some cues that will show you when you are fused with your thoughts:

■   Your thoughts feel old, familiar, and lifeless

■   You submerge into your thoughts and the external world disappears for a while

■   Your mind feels comparative and evaluative

■   You are mentally somewhere else or in some other time

■   Your mind has a heavy "right and wrong" feel

■   Your mind is busy or confusing

If you are not behaving optimally and any of these cues are present, look for a fused thought, and if you can find it, use one of your defusion techniques.

The next step in the process is for you to learn how to maintain a mindful stance toward your thoughts, feelings, and bodily sensations. The next two chapters of this book will teach you what mindfulness is and how to stay in contact with the present moment.

CHAPTER 7

If I'm Not My Thoughts, Then Who Am I?

In chapters 5 and 6 you began to learn how to distance yourself from your thoughts. In certain contexts, such as literality (taking "I am an anxious person" to be literally true, even missing that this is just a thought), reason-giving ("I am anxious because I had experiences in childhood that lead me to be anxious"), or emotional control ("I have to get rid of this anxiety before I can live"), thoughts can become entangling.

The kinds of thoughts that tend to be most entangling when they are in the wrong context are evaluations and self-conceptualizations. You will remember that evaluations and self-conceptualizations are two particularly fused ways of thinking. Evaluations are subjective judgments you make about internal or external events. They are particularly troublesome because they lead so readily to useless forms of avoidance.

Thus, achieving the goal of acceptance is not possible when cognitive fusion dominates your thinking processes. You will recall that cognitive fusion refers to the tendency to look *from* your thoughts rather than *at* your thoughts. When you engage in cognitive fusion, you take your mind's statements as literal truths, but without even being aware of these statements as the products of an ongoing cognitive process.

CONSIDERING YOUR SELF-CONCEPTUALIZATIONS

Self-conceptualizations are statements that your mind makes about you as a person that you implicitly take as literal truths. Self-conceptualizations are troublesome for a slightly different reason. Self-conceptualizations enhance psychological rigidity.

For example, consider the following questions. Please fill in the blank lines below with whatever responses come to your mind. If you wish to give multiple responses, feel free to do so.

I am a person who _____

_____

_____

I am a person who does not _____

_____

_____

My favorite part about myself is _____

_____

_____

My least favorite part about myself is _____

_____

_____

I have been wronged because other people have _____

_____

_____

I am a person who is bad at _____

_____

_____

Consider one of your negative responses. Focus on it. Now, suppose a miracle could happen and, without requiring any change in your history or circumstances, this problem would simply disappear while you go about living your life. For example, suppose you wrote the words "is an agoraphobic" in response to "I'm a person who ..." If that agoraphobia suddenly disappeared, without needing you to have a different history, be a different person, or have a different set of current circumstances, ask yourself this question: Who would be made wrong by that disappearance?

If the question doesn't make sense to you, sit with it for a few minutes. Then repeat the question and ask yourself to answer it again. Who would be shown to be incorrect?

Can you see that you are invested in your labels and stories and reasons? Even if you *hate* the label (e.g., you may hate the idea that you are an agoraphobic), if you apply it to yourself or your behavior in a fused way, you have made an *investment* in the label. If the evidence supports its use, at least you are *right*. Perversely, this also means that your mind gives you a secret investment in things remaining rigidly the same, even if you are suffering terribly right now.

The problem with identifying with any particular aspect of who you are is that once you become attached to that particular aspect of your identity, you set yourself up to distort the world in order to maintain this vision of yourself. This is as true of positive aspects as it is of negative ones. For example, suppose you said, "that I'm kind" in response to "My favorite part about myself is ..." That's fine, but are you *always* kind? *Everywhere?* To *everyone?* ... Liar!

Human beings are complex. Whenever you say, "I am x," you simply can't be telling the whole truth. Surely there are times you aren't x. It doesn't matter if the x is positive or negative. If you wrote "I am a person who is anxious," surely you can think of at least one moment when you weren't anxious. But notice how it feels when you realize that x is not 100 percent true. For most of us, such realizations come with a sense of disquiet.

That disquiet doesn't come just from perhaps being "wrong." It also comes from the need to know who we are. Consider one of the negative self-conceptualizations that you wrote above once again. Focus on it. Now, using the defusion techniques you learned in chapters 5 and 6, distance yourself thoroughly from the content of this negative self-conceptualization. That is, defuse from your thought and look at it in a mindful posture. Observe it without judging it.

To do this, you can use any of the techniques that you liked provided in earlier chapters. For example, suppose you wrote the words "is depressed" in response to "I'm a person who ..." and suppose you do well with stating your thoughts as thoughts, acknowledging them, and allowing them to float on by. In that case, use these methods with the thought, for example, "I'm having the thought that I'm a person who is depressed. Thanks for the input, mind!" and then allow it to float down the stream like a leaf, as you did in chapter 6.

If you can do this, follow through with some of its implications and you may become able to see where another form of rigidity and attachment emerges. Suppose you were defused from *all* categorical self-conceptualizations? Suppose each and every one of the self-conceptualizations above (and the myriad other varieties that can be evoked by other questions) were, to some significant degree, simply ongoing thoughts. No more and no less. If that were so, then there is something else that needs to be faced.

I (SCH) once worked with an anxious client who was defusing from self-conceptualization after self-conceptualization. Most of his self-conceptualizations were very negative, and as we went through this work, initially, the mood in the room lightened up as the client began letting go of attachment to one feared self-evaluation after another. After some time, however, as real progress began to be made, the mood changed. The client began to tear up. Finally, he asked, with a real sense of fear in his voice, "If I am not my thoughts, then who am I?" It was as if he were dying. And, in a sense, he was.

THE THREE SENSES OF SELF

According to the theory of language that underlies ACT, there are at least three senses of self that emerge from our verbal abilities: the conceptualized self, the self as an ongoing process of self-awareness, and the observing self (Barnes-Holmes, Hayes, and Dymond 2001).

The Conceptualized Self

The *conceptualized self* is you as the object of summary verbal categorizations and evaluations. It is the verbal "I am" self, as in: I am old; I am anxious; I am kind; I am mean; I am unlovable; I am sweet; I am beautiful; and so forth. The conceptualized self is brimming with content; this *content* is the story about you and your life that you've been selling to yourself. It contains all the thoughts, feelings, bodily sensations, memories, and behavioral predispositions that you've bought into and integrated into a stable verbal picture of yourself. This is the self you are probably the most familiar with because it is the product of normal applications of language to you and your life.

In terms of trapping you in your suffering, the conceptualized self is the most dangerous. That's because the conceptualized self fits into a story that provides reasons for your actions and a self that provides coherence for your experiences. It is a kind of comfortable but suffocating coherence that leads relentlessly toward "more of the same." Have you ever noticed that if someone thinks he is unimportant, most events in his life appear to confirm that view? Or have you ever observed that if someone sees herself as a victim, somehow she keeps ending up (in her mind or in actuality) being victimized?

If you are suffering with anxiety, depression, or stress, your identification with these disorders is almost certainly part of your conceptualized self. Your emotional problems have become part of the story that you've been telling yourself about your life. This is not meant to suggest that the facts as you know them aren't real. Most of your facts are probably roughly correct. But the story of your anxiety or depression doesn't tell the *whole* story of your life and, furthermore, it tells more than you can possibly know.

EXERCISE: Retelling Your Own Story

In the space provided below, write the story of your suffering as you might have written it before you began working with this book. Be brief. Describe your main problems and the historical, situational, and personal reasons for their presence in your life.

_____

_____

_____

_____

_____

_____

_____

_____

_____

_____

_____

_____

_____

_____

_____

_____

_____

_____

_____

_____

_____

Now, go back and read what you wrote and underline several facts. Facts are descriptions, not conclusions. Leave out any causal analyses. (Causal analyses can be identified by the use of words like "because." If there are any causal analyses, do not underline them.) Now take the facts you can extract from what you wrote, and write an entirely different story with an entirely different ending using all of these facts. This is not a promise, prediction, or evaluation. It's just an exercise. See whether you can take these objective facts and integrate them into a very different story.

_____

_____

_____

_____

_____

_____

_____

_____

_____

_____

_____

_____

_____

_____

_____

_____

_____

_____

_____

_____

_____

_____

Now, observe how the meaning of the same facts in the two stories changes and becomes different. If this process feels difficult, or you don't see the point yet, take the same facts and write still *another* story that integrates all of these same facts in a different story. Then, once again, note how the meaning of the same facts in the two stories changes and becomes different.

In instructing you to do this, we aren't trying to make the point that anything is possible, or that life is without limits. And we certainly aren't trying to ridicule the story of your life, as you normally think about it. Rather, our point is that (a) the facts in our stories don't determine the stories in which they appear, despite what our minds tell us. Many stories are possible. And (b) the facts are significant because of the stories they are part of. This means that what really can make a difference is something that might be capable of being changed. We know the facts. They will not change. But the story about the facts, and the self-conceptualization resulting from that story, are aspects of our lives we've been prevented from changing because of our attachment to and fusion with them. Perhaps that (our story and our attachment to it) can change.

The exciting part about seeing your own conceptualized self as something you hold on to arbitrarily is that truly new narratives may be possible that are, right now, outside of the story currently being told. But it can be frightening to open up to possibilities that go beyond your conceptualized self. If you are not your thoughts, then who are you?

When you let go of an attachment to your conceptualized self, you are like a child, open to whatever is possible and willing to find out what is. But first, you must let go of your attachment to your conceptualized self. Only the bravest among us would do this without first figuring out a place to land psychologically. For that reason, we will return to the problem of the conceptualized self later in this chapter, after we've identified a critical ally within ourselves.

The Self as a Process of Ongoing Self-Awareness

Ongoing self-awareness is your fluid, continuous knowledge of your own experiences in the present moment. It is like the conceptualized self, in that you are applying verbal categories to the self. It is unlike it because instead of being summary, evaluative categories, the categories are descriptive, nonevaluative, present, and flexible: "Now I am feeling this." "Now I am thinking that." "Now I am remembering this." "Now I am seeing that."

There is a lot of evidence that this sense of self is important for healthy psychological functioning. For example, people who can't identify what they experience emotionally are said to have "alexithymia." This clinical deficit correlates with a wide range of psychological problems. And, you will not be surprised to learn, it correlates highly with experiential avoidance (Hayes, Strosahl, et al. 2004) A person unable to observe and describe her own present experience is someone who is deaf and blind to what is going on in the moment.

We've been taught to speak of our personal histories and current predispositions by locating and identifying what we are feeling. For example, a child will be asked, "Are you hungry?" by way of asking, "Will you eat food if I give you some?" Very young children sometimes have a hard time answering this question accurately because their sense of self is still developing, and they haven't yet learned what their emotions and feelings mean. As a result, they may say they are not hungry, and then ask for food minutes later; or they may say they are hungry and then pick at the food they are given because, in fact, they are not. (Every parent knows about this type of "disconnect" with young children.)

Making contact with the present moment and the experiences it produces is more likely when fusion and avoidance are undermined. Chronic emotional avoiders do not know what they are feeling because not knowing is itself a powerful form of avoidance.

This more fluid sense of self as an ongoing process of awareness is also diminished when attachment to the conceptualized self dominates; noticing reactions that do not accord with the dominant story becomes threatening to the conceptualized self. For example, a person who is supposedly "always helpful and sweet" will have a hard time admitting to feelings or thoughts that are angry, jealous, or resentful as they emerge in the present moment. Defusion and acceptance naturally support the development of the self as an ongoing process of awareness.

The Observing Self

It's likely that the observing self is the sense of self you are the least familiar with verbally, despite it being the most important aspect of selfhood, and one that's been with you for a very long time. There are many names for it: self as context, the transcendent self, the spiritual sense, the no-thing self, and the observing self are just a few. We use the latter term in this book.

Unlike the conceptualized self or the self as an ongoing process of self-awareness, the observing self is not an object of verbal relations. That is why we "know" less about it. The observing self is not a content-based sense of self that can be described directly. Nevertheless, the theory that underlies ACT suggests that the observing self emerges as a result of language use and is critical to psychological health.

When you were very young and still acquiring language, you learned to describe events from a consistent perspective. When you described what you ate, or saw, or did, you learned that you had to report relative to that consistent perspective.

Consider this question: Where is "here?" Very young children have a hard time with this idea. "Here" is not a specific site like an address or a corner of the room; rather, it is the place from which observations are made. Any other place is "there."

Consider this question: When is "now"? Very young children have a hard time with this notion, as well. "Now" is not a specific time like Monday or 6 PM, rather it is the time from which observations are currently being made. Any other time is "then."

In the same way, consider this question: Where is "I"? Very young children also have a hard time with this final idea. "I" is also a place from which observations are currently made. Observations made from another perspective are "you," not "I."

These verbal relations are deictic, which means to point out or to show. *Deictic relations* can be learned only by demonstration because they are not material things. They are relative to an observational perspective.

The sense of a place from which conscious observations are made is a strange sense because, for the person experiencing it, it has no known boundaries. You can never consciously know the limits, because all verbal knowing is with reference to you as a knower. Go back in your memory to your early childhood. Think of a memory. It can be either a fond memory or a painful one. Relive this memory for a few moments. See if you can connect with a sense of looking out at the world from behind your eyes as they were then. Now answer this question and see if you can get to it experientially (not just logically): Who was it who saw those events as they were unfolding?

Now answer another question: Who was it who ate your breakfast this morning? Picture breakfast and once again see if you can connect with a sense of looking out at the world from behind your eyes.

Now notice who is reading this book. Again see if you can connect with a sense of looking out at the world from behind your eyes. Notice that you are here in this moment reading, and notice too that the person behind these reading eyes was there when you ate breakfast this morning and was there when you were a child. You've been you your whole life, though there have been many changes in your thoughts, your feelings, your roles, and your body. At the very moment that you gaze at these lines of ink on paper, notice who is gazing.

Hello.

You have been you ever since you showed up in early childhood as a conscious human being, and your infantile amnesia fell away (about the same time that these deictic frames of I/you; here/there; and now/then made their appearance). This "I" is what some call the observing self (Deikman 1982). It is a sense that transcends both time and space, not literally but experientially since this sense is everywhere you go. Whatever happens to you, it is this "I" that will be part of your verbal knowledge of that experience.

This "I" is boundless in that you cannot experience anything that you know about (or to be very precise, that you know you know about) without "you-as-perspective" being in it. Why? Because without this sense of locus there is no continuity of consciousness itself; there is no psychological perspective from which to view what is known.

If this sense of self is experientially boundless (that is, as experienced by the person experiencing), it is also not experienced fully as a thing. That is unique. Almost every event we can describe is experienced as a thing: as an event with known boundaries. Yet here, right in the middle of verbal knowledge itself, is a "no-thing" self. We may *believe* this sense of perspective has boundaries (e.g., we believe we are sometimes unconscious), but we cannot directly experience them (e.g., we are not conscious of those times). Here, right in the middle of verbal knowledge itself, is an event without distinction. Events without distinction include no-thing (or as our language community came to write it later "nothing") and they include "every-thing." That's it. That is why Eastern philosophies call this sense of self "everything/nothing" and point to it with odd sayings like "Wherever you go, there you are."

You may have started feeling some contact with your observing self when you worked through the defusion exercises in the last chapter. You may have been able to watch your thoughts float down the stream of your mind without becoming attached to them. But who is the watcher who observes you thinking your thoughts? Don't try to answer this by turning this sense of self into a *thing*. That is precisely what it is not. You know about this sense of self indirectly, for example, by a sense of calm transcendence, or peacefulness. For some, this sense can feel frightening because it may feel as though they are falling into nothingness. And in a nonpejorative sense, that is quite true.

It is this observing self that we hope to bring you in closer contact with in this part of the book because it is the place from which it is fully possible to be accepting, defused, present in the moment, and valuing. It is immutable and solid, not because it is a thing that does not change, but precisely because it is no-thing at all.

BEING THE OBSERVING SELF

Getting in contact with the observing self is a matter of experience. There isn't a simple formula we can give you to locate this greater sense of consciousness and presence. The route is, and must be, indirect for the reason we just discussed: this sense of self is not a thing (at least, not as experienced from within). What we *can* do is provide exercises and metaphors that will help point you in the right direction. For most of you this should be enough, because this is a sense that has been with you your whole life. It just was overwhelmed by the content of consciousness. Thus, we are neither trying to establish something nor to discover something. It is more as though we are trying to remember something we know full well, like remembering a song that you've been humming in the back of your mind for years.

The Chess Metaphor

Imagine a chessboard stretching out to infinity in all directions. On this stage different pieces start to enter. Some are black and some are white, just as in the game of chess. They come close to the center of the board and they begin to align themselves into two separate teams on the different spaces of the board.

Now imagine that each of the pieces represents a different emotion, cognition, memory, or sensation. Some of the pieces are positive, such as happiness, joy, pleasureful feelings, and loving memories. They hang out together as a team. And some of the pieces represent your pain, fears, and failings. Perhaps you are deeply depressed, or perhaps you have been diagnosed with an anxiety condition. See if it isn't true that the negative thoughts and feelings associated with these conditions hang out together as a team, as well, but this team is quite different from the positive team.

Now imagine that the various pieces start doing battle. It is a long, bloody war and pieces are being hewn and smashed to bits all around you. This battle has been going on for years. The black pieces are fighting with the white pieces edging in for the advantage while the white pieces desperately retaliate, trying with all their might not to be taken over by the enemy. They must fight because from the perspective of each "team," the other is life-threatening.

In the introduction, we began this book with a similar scene, but you yourself were in the battle. We suggested that this book was about learning how to leave the battle, not learning how to win the war:

> Unknown to [that] person, however, is the fact that, at any time, he or she can quit the battlefield and begin to live life *now*. The war may still go on, and the battlefield may still be visible. The terrain may look very much as it did while the fighting was happening. But the outcome of the war is no longer very important and the seemingly logical sequence of having to win the war before beginning to really live has been abandoned.

When you first read this, it was probably just an abstract idea to you. Now you are further along, and you can begin to consider the possibility that it was only an illusion that took you into battle in the first place. You've been acting as if your favorite emotional and cognitive team must win this chess match. But that makes sense only if the white pieces are you and the black pieces are not. In that posture, you *must* fight because such polar opposites are direct threats to your survival.

If "I'm a bad person" is 100 percent true, then "I'm a good person" is destroyed, and vice versa. Thus, leaving or abandoning the battle is not an option. It is a death sentence. The war must go on and you must win it, because you've jumped on the back of the White Queen and nominated her to be you. She (and thus you) cannot afford to stop fighting.

But suppose none of these pieces is you? In this scenario, who are you? You can't be the chess player: that is still someone trying to win the war and defend certain pieces over others. There is only one part of the metaphor that is in contact with *all* of the pieces. If you are not the pieces—if you can still be you and not have a huge investment in the outcome of the war—then who are you?

Being Who You Are, Not Who You're Not

What if you were the board on which this game was being played? Think about that. How does that fit for you? What if you aren't defined by your pain, but rather you are the conscious container for it. What would this mean for you?

To start seeing matters from the perspective of the board is to get in touch with the observing self. At the level of the board, all of the pieces are held as they play out their endless game. There are only two things the board can do while staying at "board level": (1) hold the pieces (all of them) and (2) take them all along for the ride as the board itself moves on. In order to move certain pieces around, you must go from who you are (a conscious human being aware of all of these reactions, that is, from board level) to who you are not (identifying solely with specific emotions, thoughts, or memories and not others). Said another way, you never really were in this war to begin with. It was all an illusion.

The next exercise will help you to momentarily contact your observing self. We say "momentarily" because the observing self cannot be looked at, by definition. For one thing, it is not experienced as a thing. For another, if you could look *at* it, who would be looking? You can only catch glimpses, like an afterglow. But at another level, wordlessly, you've been present all along, as concrete and certain as the chair you are sitting in or the floor beneath your feet. The battle finally will recede as you settle in to the vitality that comes from *being* who you experience yourself to be (the observing self) without demanding evidence from your mind that would consist of *seeing* your observing self. The battle can begin to recede in importance when you operate from the basis of who you are, rather than who you are not.

EXERCISE: Experientially, I'm Not That

This is a meditation exercise. The instructions are simple so you will be able to memorize them and then do the exercise without having to look back at the book. Simply get seated comfortably in a chair in front of a small desk near a wall. There should be several objects on the desk. Take a couple of deep breaths and then start by looking at a spot on the wall while breathing deeply and regularly. Keep your eyes on one spot for *at least* ten to fifteen seconds or thereabouts.

At some point after that (don't rush it), it will occur to you experientially that *you* are looking *at* the wall, and thus at an experiential level (in some sense of the term) *you* are *not* the wall. This is a distinction that is available in direct experience. We are not talking about the verbal *belief* that you are not the wall. If that were the point, we wouldn't need a meditative exercise since few of us believe we are the wall.

If your mind begins chattering to you about the truth or falsity of this belief ("Well, in one sense you *are* the wall. After all, you are the sum total of your experiences ... blah, blah, blah"), just thank your mind for the thought, notice that the person observing even *that* thought is not itself the thought you are observing, and then turn your attention back to the wall. Don't let your mind rush you through this, and don't collude with your mind to try to figure this all out. This is not a verbal exercise, it is an experiential one.

When that experiential distinction between the observing self and the events observed comes into awareness, just notice it and gently file it away (do not try to *believe* the distinction or your mind will start chattering away, arguing, interpreting, and so on). Now turn your gaze to an object on the desk. Repeat the same process with the new object (look at the object until the distinction between you, the conscious observer, and what you are conscious of occurs to you experientially, not merely as a matter of belief or disbelief). Continue doing this until all of the objects have been looked at (do not rush it!).

Then close your eyes and notice one at a time whatever pops up in your consciousness (bodily sensations, thoughts, and so on) in exactly the same way as you did with external objects. After you have done this several times (do it as many times as you like), finish by opening your eyes and repeat looking at the wall until the experiential distinction between looker and what is looked at becomes apparent.

Contact with the Present Moment

As you begin to experience this "board level" aspect of yourself, it will become more possible to feel what you feel, think what you think, and remember what you remember. Pieces become less threatening. Of what threat are the pieces to the board? What does it matter if the pieces are crowded into one area of the board or the other?

Simply holding the pieces is something that is possible only at "board level." Defusion, acceptance, and being who you are can thus be deepened by getting in touch with what is going on right now *in this moment*. The remaining exercises in this chapter and the next were developed specifically to help you get in touch with the present moment.

Traditionally, these exercises are referred to as "mindfulness" techniques, and we will use that term in the chapters that follow. However, we want to be clear that the word "mindfulness" used in this context doesn't have much to do with the mind we've been urging you to defuse from throughout the course of this book. Here, we are referring to what some Eastern traditions call "big mind." "The observing self" that was just contacted is part of "big mind" in the sense that it is without distinction ("no-thing/ every-thing").

Mindfulness is the defused, nonattached, accepting, nonjudgmental, deliberate awareness of experiential events as they happen in the moment. It involves every aspect of the things we have already worked with.

Because there are so many things to be mindful of and so many different ways to practice, the remainder of this chapter focuses on some fairly simple, one-dimensional exercises. In chapter 8, we will focus on more sophisticated exercises that ask you to take into account a multitude of sensory and emotional experiences. But before you begin, we would like to offer a few words on how to practice.

How to Practice

Some tips that will come in handy as you practice mindfulness follow.

If you lose yourself in a thought, just gently come back to the exercise. As you start to be mindful of the thoughts and sensations that are going on in your mind and body, you will notice times when you start following the thought rather than just watching it. Do you remember watching the mind-train in chapter 5? Just about anyone who does that exercise ends up in one of the trains at some point. You probably had this experience yourself. This is perfectly natural. For the purpose of practicing these exercises, when you find yourself being drawn into a thought and following where it goes, simply observe what is happening and gently bring yourself back to the position of the observer. Then continue with the practice.

Defuse from your judgments. As you practice mindfulness, one of the things you will notice immediately is that your mind will start producing judgments. If you become trapped in your thoughts as described above, you might tell yourself, "Damn. I'm such a failure, I can't even do these damned exercises correctly." Or when you are feeling particularly mindful, you might hear yourself "say," "Wow I'm really doing it, I am good at this mindfulness thing!" Or it perhaps you'll think these exercises are a waste of time. You might think to yourself, "Why am I wasting my time on this crap? I have so much to do." These are just some of examples of the millions of judgments your mind could come up with.

Any of these statements offers you some important information. They tell you that you've just become wrapped up in your word machine. It isn't the form of the judgment that's important, or the evidence for its truth or falsity. It's that you are becoming *entangled in judgment* that's important.

When you find yourself getting caught up in judging, gently notice that your mind is producing judgments, acknowledge your mind for all of its efforts on your behalf, and then go about the exercise just as before.

Accept your emotions. As you do these exercises, you will encounter some of the negative emotions you have been struggling with all this time. In fact, some of the exercises are designed to bring you into contact with these emotions. If you are suffering from depression or anxiety, for example, this may be difficult at times.

Or perhaps you have a panic disorder, and you already spend a great deal of your time and energy tracking your bodily sensations. Perhaps you are particularly worried about the speed of your pulse. Some people who suffer with panic are often completely convinced they are having a heart attack when no such event is taking place. You may be caught by this fear while you do these activities.

It may be that you are depressed and you struggle to keep yourself free from the cycles of obsessive negative rumination. When you come in contact with negative emotions or thoughts, you may start to get stuck in them. You may start to believe that your negative thoughts and emotions are the *only* thing that's happening in the present moment.

The purpose of these exercises is to help you see that the present is an ever-changing event, an ongoing process that occurs from moment to moment. When you start to struggle with panicky feelings about having a heart attack, or you become trapped in negative ruminations, it is a sure sign that you are entering into the war zone again. Once again, gently notice that you are here as an observing conscious human being and try to open up to these feeling and thoughts *as feelings and thoughts*. Do not argue with them or try to make them go away.

Mindfulness is not a distraction technique. Mindfulness activities are not meant to distract you from the negative content of your mind. In fact, mindfulness and distraction are antithetical. Thinking that you can be "mindful enough not to feel the pain anymore" is just another story your word machine tells you. Using the techniques in this way is simply another avoidance measure that leads right back to the pain you are trying to avoid. Don't try to escape your anxiety, or stress, or depression through mindfulness. If negative feelings come up, just notice them and keep on moving.

Practice. Mindfulness is probably not a stance that you are used to taking. In order to develop the skill, you need to practice it. As you begin to understand the basic underpinnings of mindfulness practice, you will naturally take it with you into the real world. Mindfulness is a practice you can engage in every moment of every day and, indeed, ACT gives you tools that will help you do just that.

GETTING STARTED

Now that you have some idea of the pitfalls to watch out for while you are practicing mindfulness, let's get started with some exercises. What follows can be thought of as "Mindfulness 101." These are some basic techniques that will give you a feeling of what it is like to observe what is going on in your mind and body without getting attached to your thoughts or feelings.

EXERCISE: Tracking Your Thoughts in Time

Because there are so many things to be mindful of, and this practice is not easy to develop, we want to start off small. We would like to begin by having you track your thoughts along a single dimension—time.

When thoughts, feelings, or bodily sensations arise, they tend to be associated with a certain time period in your life. Some lie in the past, some in the present, and some in the future. Even fantasies that have no basis in reality at all are generally associated with a particular time frame.

To see this more clearly, we would like you to take the next five minutes and track where in time your thoughts lie. Take a moment to center yourself. Breath deeply from your abdomen a few times. When you are relaxed, just let your mind wander at its will and watch what comes up. If you wish, you can use the "Floating Leaves on a Moving Stream" exercise you learned in chapter 6 to help you observe your thoughts, feelings, and bodily sensations.

While doing this, put your finger on the time line below. As your thoughts and feelings arise, slide your finger to the point on the time line that the thought or feeling corresponds to. You will notice that there are five points on the time line: distant past, recent past, present, close future, and distant future. You can choose any of these points for any thought that arises. However, note that this is a continuum, and if there is a point in the middle that makes more sense, feel free to place your finger on that point instead. Try to be accurate about what is happening without judging what comes up. Just watch it and note where in time the thought, feeling, or sensation lies.

Now, take the next five minutes, let your mind go, and track your thoughts in time.

Time Line: _____

| Distant Past | Recent Past | Present | Close Future | Distant Future |

What did you notice about your thoughts? Was there a specific time that kept coming up, or did your thoughts move throughout time? Write a few notes on your experience below:

_____

_____

_____

_____

_____

It is likely that your thoughts moved around throughout time. If they kept moving back to one place that's fine too. The point is simply to notice the thoughts and where they occur in time. There are no judgments that need to be made based on this information.

Learning to be mindful of where in time your thoughts are can be helpful in shifting your focus to the present moment. Let's repeat the exercise with a slightly different intention. This time do the exercise with the (gentle, defused) intention to stay more in the present. When your mind drifts and your finger must move to the right or left, just notice what is actually happening in the present moment. If you are drifting, notice that. If you are having a thought about the future or past, notice that you are now having a thought. Voila! When you do that, you are back in the present and your finger will be able to drift back toward the middle.

Notice that if you get too intentional ("I must go for the next five minutes with my finger on the word 'present'"), you will actually enter the verbal future, or past ("I haven't been doing it!"). If that happens, notice that you are now having a thought, and let go of your fusion with the content of that thought.

With practice, you can stay in the present for a large percentage of the time, and your finger will serve as a kind of biofeedback meter to train you in all of the methods your mind uses to knock you out of the present. This exercise can be done anywhere, anytime. For example, put your finger on your pant leg, and let it drift left, as if to enter the past, or right, as if to think to the future. You can do it easily while walking, sitting, or standing. It's fun and a useful little form of practice.

Watching Bodily Sensations

Now we would like you to take the next few minutes to track your bodily sensations as they come and go. By having a structure, you can focus attention on a particular dimension of experience which, in turn, can help you see the distinct strands of a total naturalistic event later on.

On the next page you will find a figure of the human body. To the left of this diagram is a list of words that describe various sensations that commonly arise in the human body. To do this exercise, take a few moments to center yourself again. Then start to notice the different sensations that come up in your body. Perhaps your back aches from lifting too much at work. Or perhaps your stomach is knotted up with nervousness. Just notice how your body feels.

As the feelings arise, use one finger to point to the word that most accurately describes your feeling on the left-hand side of the page. With your other hand, point to the place in your body where the sensation resides. For example, if your shoulders are tight, you would point to the tightness with your left index finger and to the shoulder in the diagram with your right index finger. Take five minutes to notice bodily sensations as they come in and go out of your body now.

This exercise will be awkward at first (especially since initially you will need to search for the words). As you repeat it, however, it will become more fluid and you will be able to focus on observing, while allowing your fingers to do the "describing."

Tight

Loose

Achy

Sore

Light

Heavy

Constricted

Relaxed

Comfortable

Painful

Warm

Cold

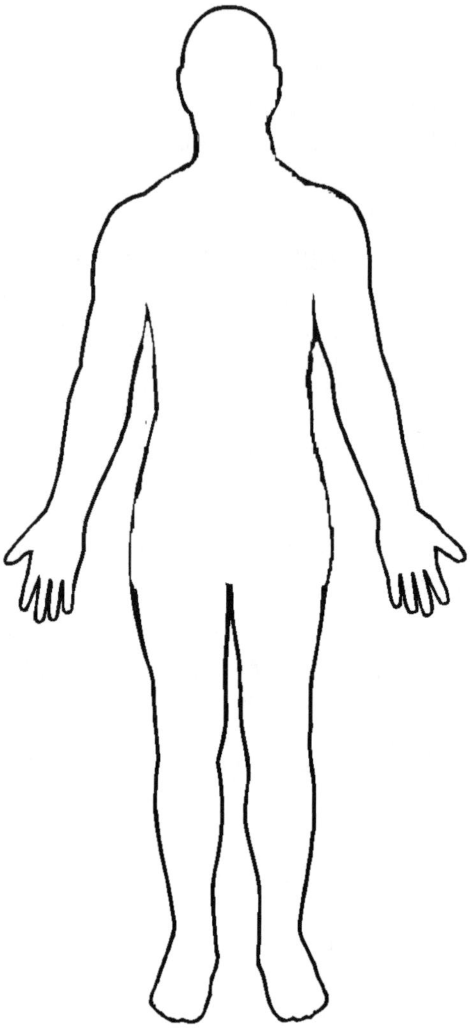

Figure 7.1: Your body.

Once you have completed the exercise, take a few minutes to jot down some notes about what you experienced.

_____

_____

_____

_____

_____

_____

_____

_____

You probably noticed that different sensations came up over the course of the exercise. Bodily sensations tend to shift from one thing to the next, from moment to moment, just like everything else does.

Defusing from Implicit Evaluations

In the exercise above you may have noticed that the experiences you were tracking had an inherent evaluation in them. Your mind automatically evaluates emotions, thoughts, and bodily sensations as they arise. For example, if you had a comfortable bodily sensation, you might have thought "good." If you drifted into the distant future in the time exercise, you might have thought "bad." Just as the whole point of mindfulness is to stay in the present, it is also the point to defuse from such evaluations.

You just practiced detecting when you drifted from the present; now we would like you to practice detecting when you are drifting into evaluations. That's relatively easy to do when the evaluative thoughts are explicit. It is harder when they are implicit. When they become combined with other experiences, they are easier to miss. The purpose of the next exercise is to learn to detect implicit evaluations, so that you can let them go and defuse from them.

Psychologists have shown that evaluations can occur reliably only along a limited number of dimensions. Good-bad and strong-weak are two of these primary polarities. Take a look at the box below. Notice that there are four terms in different areas surrounding the box. Think of this as a grid on which you can physically take note of where the nature of your evaluations lie in terms of how good or bad the evaluation is, or how strong or weak. Thus, in this exercise, simply sit quietly and become mindful of what is in the present moment. As you notice your experiences, see whether you are noticing them nonjudgmentally. If you find that you are implicitly evaluating, note the nature of that evaluation by placing your finger wherever your mind went, and see if you can let go of any attachment to the evaluation.

For example, suppose you have the thought "I'm anxious." You might have just noticed that feeling nonjudgmentally and, if so, that's fine. Do nothing but continue to observe. You also, however, might have noticed that, in the background of your thought, you were buying into the idea that this feeling is bad or too strong. If you sensed that implicit evaluation, place your finger in the upper right section of the box below. Then see if you can let go of this judgment. If you defuse from evaluations, you will find that you move your finger down into the bottom-middle part of the box (weak; neither good nor bad) and then move it out of the box altogether.

Now, please take the next several minutes to simply watch your own experience, detecting implicit judgments when they show up, and placing your finger in the box below as a kind of description of what is happening. Use the feedback this process provides to help you let go of fusion with the judgment altogether. See if you can gently create longer periods of time without having to buy into any evaluations that may appear.

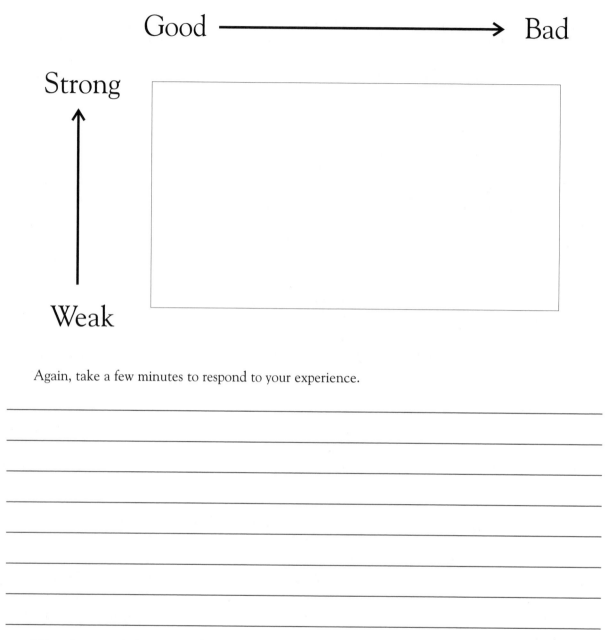

Again, take a few minutes to respond to your experience.

_____

_____

_____

_____

_____

_____

_____

_____

What happened for you in this exercise? Did you notice that your evaluations moved around as your mind moved from one thought to the next? Were you able to dig out implicit evaluations that, normally, you might miss? Were you able to let go of these judgments?

TAKING THE NEXT STEP

These exercises are meant to begin the practice of observing defused and nonjudgmental moments in your present experience. In the next chapter, we will provide you with some more formal mindfulness exercises. Now that you have a basic feel of how to track single events, we are going to help you learn how to be aware of many different thoughts, feelings, and sensations as they come and go over time.

CHAPTER 8

Mindfulness

Mindfulness is difficult, not because it is hard but because it is elusive. We are constantly being hooked by our verbal predictions and evaluations. Furthermore, life is complex. There are many, many things to be mindful of and, as events become more complex, it is easier to lose our way. You could practice focusing on only one aspect of your experience the way you did in the last chapter, but ultimately that would severely limit the breadth and richness of your actual experience.

Practicing mindfulness isn't going to do you much good if you just do the exercises written in this book and then forget about them. You need to make an effort to bring your attention more completely to the many moments in your life, fully, without defense, nonjudgmentally, defused, and accepting. Formal practice can help you acquire the skills, but it is informal practice, using these skills in your day-to-day life, that is most important.

This chapter will help you develop ways to deepen your experience with mindfulness by asking you to pay attention to many different types of experiences as they enter your awareness. It will also give you some concrete ideas on how you can institute a mindfulness practice into your daily life.

DAILY PRACTICE

Before moving on to the next battery of mindfulness techniques it is worthwhile to take some time to speak about when to practice mindfulness. Ultimately, the answer is "all the time." The problem with this answer is that you probably aren't accustomed to practicing mindfulness. It's unlikely that you will randomly remember to apply mindfulness skills to day-to-day moments until they have become well established.

To deal with this problem, it's a good idea to set aside some time to practice mindfulness every day. Once it becomes second nature (if it ever does), you can reconsider whether this is still necessary. Practicing mindfulness every day may sound like a daunting prospect but it becomes worthwhile immediately and, after a while, many people find that they really like doing it. However, regardless of whether you like or dislike it, these preferences are just more content your mind produces, and the whole point is to take back control over your life from your personal word machine. Given that, it is far more effective just to make the decision to practice every day, and then go for it. Here are some ways that you can institute a daily mindfulness practice:

1. **Set aside the time.** In the beginning, it can be useful to set aside a designated amount of time every day or every week to practice mindfulness skills. The section below on sitting meditation has some specific examples related to that particular exercise. However, you can use the same basic principles for any of the mindfulness practices you choose to engage in.

    The first thing you will want to do is figure out how many times a week you want to practice. We recommend that you practice some form of mindfulness every day. If you absolutely can't seem to fit that into your schedule, then figure out how much you can manage.

    Second, it's a good idea to set a time limit to your practice. Something between fifteen and thirty minutes at a time is a good starting point. You can adjust this as you choose, once you become accustomed to the practice.

2. **Relaxation and distraction.** People are often tempted to use mindfulness practice as a time to relax. That is a mistake. If you are relaxed, that's fine, but if you are tense, that's okay too. The point, however, isn't to relax. The point is to be aware of whatever is going on for you without avoidance or fusion. It is a matter of acquiring and strengthening skills that can be useful when your verbal repertoire begins to dominate your other forms of experience.

    Initially, it is a good idea to find a place in which you can practice without having to do other tasks, but that doesn't mean eliminating the distractions your mind presents to you. If you are distracted, that is simply another fact to notice. See it, note it, and then move on with the practice.

3. **Feeling too bad to practice.** There is no such thing as feeling too bad to practice. In some of the exercises below, you will find that when you are actually doing the work, negative content comes up for you. But this is only another set of experiences to be mindful of. It is not a problem; it is an opportunity. Presumably, you bought this book partly because you are already dealing with negative experiences. Learning what to do when such experiences show up is thus vital to your purpose. Practicing with, say, an irritating itch is in principle not any different than the same skills applied to, say, anxiety or depression.

    This doesn't mean to persist in the face of impossible circumstances. If you have a pain in your back that must be attended to, then do that. Persistence without self-awareness is just a different kind of trap. Over time, you will see that if you use pain as an excuse to run away from the practice, and if you detect that is how you are using pain, then you can learn how to do something new with pain.

Ultimately, mindfulness should be practiced as moment-to-moment awareness in real-time. It is not a special state that you "enter into" like a trance, or self-hypnosis. These guidelines are meant simply to get you to start practicing the techniques. Once you see mindfulness entering into your daily life, you can decide whether to continue with a regimen of this nature.

THE PRACTICE

The practice of mindfulness is about getting in touch with your own experience moment to moment in a defused and accepting way. In earlier techniques we've discussed, you were asked to be mindful of specific areas of your experience (i.e., thoughts in time, bodily sensations, defusing from implicit evaluations). In this chapter, there will be other things you are asked to notice, but your responses needn't be guided by anything but by the experiences that appear.

At times, many things may come up for you at once. There are different ways you can handle this. Sometimes, you might alternate back and forth between different sensations. Sometimes, you will be able to hold a number of different things in your awareness at one time. Some of the exercises actually ask you to be mindful of more than one thing at a time.

Part of the elusiveness of mindfulness is that it is purposive, and thus evokes evaluations, but the whole purpose of being mindful is to learn how to defuse from your evaluations. The best way to think about it is that there is neither a right nor a wrong way to be mindful. Simply be who you directly experience yourself to be (a conscious observing self) in the moment. If evaluations show up, then observe the evaluations but do not believe or disbelieve them. If you take your verbal judgments about your progress literally, that will be yet another instance of fusion with the verbal story your mind generates. Buying into thoughts that judge you as good or not good at being mindful is just the word machine taking control once again.

As you practice, allow yourself to become more mindful of the sensations, thoughts, and feelings that are happening for you. Be gentle and nonjudgmental (even with your judgments!). This isn't a test. It's just living.

Now, let's dive into the exercises themselves.

EXERCISE: Be Where You Are

After you've read through the following script a few times, close your eyes, and follow the instructions given. If you are comfortable with this, have someone close to you read the script aloud while you do the exercise. You can also record these instructions on an audiocassette tape and play it back to yourself while you practice. Remember not to panic if you become distracted while doing this exercise. Just bring yourself back to the present moment and continue to follow the script. (Note that you can abandon the script once you have the basic principles of the exercise memorized.)

Find a comfortable position. You can be seated in a chair or lying down on the floor or your bed. Close your eyes and take a few deep breaths. Relax. Don't let yourself drift off to sleep, but allow your body to rest.

Now slowly bring your awareness to the tips of your fingers. Feel your fingers. Rub your fingertips together. How do they feel? Can you feel the small indentations on your fingertips that are your fingerprints? Take your time and try to feel them. What are they like? Are your fingertips rough from lots of work or are they smooth and silky? How does it feel to rub them together? Notice the feelings and then move on.

Now rest your fingers where they were before. What are they touching? Are they resting on the blanket on your bed, or are they resting on the arm of your chair? What does that feel like? Is it soft or hard? Does it have any other distinguishing features? Is the blanket furry with cotton? Does the armrest have any markings or is it smooth? Take the time to completely absorb the way these objects feel to your fingertips.

Now bring your attention to your hands and arms. What do they feel like? Perhaps they are relaxed and heavy. Perhaps they are still tense from a long day's work. Either way is okay. There is no need to judge, simply observe the feelings in your arms and hands. Are there any aches or pains? Take note of these, but do not fixate on them. Simply note the pain and move on.

Move your attention down to your toes. Wiggle them around a little. Are they in shoes or socks? Are they free to move about? Squish your toes back and forth feeling whatever is beneath them. How does it feel? Can you tell what it is just by the feeling? Would you be able to tell only by touch? Just notice the sensations as you bring your awareness to your feet.

How is your head positioned? If you are sitting, is your head aligned with your spine or is it drooping, resting on your chest. Without trying to change the position of your head, simply note where it is positioned. There is no right way for your head to be. Just let it be where it is. Now think about the sensations in your head. Do you have a headache? Is your head relaxed?

What about your face? How does your face feel? There are all kinds of sensations to explore in your face. Think about your brow. Is it smooth and flat or is it crinkled up with stress? Again, don't try to change it, just notice it. Now bring your awareness to your nose. Can you breathe freely or are you plugged up? Take a few breaths in and out through your nose. How does that feel? Can you feel cool air flowing into your lungs or is the air warm? Pay attention to the feeling for a moment. Then think about your mouth. How is your mouth positioned? Is it pursed? Is it open? Is it closed? What about the inside of your mouth? Is it wet or dry? Can you feel your saliva coat the inside of your mouth and throat? Explore all of the sensations throughout your face. Perhaps you can feel oil on your skin. Perhaps your skin is dry. Perhaps there is no feeling at all. Just note it and move on.

Now bring your attention to your chest and belly. Place one hand on your chest and one hand on your belly. Can you feel yourself breathing? What is that like? Are you breathing fast or slow? Are your breaths going into your abdomen or into your chest? Breathe in through your nose and out through your mouth. How does that feel? Now invert the pattern. Spend some time with your breath, then place your hands wherever they were before.

Now think of your whole body. Where are you sitting or lying? Can you feel the back side of your body touch the chair or bed in various places? Be mindful of the way your body is positioned. There is no need to move, just observe.

Now think about the room you are in. Where are you positioned in the room? Do you have a sense of where the door is? What about the ceiling? Can you feel your body in the context of this larger space?

When you are ready, open your eyes and take a look around the room. You can move if you wish. Notice where the various pieces of furniture are. What do they look like? You can spend as much time as you like investigating the different aspects of the furniture. Remember not to judge, just notice.

Whenever you are ready, you can stop this exercise and carry on with your day.

When you have completed the Be Where You Are exercise for the first time, take a few minutes to comment on it below. If you wish, you can continue this practice of writing your responses in a journal after each session, but it is not necessary.

_____

_____

_____

_____

_____

_____

_____

EXERCISE: Silent Walking

Many cultures have developed different forms of walking meditations. This exercise is a variant on some of these.

Take ten minutes (or longer) and walk silently. You might walk around in a circle in your yard, you might walk around the house, or you might take a walk around the neighborhood. Try to remain silent throughout the course of the entire walk so that you can "listen" to the content your mind is producing.

As your attention is drawn to particular objects in your environment, thoughts in your mind, or feelings in your body, call these out by saying them three times. The purpose of the brief word repetition is to support you in defusing from your thoughts about the event. For example, if you are walking around the neighborhood and you see a car go by, say aloud, "Car, car, car." If you start to feel stressed out during the walk, you might say "stress" three times. Notice what happens as you do this.

Notice each time your attention is repeatedly drawn to something. For example, if you notice that you keep coming back to certain thoughts or feelings during your walk, you might want to gently file this information away. You might want to focus on these matters with other skills that were presented in this or previous chapters.

EXERCISE: Cubbyholing

In this next exercise, you will be asked to note the category of your psychological content as it comes up. This exercise can be done on its own, it can be done in conjunction with just about any other exercise in this book, or it can be done as you carry on with your normal day. As thoughts, feelings, or bodily sensations arise, mindfully note into which category they fall. Do this aloud if you are in a place where you can do that. Do not call out the specific thought or emotion; the point is to focus only on the category to which the content belongs.

Here is a list of the different categories from which to choose. Undoubtedly, there are many more categories, but for the purposes of this exercise, stick to the ones listed below.

- Emotion

- Thought

- Bodily sensation (just say "sensation")

- Evaluation

- An urge to do something (just say "urge")

- Memory

When you do this exercise, lead-in your labeling of the content with the word "there's." For example, if you start to feel your heart beating really fast, say, "There's sensation." If you respond to your fast heartbeat with the fear that you are going to have a panic attack, you could say, "There's emotion." If your fear is so great, you feel compelled to call a doctor, you could say, "There's an urge."

You can do this exercise while sitting, but you can also do it on long drives, while lying in bed at night, on walks, and so forth. Once you start it, try to stay with it for at least several minutes, more if you are able. If you catch yourself in long periods of silence, see if you haven't been hooked by a thought or feeling you've been following. Then come back to the exercise.

Labeling psychological content by type will help you to learn to deal with content in a defused way. For example, if you have a thought about what you need to do later on, staying with the label "there's a thought" supports you in staying present with what is actually happening. The thought may be about the future, but that is pure content. In fact, the thought is occurring now, and noticing that is a powerful habit of mind. Cultivating this habit can be helpful when even more difficult content appears (e.g., a thought that you may have a panic attack later).

EXERCISE: Eating Raisins

Raisins are funny little fruits and when we eat them, we tend to just pop them into our mouths without much thought. You might be amazed to discover how much deeper your experience of a raisin can be if you treat it mindfully.

First, take a raisin and eat it the way you normally do, that is, just pop it into your mouth. Now, get another raisin. Put it down on the table in front of you and examine it. Notice the wrinkles on its skin. Look at the various shapes the wrinkles form. Take out a second raisin and place it next to the first, and notice how unalike they are. No two raisins are identical.

Are the two raisins the same size? Think about the raisins in terms of the space they take up in the room, in the world, in the universe. Think about their size in relation to one another.

Now pick up one of the raisins and roll it around between your fingers. Feel the texture on the outside of the fruit. Feel the slightly sticky traces it leaves on your fingers as you move it back and forth.

Place the raisin in your mouth. Roll it around inside your mouth, over and under your tongue. Hide it in the crevices between your jaws and your cheeks. Don't chew it for at least thirty seconds or so. When you are ready, eat the raisin and note the way it tastes. Note the way it feels on your teeth as you chew. Feel it as it slides down your throat when you swallow it.

Now eat the second raisin, but this time, eat it super slow. Chew the raisin as many times as you can, until it turns into liquid mush in your mouth. Is the flavor different when it is eaten this way than it was last time? How is it different? What does it feel like in your mouth as it falls apart? How does it feel as you swallow it? How does it compare with the last raisin? What's different when you eat the raisin mindfully rather than simply popping it in your mouth and slurping it down? Write down your answers to these questions in the space below:

_____

_____

_____

_____

EXERCISE: Drinking Tea

Now we will try a similar exercise with a cup of tea.

1. Boil a pot of water.

2. Get a tea bag or a tea-leaf strainer filled with tea leaves and put it into a cup.

3. Pour the boiled water over the tea bag or the strainer. Fill the cup.

4. Let it steep.

As the tea steeps, watch the water change colors. When you first pour the water over the tea, the water will turn a light brown, green, or red (depending on the kind of tea you are using). Soon it will darken. Let it steep for a few minutes and remove the tea from the water. Look closely at the color of the tea. Is there anything you didn't notice about the color before? If so, you might want to jot down your observation below:

_____

_____

Now place your hands around the outside of the warm cup. Have you ever felt a cup of tea like this before? How does it feel? Is it quite hot, or just warm? Note the temperature.

Bring the cup to your lips. Feel the steam as it touches your face. Blow into the cup and feel the steam rise up to your lips. Smell the tea. Take a good long whiff. Ninety percent of your sense of taste is controlled by your nose. If you aren't smelling your tea, you aren't tasting it.

Now take a sip. Does it burn your lips? Is it too hot? Or is it nice and warm? What does it taste like? Try to note your experiences without judging them. Then, describe your experience below:

_____

_____

_____

_____

If you don't like tea, that doesn't really matter. Just try the exercise. Note how much you dislike tea as you taste it. And write down that experience. It's folly to think that you should practice present awareness only in moments of pleasure. That would eliminate half of your life. You know that you will have some unpleasant experiences, so you might as well experience them fully and take them for what they are worth.

Mindful Eating

The exercises above are actually tiny subsets of a much larger practice that is known as mindful eating. There are as many ways to practice mindful eating as there are schools that practice mindfulness. Some ways require you to eat slowly, some to chew each mouthful of food fifty times, some to eat a limited number of meals, some ask you to test for your hunger responses while you're eating, and so forth.

In many Western cultures, and particularly in the United States, we don't pay a great deal of attention to the food we eat. In a world where everything is supersized and the burger is king, we tend to think of food as not much more than a necessary factor of survival. What's worse, we tend to believe that this factor is as much a given as the air we breathe. We take our food for granted.

In the context of this book, the point of eating mindfully is not the activity of eating itself. It is used as a means to practice mindfulness. Becoming aware of your eating behavior rather than just rushing through it is an excellent way to bring yourself back to the present moment. Observing yourself while you eat is a great way to practice removing yourself from the conceptualized self. It doesn't matter whether you like the activity of eating. The important thing is to practice connecting to the present moment.

To practice eating mindfully, you can use many of the same techniques and much the same attitude as you did while doing the exercises above, only you continue the practice for an entire meal. Set aside some extra time for yourself at your next meal and try it out.

EXERCISE: Eating Mindfully

To start, move through the meal slowly. Take your time performing every action and notice what your experience is, as you go through it. When you lift a fork or cut your meat, note what that is like for you. As you place a bite of food in your mouth and chew it, think about the flavors and the texture of the food. Is it enjoyable or repulsive? Don't get hung up in judging it. Just notice it.

Do you find that particular thoughts or feelings come up during the course of the meal? If so, simply note those as well. You might want to use some of the techniques used throughout this book to help you do that.

Are you eating with a friend or partner? Are you eating alone? It may be interesting to watch your mind as you interact with the people with whom you take your meals. It may also be interesting to note the kinds of thoughts and emotions that come up when you are eating alone.

Because we all have to take the time to eat in order to live, eating mindfully is an excellent way to practice staying in contact with the present moment and make the most of your time.

EXERCISE: Listening to Classical Music

This is an interesting exercise that may provide insight into the way you can focus your attention on specific aspects of complex sets of stimuli, concentrate on several things at the same time, or simply allow all of your experience to become wrapped up in one flowing song. Classical music can act as an interesting metaphor in this regard. Moreover, listening to classical music can be a good exercise in mindfulness in itself.

Pick a piece of classical music. You can choose a favorite symphony, concerto, or string quartet. It doesn't matter what you choose, as long as you choose a piece that has a number of different instruments playing together. Solo piano or violin sonatas won't work for this exercise. (Even if you don't "like" classical music, try the activity anyway. It can be done with other forms of music, too, but we've found it is a little easier to draw attention to certain distinctions that are heard more clearly in classical music than in other genres. Of course, you can also do this exercise at a concert hall.)

Turn on the music and begin by listening as you normally would. After you have warmed up to the music a bit, bring your attention to one particular sound or set of instruments. If it is a symphony, you might start by listening for the string section. Focus on that part of the music. Be mindful of the strings. Can you distinguish between the sound of the cellos and the sound of the violins? What about the bass? Can you separate out the sound of the double bass from the other strings?

Now shift your attention to a different instrument or section of the orchestra. Can you hear horns? What about percussion? How about woodwinds? Try to name the different instruments as you listen to them. If you aren't especially familiar with classical music, simply note the different types of sounds.

Do you notice anything happening as you shift your focus back and forth between the different instruments? Do you start to focus on the sound of only one instrument or section? If you do that, where do the other sections of the orchestra go? Experiment with this by shifting your focus back and forth between the different sounds.

Now try to hold two sets of sounds in your mind at one time. For example, you might try to track the strings and the horns. Try not to get "wrapped up" in the music. Mindfully notice and label the sounds. You might further this experiment by trying to track other sets of instruments as well. Or you might watch the way your mind shifts back and forth between the sounds. At what point are you aware of only one sound? At what point are you aware of multiple sounds? If you wish, you can play around with this a little.

When you are done experimenting with hearing single sounds as opposed to hearing multiple sounds, bring the entire piece of music back into focus. Be mindful of all the instruments playing at the same time. Do you find yourself noticing certain sounds more than others? Can you hear all the different instruments while listening to the piece of music as a whole? What happens when you listen to all the instruments together? Does it change into a different, bigger sound? Try to identify the point when single sounds are subsumed by the total piece of music. Mindfully watch the way you interact with the sound.

If you are a music lover, this can be a particularly revealing exercise. That's because, in some ways, the way we listen to music mimics the way we listen to the word machine we call our mind. During passionate crescendos our observer self is often swept up into the music. We are carried away on a verbal journey. However, if we can maintain a mindful posture while listening, we can enrich the experience in so many ways. What a pleasure it is to be able to recognize the individual sounds the different instruments make, and still have the choice of being carried away by a passionate passage.

Perhaps you can learn to view your depression or anxiety as you would a symphony. There are many melancholy pieces of music that are quite compelling. Try to be mindful of your feelings, thoughts, urges, and sensations the way you might be mindful of the different instrumentation. Can you pick out different notes and chords being struck? It can be fascinating to note mindfully the music your experiences make.

EXERCISE: Be Mindful of Your Feet While You Read This

Bring your focus to your feet. Think about how they feel just where they are. Try to remain mindful of your feet while you read the next few lines.

Mary had a little lamb

Whose fleece was white as snow.

And everywhere that Mary went

The lamb was sure to go.

He followed her to school one day

Which was against the rules.

It made the children laugh and play

To see a lamb at school.

Were you able to remain mindful of your feet while reading this nursery rhyme? Did you notice that your awareness was shifting back and forth between the content of the passage above and your feet? Did you become mindful of your feet only occasionally, when you remembered them? Or were you able to hold onto your feet mindfully while reading the passage above? Take a few minutes to answer some of these questions.

_____

_____

_____

This exercise is particularly interesting on a number of levels. In the first place it asks you to divide your attention in half by asking you to remain mindful of your feet while reading a nursery rhyme. The other interesting thing about this exercise is that it mimics the way we sometimes can get so wrapped up in our own stories that we forget about other things that are going on for us.

When you get scooped up into the story of your depression, your anxiety, or your low self-esteem, often you may forget that there are many other things going on for you. That story may be the only matter you take notice of. You might also pay attention to your feet, your hands, the quality of the air around you, or millions of other factors that are taking place within you and in your environment, at the same time your psychological distress stories are being generated. Remember, though, the goal is not to think of your feet as a means of forgetting about or ignoring the pain you are in. Rather you can focus on your feet to practice being able to attend in the moment, deliberately and flexibly, as you wish.

You can do this same exercise while reading the newspaper, or indeed this book. Pick out something specific to attend to and see whether you can focus in on it while simultaneously being very focused on your reading.

Meditation

All the major religious and philosophical traditions have explored the concept of the observing self. Many practices have been developed to help people train themselves to become more mindful. One of the oldest of these is called mindfulness meditation.

In our culture, the problem with meditation is that it's gotten a bad rap. In the West, people look at meditation from one of two perspectives. One perspective sees meditation as some kind of weird metaphysical practice that is too hard or too esoteric to be practiced by normal people. The other seems to see meditation as a time to sit quietly and allow the feeling of peacefulness to roll over the body like a gentle wave, enlightenment only a step away. Light another incense candle for us all!

Neither of these perceptions is useful. In Zen Buddhism there is a form of meditation called Zazen that many practitioners in the West refer to as "just sitting." That's it, just sitting. There is no waiting for a wave of peace to wash over you, and there is no mystical component. There is just sitting.

However, the "just" can't be taken literally. There are many things that happen when you just sit. You can't stop breathing for example. You can't stop being hungry. And, by now, you ought to be able to guess at one other thing you can't stop doing. Yes, indeed, you can't stop thinking. This is one of the greatest misconceptions that many have about meditation. They seem to believe that meditating is a way to stop thinking or feeling while residing in some peaceful place. That is not the case at all. Painful emotions, thoughts, and bodily sensations abound in meditation practice. But you are taught to simply watch them come in and go out.

To sit still for extended periods of time and simply watch what your mind and body produce for you is an excellent way to practice acceptance, defusion, and being present. Used in conjunction with some of the other activities in this chapter, just sitting can be a particularly compelling way to develop your mindfulness practice.

Rather than read about it, why not experience it directly? What follows is an exercise that should help you begin your own meditation practice.

EXERCISE: Just Sitting

Many different forms of meditation are practiced all over the world. Some are focused or guided meditations where you either direct your consciousness to focus on a particular point, thought, or word, or you guide yourself on a "journey" through a predescribed set of instructions. Sitting practice is simply sitting quietly in a position that you maintain for the duration of the meditation, without moving much at all, while watching what comes up for you in an accepting, present, and defused way. There is no religious component to it (or at least, there doesn't have to be), and you shouldn't have a set of expectations going into it. The goal is to get in touch with the observing self, and simply see what there is to be seen.

The regimen. To do this, we recommend that you find a time in your day when you can consistently dedicate a designated amount of time to practice. How often you want to sit is up to you. The important thing is that you do it consistently. We suggest starting out with three fifteen-minute sessions a week. However, if this is too daunting, or you simply don't have the time, you could sit once a week. Put aside a certain amount of time, and practice when you have decided to practice. There will always be something that could get in the way and there will always be days when you don't feel like doing it. Simply look at these distractions and emotions for what they are, and practice when you've decided to practice anyway. If you sit only when you feel like it, or when it's convenient, you will find these periods disappear over time.

The place. It is also important to find a place where you can sit and not be too distracted. The point is not to eliminate distraction so much as it is to allow yourself the time and space to be able to sit quietly still for an allotted amount of time. If the kids come in every five minutes wanting to know what's for breakfast, this won't help you move in the direction you want to go. On the other hand, you will never be able to eliminate every distraction, so don't try. We live in a world brimming over with noise and activity. Part of the challenge of remaining mindful is not to become too rigidly trapped by this activity. Part of the practice is watching yourself when you do get trapped.

The amount of time. Don't begin by trying to sit for an hour at a time. It is unrealistic to expect you will be able to do this and be successful. It is far more reasonable to start out with smaller increments of time and build up as you go. If even fifteen minutes is too long to sit, then scale back and start with ten minutes, and slowly build up from there. You may want to increase the length of time you sit by two or three minutes every week, until you reach your goal time. Don't bite off too much more than you can chew. On the other hand, if you know yourself and know it will work to increase the amount of time more rapidly, then do so.

You can set your ultimate goal based on what works best for you, but few Westerners meditate for more than thirty minutes a day. This may seem like a lot of time, but if you start to practice, you may find that you *want* to do this. Meditation practice can have a dramatic impact on your life. Just do it regularly and see what works for you.

You may want to set an alarm or use some other means by which you can judge the amount of time that you will sit, without having to rely on your watch. You'll find it is very distracting to look at your watch all the time. Besides, constantly checking the time gives you a very convenient excuse to move, which is unhelpful. Once you have practiced sitting for a while, you'll find that your body will have a natural sense of how much time has elapsed. Ultimately, you can rely on that. In the meantime, set an alarm.

The posture. Shunryu Suzuki, a famous Zen teacher who lived in this country in the 1960s, often said, "The posture is the practice." Traditionally, sitting practice of the type we are discussing is done seated on a pillow on the floor in the lotus position. While in the lotus position, your legs are crossed. That is, you take your right foot in your hands and place it on your left thigh. You rest that foot on top of your thigh at the crease between your hip and your left groin. Then you take your left foot and place it on top of your right thigh, at the crease between your hip and your right groin. Your spine should be straight, chin pointed slightly downward, while the crown of your head reaches toward the sky. Your arms form a loose circle with your hands also forming a circle of their own, resting one on top of the other, thumbs touching lightly together. Seated in this position there are three points of contact with the ground: your two knees and your bottom via the pillow.

This is a somewhat advanced yoga posture. For beginners, this position is extremely difficult to get into and it is even more difficult to maintain over long periods of time. It takes a fair amount of flexibility to get your legs into that awkward position. In fact, one of the main reasons that yoga was created was as a means to slowly condition the body to be able to sit in this strange position.

We do not recommend that you attempt the lotus position unless you already have some experience with it, or you are naturally very flexible. We describe it as a means of illustrating some important points about the posture you should try to maintain when you practice a sitting meditation.

At the beginning, you will want to make a choice about sitting on the floor or in a chair. We recommend that you sit on the floor if that is possible for you. In the first place, it is an interesting experience to feel this posture. What's more, it encourages the practitioner to maintain a stable and erect posture (two of the most important components of sitting) by the very nature of the pose. We are so accustomed to sitting in chairs that we tend to slouch and relax in them. It is most important that you maintain an erect posture for the duration of your sit. In a chair, this is less likely to happen. However, if you have suffered some injury (particularly to your lower body) or you feel too much pain when you sit on the floor, sitting in a chair is a legitimate alternative.

There are three important principles illustrated in the lotus position. The first is that you must maintain an erect spine. You should be seated as straight as you can possibly sit. The second is to try to have three points touching the floor, your two knees and your bottom (on top of the pillow). This will ground you in the position more fully. If you are seated in a chair, the three points will be your feet (planted firmly on the ground) and your bottom on the chair. The third is the position of your hands and arms. If you allow your hands and arms just to hang at your sides, it is likely that the position of your spine will be compromised. Hence, you should follow the description above as to how to hold your hands and arms. If you can't do this, or you don't feel comfortable with it, place your hands in your lap.

If you choose to sit on the floor, you may want to buy a traditional pillow used for the purpose of seated meditation. These are called *zafu*. They are sold in many stores that sell Asian goods. If you can't get one, you can simply use a pillow, scrunched up under your bottom. It isn't quite as effective, but it works. You will want your bottom to be high enough off of the ground so that your knees naturally contact the floor when you are sitting.

There are three basic postures other than the lotus position that you can choose from. They are the half-lotus, the quarter-lotus, and the Burmese. In the half-lotus posture, you cross your legs and lift one foot onto your hip joint. In quarter-lotus, you sit cross-legged and lift one of your feet onto your knee. In the Burmese posture, you sit on the pillow, with both legs lying on the floor, one in front of the other, in a kind of abbreviated cross-legged position. All of the other points on posture discussed above apply.

If you choose to sit in a chair, make sure that you keep your spine straight. Do not lean your back against the back of the chair, but rather sit a little bit "out" on the chair, and let your body maintain an erect posture without the support of the chair. You will want your knees to be at ninety degrees from your hip joints. Your feet should be planted firmly on the floor, separated by about the width of your shoulders, with your toes pointing straight out in front of you. Again, all of the other points discussed above apply to this seated position.

The last point about sitting in this posture is this: *Be still*. Try not to move at all during the duration of your sit. If you find yourself shifting about, bring yourself back to the present, and sit still. Just sitting means not moving, to the degree this is possible. If you practice, you will be amazed at how still you can become.

The practice. The practice is to sit. There is no "goal" to speak of. There are, however, some things to keep in mind as you practice. Remember the exercise you did in chapter 6 where you watched your thoughts drift down a stream on floating leaves? Much of sitting meditation is about practicing this skill. You don't need to focus on anything in particular and you shouldn't try. Just let your mind generate whatever it wants to, and watch what it does with the time. Let the thoughts come in and go out. Simply watch them pass by.

Inevitably, there will be times when you get caught up in your thoughts. You may start daydreaming, or you may get trapped in your psychological pain. You may think about what you had for breakfast, what time the kids are due home from school, what movie you want to watch that night, or an ex-girlfriend you haven't seen in years. As you know, your mind is extremely adept at creating thought. It's likely you'll find when you sit quietly that it seems as if your mind's already natural talents have been amplified. You may have millions of thoughts flowing through your mind, and it's likely you'll get caught in them from time to time.

When this happens, simply notice that it has happened, and try to bring yourself back to the present moment and your observing self. Note that you have been in a thought and then return to the here and now. You've been practicing this skill over the course of the last two chapters, so you should have some sense of how to do this by now.

You may want to employ some of the defusion techniques that you learned in previous chapters. One technique that is particularly effective to use while sitting is to label your thoughts. As you watch your thoughts pass before your mind's eye, you may say, "I am having the thought that I had eggs for breakfast," or, "I am having the feeling that I am sad." It is also useful to note when you have drifted off, and even the thought that you have drifted off with: "I have been daydreaming about my ex-girlfriend. I am having the thought that I have been daydreaming."

You might also try using the exercise "Cubbyholing" above. This can be particularly effective while you sit, because it is brief but still allows you to notice your thoughts, feelings, and bodily sensations as they come and go.

Follow your breath. Another practice you can add to your sitting meditation is to "follow your breath." Simply watch your breath come in and go out of your body. This happens naturally. Feel the breath come in, feel the breath go out. Allow it to happen without getting in the way. If you want to, you can count your breaths, from one to ten. Once you have reached ten, go back to one. Just keep on watching your breath.

All kinds of content will come up when you sit. Your anger, depression, anxiety, low self-esteem—all of these may surface. Just watch them come in and go out. As they appear, treat them with kindness, the way you would pat a visiting child on the head in acknowledgment of his presence.

Physical pain. One matter that is very likely to come up while you sit, particularly when you start sitting longer for longer periods of time, is physical pain. Pain can be a very difficult distraction to sit through. Physical pain is an amazing phenomenon. It is remarkable how much your mind can focus on it.

Remember the studies we cited about chronic pain and the willingness to experience it in chapter 4? Trying to get free of physical pain can be as much a matter of experiential avoidance as trying to escape emotional pain, and, indeed, the methods discussed in this book have been shown to be helpful for people who suffer with physical pain (see the appendix). As such, we recommend that you try to sit with your pain, rather than getting up and moving around when you feel you "can't do it anymore." If you practice, you will find that you can sit with a lot more than you ever thought possible.

It is very likely that physical pain will be your greatest temptation to move. For novice practitioners, this is almost universally the case. Everyone goes through the pain of sitting at first; even the most experienced meditation teachers have had this experience. Sit with the pain for as long as you can. If you find that you absolutely can't continue to hold the position, move about just enough to adjust yourself, then resume your sit. If you give up, and avoid the experiences that pain brings, you will condition yourself not to sit at all. If you choose not to sit, that is one thing. If you allow experiential avoidance to dictate this choice to you, then you will have fallen into the same old trap.

Of course, it is necessary to take care of yourself, and if you have a real injury, you should attend to that. Be gentle with yourself. Gently press yourself forward, and continue with your practice.

MINDFULNESS IN CONTEXT

All of the material in this book works together. Many of the techniques you've learned in this chapter will be useful as you enter other components of the ACT program. Not only do you want to take mindfulness with you into your daily life, you will need to take it with you as you move forward with this book. In fact, you can take mindfulness with you and move backward in the book as well.

If you feel that you need to do some more work in cognitive defusion, try taking these mindfulness strategies with you and review some of the previous chapters.

It is also true, as noted in sections of this chapter, that many of the techniques presented here can be used in conjunction with one another. Experiment. See what works for you. Feel free to use many different mindfulness practices at the same time and combine techniques as you see fit. There are no hard rules to tell you how you "have to" be mindful. Do what makes sense for you.

There is no "right" way to be all of the time. Pretending that is true will simply lead you back into the traps that your verbal repertoire generates so well. Mindfulness is not the "right" way to live any more than anything else is. The practice is built to help you increase your psychological flexibility; to allow you to broaden the repertoire of responses that you can make to any given situation. Many studies have demonstrated that increasing psychological flexibility is very helpful for people who are suffering from the kind of distress that led you to pick up this book and work with it (see appendix).

None of the techniques in this chapter will work simply by reading about them, any more than reading about physical exercise will build your muscles. The techniques will be of value to you only if you do them, and do them repeatedly. If you have been reading this chapter for understanding, fine. You understand. Now practice. You will need these skills as we now deliberately move toward the pain that led you to pick up this book in the first place.

CHAPTER 9

What Willingness Is and Is Not

In chapter 4, we roughly defined acceptance and willingness as an answer to the question "Will you take me in as I am?" We said that to be accepting and willing is to say yes to the universe of private experience in the moment. Here is a quote from Dag Hammarskjöld, Former secretary-general of the United Nations, that expresses some of the power of saying yes to what life and your experience affords:

> I don't know Who—or what—put the question, I don't know when it was put. I don't even remember answering. But at some moment I did answer Yes to Someone—or Something—and from that hour I was certain that existence is meaningful and that, therefore, my life, in self-surrender, had a goal.

> —Dag Hammarskjöld

In this section of the two chapters that specifically deal with the concept of willingness, we will try to define what it means to say yes and we will practice doing so. First, however, you need to decide if now is the right time for you to do this. To do this, you need to be clear about what there is to be accepted. If you know what needs to be accepted in order for you to move ahead toward what you really care about in your life, then now is the time. If you aren't sure, then skip ahead to chapters 11 and 12, and return to chapters 9 and 10 after you finish working with chapters 11 and 12.

WHAT NEEDS TO BE ACCEPTED?

In some ways, acceptance of your experience is required, even when the situation calls for deliberately changing your experience. If you accidentally put your hand on a hot stove, you would immediately pull it back. If you did it quickly enough, you might even avoid tissue damage and the pain might pass in a matter of seconds. But to do that you needed to know first that you were hurting.

One of the saddest side effects of the chronic unwillingness to feel is that we begin to lose our ability to know what it is that we are avoiding. As mentioned in chapter 7, "alexithymia" (literally: "without words for feelings") is a clear example of the unwillingness to feel. If you chronically avoid what you feel, eventually you do not know what you are feeling at all. That's sad for two reasons. First, it's far easier to make mistakes in life as a result. For example, you may begin a bad relationship by missing the signs your own feelings would give you that your new love interest is very similar to past partners who didn't work out for you.

Or, by not recognizing the uneasy feelings that might have warned you, you could take a job that would be unhealthy or excessively stressful for you. Like someone who's lost the sense of pain, experiential avoiders can place their psychological hand on top of the hot stove and just leave it there to burn. Second, it is known that experiential avoiders actually tend to respond more intensely to events, both positively and negatively (Sloan 2004). In the service of keeping their distance from the pain they might otherwise feel more acutely than others, experiential avoiders also stand aloof from the joy they otherwise might feel more acutely than others.

Our general point is that acceptance doesn't mean that your emotions will change, just as defusion doesn't mean that your thoughts will change. Ironically, if change is possible at all, it is more likely to take place when we adopt an accepting and defused stance. When you avoid getting into an unhealthy relationship, for example, in a very real way you've avoided both pain and damage, just as removing your hand from a stove avoids both pain and damage. But first you had to feel the pain or you wouldn't have removed your hand.

There are other kinds of pain that are not like a hot stove. These are forms of pain that either necessarily come along with healthy actions or are historical in their nature, conditioned, and not based on the current situation. If you exercise vigorously, your muscles will be sore. If you study hard, you will be tired. If you remember a past loss, you will be sad. If you open up to relationships, you will feel vulnerable. If you care about the world, you will know that others are hurting. Most psychological pain seems to be of this type.

Anxiety is usually not based on real danger; depression is usually not based on the objective current situation. Feelings that are historical in their nature, conditioned, and not directly caused by the current situation are like that. Some of these feelings are not very good guides to action. For example, someone who has suffered abuse may be afraid of intimacy, even if that person's current partner is sensitive and kind.

In these kinds of situations, acceptance and willingness are needed for a second reason: without them, healthy action is not possible. Consider someone with panic disorder who has had several panic attacks in shopping malls and no longer dares to go inside a mall. Anxiety is, in part, a conditioned reaction. If shopping, freedom of movement, and the like are important to that person, eventually, it will be time to reenter shopping malls. That doesn't mean that the conditioning will now be magically removed. When such a person enters a mall again, guess what this person will then face? Anxiety. If that is unacceptable, the person now has an insurmountable barrier.

Ironically, as discussed earlier, anxiety is only exacerbated by trying to get rid of it directly. If this person decides to wait until the anxiety disappears until beginning to live again, he or she is likely to wait a very long time.

When we say "acceptance" or "willingness" in this book we are *not* referring to accepting situations, events, or behaviors that are readily changeable. If you are being abused by someone else, "acceptance of abuse" is not what is called for. What may be called for is acceptance that you are in pain, acceptance of the difficult memories that have been produced, and acceptance of the fear that will come from taking the necessary steps to stop the abuse.

If you have an addiction problem, acceptance of substance abuse is very likely not what is called for. What may be called for is acceptance of the urge to use drugs, or acceptance of the sense of loss that may result from giving up your favorite coping strategy, or acceptance of the emotional pain that will arrive when you stop relying on drugs or alcohol to regulate your emotions.

You may know right now what you need to accept in order to move ahead. If that is so, then this chapter and chapter 10 should be read next. Now, look at the following questions and see what comes up for you. If you have no idea what to write, just skip to the next question.

EXERCISE: What Needs to Be Accepted

The memories and images I most avoid include:

_____

_____

_____

Avoiding these memories and images costs me in the following ways:

_____

_____

_____

The bodily sensations I most avoid include:

_____

_____

_____

Avoiding these bodily sensations costs me in the following ways:

_____

_____

_____

The emotions I most avoid include:

_____

_____

_____

Avoiding these emotions costs me in the following ways:

_____

_____

_____

The thoughts I most avoid include:

_____

_____

_____

Avoiding these thoughts costs me in the following ways:

_____

_____

_____

The behavioral predispositions or urges to respond that I most avoid include:

_____

_____

_____

Avoiding these behavioral predispositions and urges to respond costs me in the following ways:

_____

_____

_____

We just listed five domains of avoidance (memories and images; bodily sensations; emotions; thoughts; and behavioral predispositions and urges to respond), and we've asked about the costs in each of these domains. If you were able to respond to the questions in two or more domains of those listed above, and if two or more of these have clear costs, then you are ready to proceed. If not, go on to chapters 11 and 12 and then return to this chapter.

THE GOAL OF WILLINGNESS

The goal of willingness is flexibility. When you are able to be fully present in the here and now without being judgmental or without pushing away experiences (thoughts, feelings, emotions, bodily sensations, and so on) you have much more freedom to take needed steps to action. If you are willing to have an emotion, feeling, thought, or memory instead of attempting to control it, then the agenda of control is undermined, and you are free from the inevitable by-products of this agenda. These by-products are fairly predictable. First, you lose the war with your own internal content. If you refuse to have that internal content, you've got it. If you aren't willing to lose it, you've lost it. Next, you lose the ability to control your own behavior in a flexible and effective way.

What Willingness Is Not

It's not easy to be willing. That doesn't mean it takes a lot of effort. Willingness is hard in the sense of "tricky," not in the sense of "effortful." It's tricky because it's an action that humans can learn but minds cannot. Our minds cannot fully understand willingness, because willingness is nonjudgmental and exists in the present, while the way that minds work is based on temporal relations and evaluations. (Remember in chapter 2 how we used our minds to figure out how to remove the screw from the board?) For that reason, to begin willingness work, it seems to help by becoming clear about what it isn't. That way, when your mind tells you that willingness is something that it isn't, the message can be taken with a grain of salt.

Willingness Is Not Wanting

In ACT, the first few times patients are asked whether they are willing to have a particular private experience (for example, a negative feeling), the most common response is "No, I don't want it." But that answer is quite revealing. Willingness is not a matter of wanting.

"Wants" are desired things we miss not having. (Originally, the word "want" meant "missing," and it is still occasionally used that way, as in "he starved for want of food."). If you look at the items you wrote down a few minutes ago—the memories, images, bodily sensations, emotions, and thoughts to be avoided—you weren't saying you "missed" them. If willingness meant wanting, no one would be willing to have pain. Someone with an anxiety disorder will never leap out of bed in the morning, saying, "Hey, I'm missing my panic attack!"

You can think of willingness in the same way you would think of welcoming a guest. Suppose you wanted to invite your entire extended family to come to your home for a feast. Everyone decides to come: your favorite Uncle Milton, your second cousin Jacques, your dear sister Sue. Dozens of relatives arrive at your house and everybody, including you, appears to be having a great time. As you look around, you're overjoyed to see that everyone came and they all seem to be getting along so well. Then, when you see a certain car pull up in front of your house, your heart sinks. It's your cranky old Aunt Ida. She rarely bathes. She doesn't have any kind words for anyone, but especially not for you. She likes to wolf down your food but will rarely say so much as a thank-you. But you told your whole family, "Everyone's welcome!"

The question is this: Is it possible truly to *welcome* Aunt Ida, even though you actually didn't *want* her to be there? Most of us have been in this situation and we know the answer: Welcoming is not the same as wanting. At its most basic level, you would welcome Aunt Ida by allowing her into your home, acknowledging her presence, asking her how she's been, and letting her join the party. You do so because you care about the family, and Aunt Ida is family. None of that requires you to first decide, "This party is missing Aunt Ida." Wanting her to come to your party is not the issue. Being willing to have her come is.

Now, suppose you decide, "Hell no! I'm not letting her in!" You slam the door shut in her face, and when she knocks, you grip the doorknob and yell, "Go away!" Several things would be likely to happen. First, this is no longer much of a party. You aren't doing fun things anymore. You're just trying to keep Aunt Ida out. Second, the other guests are affected by all of the commotion. They might become agitated, argue with you about your course of action, leave entirely, or withdraw into a distant part of the house. As they begin to leave the living room, Aunt Ida becomes more and more the center of attention. Third, you are no longer able to move. You are stuck to that door. For you, at least, the party is over.

Suppose that instead of trying to keep Aunt Ida out, you decide to let go of your attachment to your wants. You hold to your original decision to welcome all your guests. You show Aunt Ida where the punch bowl is. You offer her a few tasty appetizers. Now, even though you still don't want Aunt Ida to be there, you and your other guests can have a good party. You can mingle. You are free to come and go. So is Aunt Ida.

Willingness is exactly like that. Here is a quote that expresses this idea succinctly:

A joy, a depression, a meanness, some momentary awareness comes as an unexpected visitor. Welcome and entertain them all!

— Jelaluddin Rumi, translation by Coleman Barks (1997)

What this metaphor is about, of course, is all the feelings and memories and thoughts that show up that you don't like. There are many Aunt Idas at your door. If you wait for them to go away before the party begins, it will not begin. The issue is the stance you take with regard to your own experiences.

Willingness Is Not Conditional

There are effective and ineffective ways to limit willingness. First let's get really clear on the ineffective way. Learning to be willing is like learning to jump off of something. Jumping off of things has this quality: you put your body into space and gravity carries it down. You can jump off of a sheet of paper on the floor, or a very thick book, or an armchair, or the roof of your house, or an airplane. The action is exactly the same, only the situation is different. So, even when you are jumping off of a sheet of paper, you are learning how to jump and the same actions will be what is needed to jump from a book, chair, house, or airplane.

Now suppose you said, "Well I want to learn to jump ... but it's pretty scary, so I'll just step down instead. That way, I'm in control at every point." That makes good sense but it won't work because it can't generalize except to a few situations. You can step down from a sheet of paper, or a book, or even a chair, but you can't step down from your rooftop or from an airplane. So when you step down from a sheet of paper, you aren't learning how to jump, and you aren't learning something that will apply whenever you need it. It's just not the same thing.

When we discuss this concept with clients, they usually can think of elements in their lives that are like that. A rock climber who was in therapy once said, "It's like doing my climbing moves. I know if I do a move halfway, that I will come off the wall and be hanging there, dangling on the rope. If I have a move to practice, I have to practice all the way." An ice-skater explained that if she did even a simple jump half-heartedly, she was likely to trip and fall. She had to do simple jumps and difficult ones in the same way: as full jumps requiring her full attention. A dancer talked about how he had to let go and just dance, or he would be nothing but a pair of left feet.

Now, think of your own life. Have there been times when half-measures simply wouldn't work? List an example or two here:

_____

_____

_____

_____

Now consider the possibility that willingness is something like what you wrote down.

That doesn't mean that willingness cannot be limited. You can limit it by choosing your situations and times. You can be willing to go into the 7-11 with your anxiety, but not to go to the mall. You can be willing to talk to your brother about a past painful event, but not your mother. You can be willing to go into the mall for ten minutes, but not for twenty.

This is how to recognize the difference between being willing with appropriate conditions set on that willingness and not being willing at all. It is *not* safe to limit your willingness based on the degree or the quality of the painful private experience that might come up for you. "I am willing if it doesn't get too intense" is not safe. It isn't safe because basically it means "I am not willing at all." Judging how much you will allow yourself to feel before moving ahead is more like stepping down than jumping. However, to say, "I am willing for the next five minutes" is safe. You have set a limit, but it is not one of quality, rather it is a limit of time, of duration—or situation.

Willingness Is Not "Trying"

When clients are asked whether they are willing, often the response is "I will try." This is a sure sign of being only halfway willing.

The word "try" comes from a word that originally meant "to sift through or pick out." That's why a legal trial is called a "trial." "Try" and "trial" come from the same root. The problem with "trying" is that sifting through is a matter of conditional judgments and evaluations. (Note that we call the results of a legal trial a "judgment.") But willingness is the exact opposite of a conditional judgment and evaluation. Willingness is an active leap into the unknown. "Trying" has the quality of "weighing" or of "seeing if." It is full of passivity and judgment.

Sometimes we help clients to see the passive quality of "trying" by putting a pen on the table and saying, "Try to pick this up." If they pick it up, we shout "No, No! That's really picking it up. *Try* to pick it up."

The other connotation of "try" is "with great effort." This definition also does not apply because willingness, properly understood, has nothing to do with effort. You can try to move a large rock in the sense that you will use great effort, but you cannot guarantee the outcome. This doesn't apply to willingness because willingness is simply answering yes to your actual present experience. That is not a matter of effort or of seeing whether effort will produce a result. It is a mere yes or no. If willingness is applied to a feeling, we aren't talking about feeling what you do *not* feel, we are talking about feeling what you *already* feel. If there is any effort involved, it is in the opposite direction.

To see this clearly, take a minute to move your right hand to touch your left arm. Notice what it feels like.

Now move your right hand to touch your left arm and feel absolutely nothing.

Which of these two options took more effort? Did you have to "try" to feel what it already feels like, or did you simply feel it automatically?

Willingness Is Not a Matter of Belief

When clients are asked whether they are willing, at times, the answer is "I don't think I can." Since we've already spent so much time on defusion you can probably see the trap that is being laid. Willingness is not a matter of belief. Let us explain.

Let's return to feeling what it feels like to touch your arm. Repeat these words over and over again out loud: "I cannot touch my arm. I cannot feel my touch." Keep saying those sentences over and over again. Now, while still saying that you cannot, move your right hand to touch your left arm and notice what it feels like.

Our guess is that you felt your arm, regardless of what you were saying about it. Feeling what you already feel is not a matter of belief. It's fine to think that you cannot do it, and it's fine to think that you can. In any given moment, the issue is the same: Will you feel what you feel when you feel it? This is a yes or no question. It can be answered in only two ways: yes or no.

In exactly the same way, willingness is not something you hope to do, wish you could do, will try to do later, and so on. Willingness is a yes or no question in the moment.

Willingness Cannot Be Self-Deceptive

Sometimes clients secretly don't answer yes to the willingness question, but they go through the motions of saying yes in their efforts to deceive themselves. The sure sign of their secret unwillingness is that after they say the word yes, they say the word "if," and what follows the "if" is not something that can be voluntarily controlled. Such efforts at self-deception are doomed to failure.

This situation is like having a child who throws temper tantrums to get his way. Suppose you have a rule in your house that no video games can be played until all homework is done. Your child screams and cries and calls you a terrible parent. Now suppose you think to yourself, "I'm willing to let him have a tantrum without giving in … unless he uses foul language." Now, suppose your mind was like an open book, that your child can, in fact, hear your thoughts just as if you had said them aloud. Guess what you would get? You'd get swearing that would make a sailor blush. Now suppose you think to yourself, "I'm willing to let him have a tantrum without giving in … unless he has a tantrum for more than five minutes." If he could read your mind, guess what you would get? You'd get a tantrum that lasted just over five minutes.

Making deals with thoughts, feelings, sensations, and so on isn't workable because your mind has plenty of room for both the avoided event and the deception. It's exactly like the tantrum situation. Suppose you are willing to experience anxiety but you exempt one of these unsafe conditions in your willingness answer. You don't answer "yes" but "yes if," and the "if" isn't anything you can control. Let's say your answer is "yes, if the anxiety doesn't go over 60 on a scale of 1 to 100." Guess how high the anxiety will go?

Willingness as a Manipulation Is Not Willingness at All

This is the concept that minds can never get. According to your mind, the content of your pain is the source of your suffering because the pain is bad. Thus, you can measure suffering by the amount of the (bad) pain. For someone struggling with anxiety, a "good day" is a day with less anxiety. For someone struggling with depression, a "good day" is a day with less depression. And so on.

Willingness means abandoning that measurement. Suffering is no longer synonymous with the content of your pain. It is now synonymous with the postponement of living your life in the service of winning the struggle.

When you truly answer yes to the willingness question, it becomes a new game altogether, and the old measurements like "how anxious or depressed are you?" are no longer relevant. It's like a person who's been losing game after game of football suddenly sitting down in the middle of the football field, still in full football regalia, and painting a picture instead. Questions like, "How many points are there?" or "Are you winning?" would simply be no longer relevant.

In a real sense, willingness means shifting your agenda from the content of your pain to the content of your life. If that is true, willingness as a method of self-manipulation is not willingness at all. Minds can never learn this. Fortunately, people can.

One ACT client who had struggled for years with panic disorder and who had transformed his life as a result of therapy put it this way:

> I mainly notice when I'm in situations where I used to be locked into struggle, that the choice to struggle is almost gone. I've done that and know how that works. In a situation where I used to struggle, run away, or whatever, I still feel the lure to go ahead and struggle. I just try and get back to a more spiritual level, and kind of see it for what it is, and then just go with that.
>
> The agenda itself has actually shifted. It used to be about anxiety. The new deal is that it is about the struggle, and even the struggle with struggle. I look at it more as just a philosophy, or as a way of life. I don't really see it as just a therapy for a phobia. So, I see it more as just a life philosophy. It's like I've been given color. I was seeing black and white my whole life, and it's like I see rainbows now and stuff. A lot of the emotions I thought I couldn't have and wasn't willing to have … I can get as much enjoyment out of those now as anything else.
>
> Sadness was one, embarrassment was another, and then anxiety. And the anxiety is one that I still focus on the most, because it does have that life-threatening quality sometimes. I'm very in touch now with mortality, and like I said, you get a stabbing chest pain, numbness, and can't breathe, and you know that catches your attention. But in one sense I enjoy it all. So sadness, sadness used to be a thing that was awful.… It was so overwhelming in some areas that it almost felt life-threatening in itself. I would come up against issues in my life, and it was so sad that I thought if I was to have that or feel that fully, that I really wasn't sure what would happen. I couldn't conceive of being that sad.
>
> Now it's a whole new light. It's like I said—it's colors with better vision. I mean I see things in my past and the present so differently than I did just a few months ago, it just never

ceases to amaze me. So, I feel like I'm still growing all the time. My life is not just about agoraphobia. It's about living and people and myself and understanding.

What Willingness Is and Is Not

Willingness is:

- Holding your pain as you would hold a delicate flower in your hand

- Embracing your pain as you would embrace a crying child

- Sitting with your pain the way you would sit with a person who has a serious illness

- Looking at your pain the way you would look at an incredible painting

- Walking with your pain the way you would walk while carrying a sobbing infant

- Honoring your pain the way you would honor a friend by listening

- Inhaling your pain the way you would take a deep breath

- Abandoning the war with pain like a soldier who puts down his weapons to walk home

- Getting with your pain like drinking a glass of pure water

- Carrying your pain the way you carry a picture in your wallet

Willingness is not:

- Resisting your pain

- Ignoring your pain

- Forgetting your pain

- Buying your pain

- Doing what pain says

- Not doing what pain says

- Believing your pain

- Not believing your pain

Given that willingness is not something minds can understand, those words are unlikely to have had much impact in and of themselves. To get you started doing willingness as an action, we will have to sneak up on it with a combination of metaphors and exercises in the chapters that follow.

Let's say that the image of the head that follows is yours. Inside this head, write down a single troublesome emotion, memory, thought, sensation, or behavioral urge that you've been struggling with. Now look at what you've written. Does it evoke other strong and difficult feelings, thoughts, or other experiences that are themselves the targets of struggle? If so, write them down inside the head, too, because they are "fellow travelers" with your initial pain. Continue doing this until you have everything written down. If you can't fit everything you would like to on this sheet of paper, you can photocopy the blank form and fill in as many "empty heads" as you would like. When you have all the pain and chatter written down, make a copy of the page with all the pain you have floating around in your head.

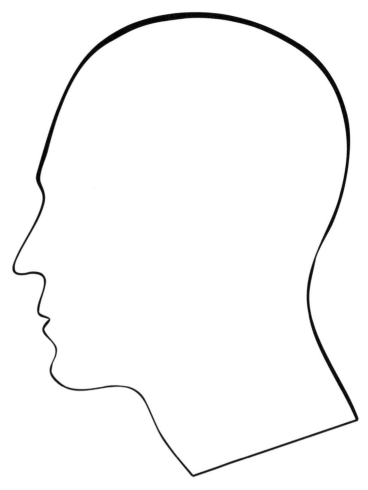

Figure 9.1: The pain in your head.

As we said at the beginning of this chapter, acknowledging that you are struggling with a head full of these issues is itself a kind of willingness. Willingness is the answer "yes" to the question "Will you take me in as I am?" Metaphorically, willingness is like taking the copy you made of the image of your head with all the pain in it, and putting it into your pocket to carry as a gesture that states, "I can and will carry this with me, not because I have to, but because I choose to." Before you actually do that, however, let's see if it is clearer now what willingness is not by answering the questions that follow.

Must you want to have this head full of all your issues in order to put it into your pocket? Hopefully, it is clear that the answer is no. Willingness is not wanting.

Must you first change what you've drawn in order to put it in your pocket? Hopefully, it is clear that the answer is no. Willingness is not conditional, except that you can choose to limit it by time and situation (for example, you could put the picture into your pocket for a single minute or a full week, or you could carry it with you at work or only at home).

Is putting what you've drawn into your pocket something that takes a lot of effort, so that you will have to try to see whether you can do it? Hopefully, it is clear that the answer is no. Willingness is not a matter of trying.

Must you believe something about this drawing in order to put it into your pocket? Hopefully, it is clear that the answer is no. Willingness is not a matter of belief. Beliefs are just more issues that could be drawn inside the head.

Is pretending to put the paper into your pocket the same as putting it into your pocket? Hopefully, it is clear that the answer is no. Willingness is not self-deceptive.

If you spent some time on it, you might end up with a head that looks something like figure 9.2.

The head looks very busy. But must it be your enemy?

As a physical metaphor for a real change in direction in your life, are you willing to put your head on paper into your pocket and carry it for a while? We suggest carrying it one hour or more a day, but if that is too much for you right now, specify the amount of time you will carry it and commit to doing so.

If the answer is "yes, if ... " and the "if" is something you do not control, try again. If the answer is no, dig into what that answer is in the service of, and see whether it is really in your best interests. If your answer is a good, clean yes, then put it into your pocket.

Go back to the bulleted list of things that willingness is, and see if you can carry this paper that way. During the time you choose to carry it, pat your pocket periodically to remind yourself of what you are carrying. In this physical meta-

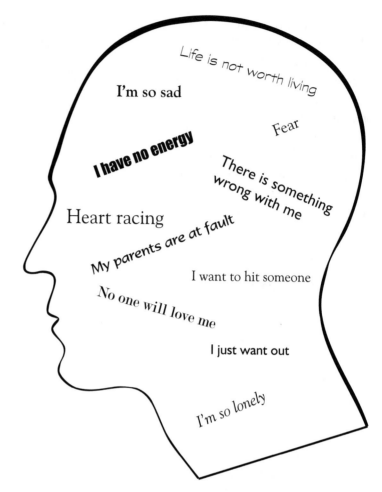

Figure 9.2: What the pain in your head might look like.

phor, see whether it is okay to have all that stuff on the paper and still do whatever you need to do in your life as you go about day-to-day living. Let carrying the picture of your head stuffed with your issues be a way of asking yourself whether the stuff on that paper really stands between you and living a powerful, vital life, or whether you can, in fact, carry it gently, lovingly, and willingly, as it is and not as it says it is.

CHAPTER 10

Willingness: Learning How to Jump

Life is asking you a question. The question was once mumbled, misunderstood, or nearly inaudible. It's not surprising that you haven't answered yes, but, unfortunately, failing to answer or answering no have nearly the same results, and they have those results whether you know that you are being asked a question or not.

One purpose of this book is to help you hear the question. Another is to figure out whether it's really in your best interests to continue giving life the same answer or nonanswer. If it isn't in your interest to continue with a negative or nonanswer, then the purpose of this book is to help you get to saying yes to life.

The question is complex in its form but simple in its essence. We call it "The Life Question." Now read through the following multipart question several times until you can hold on to it as a single question:

- Starting from the place in which there is a distinction between you as a conscious, mindful human being on the one hand, and all of the private experiences you are conscious of and struggle with on the other hand,

- are you willing to feel, think, sense, and remember all those private experiences,

- fully and without defense,

- as you directly experience them to be, not as what your mind says they are,

- *and*, do whatever it takes to move you in the direction of that which you truly value,

- at this particular moment, and in this particular situation?

- YES or NO?

It's time to begin to jump. Using all of the skills you've learned so far, now's the time. Answering yes to the life question, no matter how narrowly it's cast, is such a jump. It is a jump into the unknown. It is a jump into a world in which getting rid of or managing your own history is no longer required in order to begin to live the life you truly want to live. It is a world of self-acceptance, openness, ambiguity of content, and clarity of purpose. It is a world of psychological flexibility, in which you let go of the struggle, give up and live, less concerned about being right than being alive.

You do not *have* to say yes. Life will accept either answer. There is, however, a cost to silence or to saying no. Indeed, you've been experiencing those costs. Your pain is your biggest ally here. Have you suffered enough? Have you?

We don't want to scare you. You don't have to begin by jumping from the Empire State Building. You can jump off a sheet of paper, or a thin paperback book. But if you are going to start, you must start. In fact, you already started at the end of the last chapter. You carried your head around with you. Did having a representation of your head on paper stop you from doing what you needed to do? Did it really determine what happened to you? If you found you were able to carry it around with you, then what stands between you and doing the same with other issues you've been struggling with?

THE WILLINGNESS SCALE

In the following exercise, you are asked to identify a thought, memory, emotion, or sensation that you tend to avoid; one that has cost you because of your avoidance (e.g., anxiety, anger, guilt, depression, confusion, and so on). You can use the issues and problems you wrote about while you were working with chapter 9, or refer to your Suffering Inventory from chapter 1, or to various other internal-content tracking exercises you've done up to this point. Any of these would provide good places to start, but feel free to change them if something else seems more doable or more important.

When you have the thought, memory, emotion, or sensation in mind, write it down here (we will call this the "target"):

_____

_____

_____

Now imagine the two radio dials alluded to in chapters 3 and 4: one easily seen, the other is less visible and harder to see. The easily seen dial is called Discomfort and it includes problems like unpleasant sensations or emotions (e.g., anger, anxiety, guilt, or depression) or unpleasant thoughts or memories. Now, imagine that this dial has a range from 0 to 10. Although it looks like an ordinary dial that can be set to any value you wish, it turns out that the Discomfort dial moves on its own; when you try to move it, it quickly returns to whatever value it goes to, regardless of your preferences.

Now, write down the intensity of the Discomfort dial associated with your target item:

_____

We think one reason why you are spending time with this workbook is that the volume on your Discomfort dial is set too high for your liking. This doesn't necessarily mean that it's a high number, although as a rule, that is the case. Sometimes, a "volume setting" of even 2 or 3 is thought to be "too high."

Remember that you learned in chapter 3 that there are two dials? The one in the back is not so obvious. We're going to call this dial Willingness and it too ranges from 0 to 10. If you are maximally open to experiencing your own experience as it is, directly without trying to manipulate it, avoid it, escape it, or change it, you've set the Willingness dial to 10. That is the setting we are after. If you are maximally closed to experiencing your own experience as it is, that's a 0.

Now, looking back at where you were when you first picked up this book, write down where you were setting the Willingness dial with your target item:

_____

Finding that your Discomfort dial reads a high value and then setting your Willingness dial to a low value is a terrible combination. Setting the Willingness dial low is like setting a ratchet. A ratchet wrench can move only one way once the ratchet has been engaged. If your Willingness dial is set low, there is no way that the anger, anxiety, depression, guilt, or unpleasant memories (the Discomfort dial) you may be experiencing in the present moment can go down consistently. For example, if you are really, really, really not willing to feel anxiety, and then, if anxiety shows up for you, that anxiety becomes something else to be anxious about. You have a self-amplifying loop.

If you set your Willingness dial at a 10, then the ratchet disengages. This does *not* mean that your discomfort will go down. It will or it won't. If you set your Willingness dial high *in order* to get your Discomfort dial to go down, it acts like a knob with a spring in it. Your Willingness dial will automatically spring back to a low level again. Self-deception, secret deals, and hidden agendas won't work here. If you set your Willingness dial high, it means abandoning the value provided to you by your Discomfort dial as a measure of progress in your life, as least in this specific instance or area.

If you can't set your Willingness dial high in order to control your Discomfort dial, then why set it high at all? One answer your own pain tells you is that not setting it high is associated with the deadening pain of your life not lived. It doesn't work. So one safe answer is simply, why not? If the alternative doesn't work, why not?

The less flippant answer is perhaps more direct, but it can easily be misunderstood. It will not be fully understood until you start to do the work in chapters 11, 12, and 13. You set your Willingness dial high in order to live an empowered, vital, valued human life.

The final reason why you might want to set your Willingness dial high is simply because, unlike the Discomfort dial, this one is your responsibility. Does your experience tell you that you control the Discomfort dial? Presumably not; otherwise, why isn't it set low all the time? It looks like a dial you can move, and you can put your hands on it and turn it, but it functions more like a passive meter than a dial you can set.

But note who controls the Willingness dial. Isn't it clear that you do? In fact, you are the only one who can. Life can yank the Discomfort dial up or down. A loved one dies: Boom. The Discomfort dial moves. You find out you have a life-threatening illness. Boom. Your spouse is unfaithful. Boom. But no matter which of these unfortunate events happen to you, the Willingness dial is something you, and only you, can turn. So which would you rather work on? The dial you don't control or the dial you do?

TAKING A JUMP

It is time to jump. Look at the target item you wrote down above, and ask yourself this question: What stands between me and resetting my Willingness dial high in regard to my target item? When you've thought about this for a while, it may occur to you that no content can take away your freedom to set the dial anywhere you choose to set it. If this is so, then it's time to take your first willingness leap.

You can safely limit your leap only by time or situation. For example, you may put down a 10 to express your willingness to experience anxiety in the worksheet below, but then add time qualifiers, such as "while shopping in the 7-11 store this afternoon for five minutes." That means you will allow yourself to feel anxiety as fully as you can experience it while shopping (without leaving the store, freezing in your tracks, separating yourself from your experience, and so forth), but you are committing to doing this only for five minutes. *Do not pick a willingness leap that is beyond you right now.* No one has a radar gun pointed at you. Speed is not the issue. It's more important to learn to leap at all than to start by trying to leap tall buildings in a single bound. However, if you know that a big leap is the right thing to do, go ahead. If you're not sure, start small. But starting small means limiting the time or context, not the setting on the Willingness dial. If you can't get the dial set to a 10, it is not worth doing even for a second.

I (SCH) once worked briefly with a patient of a close colleague of mine. I was consulted on the case. The patient felt such terrible loneliness that she believed that if she willingly allowed herself to feel its far-reaching effects, she would be destroyed by its intensity. Her marriage had broken up, she had no job, she lacked adequate education to find anything but the most menial employment, her friends had abandoned her, she was barely surviving on disability insurance, and she'd tried to commit suicide and failed. Her life seemed absolutely empty and meaningless. In a therapy session, my colleague and I asked if she would allow herself to feel her loneliness, and she kept saying no until we got her down to agree to be fully willing for one second. She agreed to feel lonely openly and without defense for one second. That was a start.

After months of working with ACT she terminated therapy. Years passed. We'd completely lost track of her but she called a few weeks ago. Now, more than a decade later, she has a degree, a job, a partner, friends, and a purpose. She has a life. She walked through hell to get there, one moment at a time. And that journey started somewhere. It started with her willingness to feel lonely, to feel it deliberately without any defenses, as you might reach out to feel a fine fabric, for one single solitary second.

EXERCISE: Willingness Scale Worksheet

Now, fill this out:

With regard to my target item, I am setting my Willingness dial at (see if you can get to 10! If not, pause and reconsider. It functions more like a switch than a dial, so anything less than a 10 might not work. See if you can get to 10!):

_____

My limitations are (only limit your willingness by time and situation, not by intensity or the presence or absence of other private experiences).

_____

_____

USING YOUR SKILLS AND LEARNING SOME NEW ONES

When you make a choice like the one you just made, various issues may come up immediately. If they do, use your skills. If your mind starts screaming, just notice your thoughts as thoughts; don't argue with them. For example, your mind may predict an awful future or it may demand reassurance that your willingness leap is not dangerous.

Any attempt to reassure your mind with literal arguments will just feed your old habits, and you will become more entangled. Just thank your mind for the input, and provide reassurance by the very act of having silent faith in yourself. That is the confident thing to do, as the etymology of the word "confidence" implies ("con" means "with" and "fidence" is from the Latin "*fides*" which means "faith" or "fidelity.") If your body starts rumbling or demanding attention in any way, just feel what you feel where you feel it. Be patient, loving, and kind with yourself.

Now that you've reached a yes, no matter how small it is (remember the woman with her one-second commitment), you need to practice applying your skills to this situation and to others like it. The rest of this chapter will present several exercises that will allow you to build your willingness skills. These will be graded exposures in which you can practice your new skills, one step at a time, as you encounter painful personal content.

As mentioned earlier when you chose your target, there is no reason to rush into anything that is immensely painful. Push yourself to work on each new step presented, but be compassionate with yourself. In the next exercise, you'll work on the item you just said yes to above, practicing willingness, so that when you implement your choice to be willing you will be better prepared for the potential outcomes of that choice.

EXERCISE: Physicalizing

When we look at objects external to ourselves, we do not take them to be self-referential. Imagine you are walking down the street and you notice an ugly pile of trash. Normally you wouldn't take it to be a sign that you are a horrible person. However, if instead of the pile of trash, you noticed a feeling of self-loathing, you might fuse with that feeling and take it as an indicator that you are a horrible person. But, as you now know, this feeling doesn't define you any more than the pile of trash you noticed. This exercise takes advantage of that distinction to help us learn to be more willing to sit with painful events.

Begin by looking at the target item you wrote down in preparation for the Willingness Scale Worksheet exercise. Get in touch with how you feel when you make contact with your target event.

Now we would like you to imagine taking this feeling and placing it four or five feet in front of you. Later we'll let you take it back, so if it objects to being put outside, let it know that you will be taking it back. See whether you can set it out on the floor in front of you in the room in which you are reading.

It may help you to close your eyes and imagine it, and when you get it out there, open your eyes just long enough to read the next question. Then close your eyes again, see what comes up in response to the question, and allow this feeling to assume the properties that come to mind. This exercise may seem a little strange, but don't let that stop you.

EXERCISE: Giving Your Target a Form

If this target had a shape, what shape would it be? (Close your eyes and let the answer come up ... try to really picture it.)

_____

If this target had a size, how big would it be? (Close your eyes and let the answer come up ... try to really picture it.)

_____

If this target had a color, what color would it be? (Close your eyes and let the answer come up ... try to really picture it.)

_____

If this target had power, how powerful would it be? (Close your eyes and let the answer come up ... try to really picture it.)

_____

If this target had a weight, how much would it weigh? (Close your eyes and let the answer come up ... try to really picture it.)

_____

If this target had a speed, how fast would it go? (Close your eyes and let the answer come up ... try to really picture it.)

_____

If this target had a surface texture, what would it feel like? (Close your eyes and let the answer come up ... try to really picture it.)

_____

If this target had an a internal texture, what would it feel like inside? (Close your eyes and let the answer come up ... try to really picture it.)

_____

If this target could hold water, how much volume would it hold? (Close your eyes and let the answer come up ... try to really picture it.)

_____

Now close your eyes one last time and picture the entire object. See if you can drop your struggle with an object made up of this exact size, shape, color, power, weight, speed, surface texture, internal texture, and volume. Try to be willing to experience it fully, without defense. Meditate on that for a few moments.

Now, see whether there are any sticky negative reactions that appear to interfere with your willingness to have this object be exactly as you experience it to be. These reactions might be things like disliking it, fearing it, judging it, or just wanting it to go away. Close your eyes and see if any reactions like that are rumbling around.

If there are not, you can end this exercise. If there are any, move the original target object off to the right and imagine taking your sticky, difficult reaction to that target and putting *it* four or five feet in front of you, next to the first one. See whether you can get *it* out in front of you on the floor in this room. For example, if you find that you hate the first thing, put "hate" out on the floor next to the first object. We will call this second one the "new target."

If this new target had a shape, what shape would it be? (Close your eyes and let the answer come up ... try to really picture it.)

_____

If this new target had a size, how big would it be? (Close your eyes and let the answer come up ... try to really picture it.)

_____

If this new target had a color, what color would it be? (Close your eyes and let the answer come up ... try to really picture it.)

_____

If this new target had power, how powerful would it be? (Close your eyes and let the answer come up ... try to really picture it.)

_____

If this new target had a weight, how much would it weigh? (Close your eyes and let the answer come up ... try to really picture it.)

_____

If this new target had a speed, how fast would it go? (Close your eyes and let the answer come up ... try to really picture it.)

_____

If this new target had a surface texture, what would it feel like? (Close your eyes and let the answer come up ... try to really picture it.)

_____

If this new target had an internal texture, what would it feel like inside? (Close your eyes and let the answer come up ... try to really picture it.)

_____

If this new target could hold water, how much volume would it hold? (Close your eyes and let the answer come up … try to really picture it.)

_____

Now, close your eyes one last time and picture the new target object. See if you can drop your struggle with this new object … with an object of its size, shape, color, power, weight, speed, surface texture, internal consistency, and volume. Try to be willing to experience it fully, without defense. Meditate on that for a few moments.

Now before taking these objects back, since they do reside within you, close your eyes and just take a peek at the first target object and see if it looks any different in size, shape, color, and so on. It may or may not change, but just take a peek. Do you see any differences? If so, note what they are below:

_____

_____

_____

Now imagine picking the new target up from the floor and taking it back inside of you, then take the first target and do the same, but also realize that it's possible to be more willing toward the things we struggle with, and notice, too, that it is how we react to these events that gives them much of their power over us. Close your eyes and bring both objects back inside you, willingly, much as you would welcome a guest into your home.

As we physicalize painful and avoided events, usually we become more able to embrace them. Many of you probably noticed that the second target was as difficult or more so than the first. Some of you even noticed, as you let go of your struggle with the second, the first target got lighter, less heavy, or smaller when you peeked back at it at the end. If this was true for you, you've discovered something really important: The power of avoided events derives more from our unwillingness to have them than from the features they have.

Taking Apart the Problem

Facing our problems is like facing a thirty-foot monster composed of tin cans, wire, and string. In this seemingly overwhelming form, the monster is very difficult to face. If we disassemble him, however, into all the separate cans, wires, and string that he's made of, each of these pieces is easier to deal with one at a time.

In the next exercise, we will walk through the multiple dimensions of your target item, and see if it is possible to embrace each element willingly. If you recall the metaphor of being in a tug-of-war with your own emotions, in essence we will "drop the rope" with each domain, one at a time.

You can do this either in workbook form or as an eyes-closed exercise. To do it the latter way, you can read it into a tape recorder (leaving long pauses where you will need time to process the instructions), and then with your eyes closed, follow the tape and do the work. Or you can have a friend read it aloud to you. Be sure to ask your friend to give you the time you need before proceeding. Setting up a signal system at each pause would be a good idea, such as your friend not reading past a pause until you raise your finger.

If you do it as a workbook exercise, do it slowly (don't rush through it just reading, for it will be unlikely to have any impact that way). Instead read a little, do thoroughly what the text asks, then read the next part, and so on. This exercise can easily take an hour or more if you take your time to do it properly, so don't start until you have the time and a quiet place in which to work.

EXERCISE: The Tin-Can Monster

In this exercise you will continue to work with the target item you've been exploring this chapter. However, you may want to copy this exercise before you start working on it, so you can do this with different targets later.

Get comfortable wherever you are seated. Now first notice your breathing and take a few nice deep breaths, with the air coming in through your nose and out through your mouth. See if you can notice those parts of your body that come in contact with the place you are sitting. Now notice any sounds that are present in or outside the room. Take at least a minute just to get centered before moving on. You can use some of the mindfulness exercises presented in the last chapter to this effect.

Start out by recalling something that happened last summer. Anything that comes to mind is fine. Remember what was happening then. Remember where you were and what was happening. See if you can see, hear, and smell, just as you did last summer. Don't remember the scene as if you were someone else looking at the scene from the outside. Do it from inside the body of the person called "you" who was there, looking out from behind your eyes. Close your eyes and take a few moments to imagine this scene.

Now notice as you remember the scene that *you were there*. There was a person behind those eyes, just as there is now. And although many things have happened since last summer, notice too that there is an essential continuity between the part of you that is aware of what you are aware of now, and the part of you that was aware of what you were aware of back then. As you know from chapter 8, we call that person the "observer-self." See whether you can do the rest of this exercise from the point of view of your "observer-self." You can let the scene you've called into memory go once you have gotten into the observer's seat.

Bodily sensations. Get in touch with your target. Take a few moments to do this. Deliberately become aware of the feelings that are attached to your target.

Now watch your body and see what it does. Just stay in touch with the feelings and watch your body. See if you notice any bodily sensations arising. If there are several, select just one to focus on. If you are doing this exercise in workbook form, write down your bodily sensation on the line below:

_____

Now focus on that single bodily sensation. If other events crowd in (thoughts, emotions, memories, other bodily sensations), let them know you will get to them later, and shift your attention back to this bodily sensation. Notice where the sensation begins and ends. Notice exactly where it is in your body. If you could make a sculpture in the shape of this sensation and put it into your body, what would it look like?

Now see if you can completely "drop the rope" with this sensation. Must it be your enemy? Is it okay to have it be exactly as it is? If you find there is still something you are resisting, create an imaginary sculpture that is 100 percent identical to the sensation and place it where the sensation was, so that everywhere the sensation used to be, you now have the identical sensation that you created. They are identical, but this one you created. See if you can allow this sensation to be there as it is, instead of running away from it. How would that be? You aren't promising yourself you will always do this, but for just this moment, see whether you can do it.

Now go back to get in touch with your target, and once again watch your body and see what it does. See if there are any other bodily sensations that pop up in association with your target. If there are, that's just one more sensation to focus on. If you are doing this exercise in workbook form, write it down here:

_____

Now focus just on *that* bodily sensation. Notice where the sensation begins and ends. Notice exactly where it is in your body. And once again see if you can give up any sense of struggle with this sensation. Is it okay to have that sensation (not "okay" as if you like it, but just "okay" in the sense that you acknowledge it and allow it to be what it is). Take a few moments and sit with that feeling until you sense that you are a little more open to having that feeling in your body.

If you find that you are talking to yourself about it, that is a thought. We aren't dealing with thoughts yet. Just come back to feeling the sensation and seeing whether you can renegotiate your relationship with it. Are you willing to sense what you are already sensing?

Now set that aside and get in touch with your original target. Take about a minute to look for other specific bodily sensations. You can repeat the process described above as many times as you wish for each different specific bodily sensation. After a while, you also can just go through and notice all the little twinges or other reactions that appear, without spending much time on each. As each one pops up, notice it and acknowledge it. It would be like waving to one acquaintance after another from across the street. Just welcome them and acknowledge them, without arguing, agreeing, doing what they say, resisting, defending, or any of the rest. You can write down any other bodily sensations that appear here, one at a time.

_____   _____   _____

_____   _____   _____

_____   _____   _____

After you have exhausted all of your physiological sensations, then you are ready to move on to your emotions.

Emotions. Go back and get in touch with your target once again. Take a few moments to do so. Deliberately become aware of that feeling.

This time, watch for emotions associated with your target. Just watch and see what they do. Stay in touch with your feelings and take a few moments to see what comes up for you. If several things come up, select one to focus on. If you are doing this exercise in workbook form, write it down here.

_____

Focusing just on this one specific emotion, see if you can actually get next to this emotion by choice, instead of running away from it. See if it's okay for you right now to feel this particular emotion.

The goal here is not to like or dislike the emotion. We aren't evaluating it. The goal is to feel it, as it is, without needless defense. Try not to let it spread out into other areas like thoughts, or behavioral predispositions. Just go into the emotion. We will get to the others later.

Is there anything in this emotion that you cannot have in this moment and this moment only? Is there anything truly dangerous, harmful, hostile, or bad that requires you to get rid of it, or considering it only as an emotion, is this something you can experience? However much you have opened up to this specific emotion, see if you can open up to it just a little bit more. Again, see if you can actually get next to this emotion by choice, instead of running away from it. See if right now you can stay with this one emotion. Take a few minutes and sit with that emotion until you sense that you are a little more open to it.

Now set that aside and get in touch with your original target. Take about a minute looking for other specific emotions. You can repeat the process as many times as you wish with each different specific emotion, but see whether you can do at least one more round. When you feel another emotion, write it down below:

_____

Now repeat all of the same steps as before. See if you can let go of any sense of struggle with this emotion.

After taking a minute or two to do that, look again, and if you sense there are other emotions present, just notice and acknowledge them. As each one pops up, just welcome them and acknowledge them. You can write down the names of the other emotions that show up below, one at a time. Don't go on to the next item until you sense that you are beginning to "drop the rope" (i.e., that you stop struggling so much) with the emotion on which you are focused.

_____	_____	_____
_____	_____	_____
_____	_____	_____

After you have exhausted all of the emotions that are attached to your target, you are ready to move on to behavioral predispositions and urges to action.

Behavioral predispositions. See if you can get in contact with the person behind your eyes, the observer you, the aware person you've been your whole life. As we have been diving into your content, that sense of self may have slipped away, and doing this exercise effectively requires contact with this more transcendent aspect of our experience. From that perspective (or point of view) get in touch with your target feeling. Take your time until you have it.

Now, see whether you can sense an urge or a pull toward action. What do you want to do when you feel this? Don't actually do it, just notice the pull to engage in this behavior. It's almost as if your muscles are starting to move. It's kind of like a bodily sensation, but it's more like the beginnings of a behavioral sequence. When you have one write it down here:

_____

This time, instead of just doing that behavior or trying to suppress it, stay exactly where you are and feel what it feels like to feel the pull to behave in this way, without actually behaving in this way. It's like standing on the ledge of a tall bridge over a river and feeling a slight pull to step back or to jump. Instead of stepping back or jumping, just feel the pull. Now ask yourself, "Is there anything in this pull that is something I cannot have? Is it fundamentally bad or something that will destroy me? Is it something that I must get rid of?"

As before, if other reactions (bodily sensations, emotions, thoughts, etc.) try to creep in, let them know you will get to them later.

Take a few minutes and sit with your behavioral predisposition until you sense that you are a little more open to its pull to act on it, without needing to act on it or make it go away.

Now set your behavioral predisposition aside. Again, get in touch with the person behind your eyes, the observer you. From this perspective, see whether you can bring the target feeling into the center of your consciousness. Watch quietly for what other behavioral predispositions may be present. As you watch, stay with your observer-self—the part of you that has always been you. Watch from there. When you have another behavioral predisposition write it down below:

_____

Then, repeat the same steps as above. Repeat this process as many times as you can with all the different behavioral predispositions that appear. Write each of them below. As you contact each, the key is to see if you can be more willing to feel this pull toward action without either compliance or avoidance. Try to stay with each one until that happens. The goal is to be more willing to have it as it is, not as what it says it is. Write down each one that appears:

_____   _____   _____

_____   _____   _____

_____   _____   _____

After you have exhausted them all, then you are ready to move on to thoughts.

Thoughts. Thoughts are very tricky, so take a moment to gently get in contact with the person behind your eyes, the observer you. You can't look *at* this part of yourself, because it is just looking *from* the I-here-now, so just touch the "big mind" part of yourself, and then look at this next domain from that perspective.

Get in touch with the target you've been struggling with and then watch which thoughts show up from this place. See if you can catch just one, much as you might catch a fish. See if you can reel it in and write its name down below. You've practiced this skill quite a bit by now, so you should have some sense of how to do this.

_____

_____

_____

Now see if you can just think that thought without trying to minimize, diminish, or argue with it. It's important that you don't try to dismiss it, because it will demand your attention and agreement if you do. See if you can really listen to it and give it your maximum attention, much as you might listen to a babbling baby: carefully but with neither disagreement nor agreement. You are not believing the thought and you are not disbelieving it. You are seeing it as a thought. (Remember "milk, milk, milk"?)

Notice that it is indeed true that your mind thinks this when coming in contact with your target. Is it okay if that thought is simply a thought?

See if you can think that thought as a choice. This doesn't mean you believe it. It doesn't mean you disbelieve it. It means allowing your mind to think that thought as a thought on purpose. Ask yourself if there is anything in there that is fundamentally bad, hostile, or harmful that you cannot have, if this thought is just a thought.

When you sense you are more willing to think the thought as a thought, set it aside and get in touch with your target. Take a moment to do that … do not rush through this. Once you are experiencing your target, go "thought fishing" again. When you catch the next thought associated with your target, write it down here:

_____

_____

_____

And thank your mind for that thought: "cool, nice thought … that's a good one." Notice whether you've seen that thought before. Do not do any of this dismissively or in a way that patronizes your mind. You are allowing it to do what it knows how to do without adding or subtracting from it. It will provide you with a sequence of words that you are going to hear and you are going to respectfully decline to struggle with these thoughts, either way. You are just going to hear them, with understanding.

If other physiological sensations, emotions, or thoughts try to creep in, let them know you will get to them later.

Sit with that thought until you sense that you can just think the thought without trying to minimize, diminish, argue with it, or do what it says in order to make it go away. Then set that thought aside. Again, get in touch with the person behind your eyes, your observer-self. From this perspective, contact the target and place it fully in the center of your consciousness; again, watch quietly for other thoughts that may be associated with it. Write down any that appear, and either repeat the process above with each thought as many times as you wish, or just acknowledge them in a defused and accepting way, and watch for the next thought to write down.

_____   _____   _____

_____   _____   _____

_____   _____   _____

After you have exhausted this domain, you are ready to move on to your memories.

Memories. Again, see if you can get in contact with the person behind your eyes, your observer-self, the person you have been your whole life. From that perspective, or point of view, get in touch with your target item.

Okay. For the last part of this exercise, imagine you have all the memories from your life on little snapshots, like index cards filed away in a file drawer, all the events of your life from your birth until the present moment. Get in touch with your target, open the file cabinet, and start gently flipping through your cards of memories. Start from the present, and flip back deeper and deeper into your past. If you find yourself pausing at any picture, stop flipping and look at that memory. Write a note to yourself that will remind you later of which memory came up:

_____

_____

_____

Now just notice, from behind the eyes of the person called "you," your observer-self:

- Who else was there?

- What were you feeling?

- What were you thinking?

- What were you doing?

- What did you want to do?

Now, see if you can let go of any struggle that might be associated with your memory. It might be a pain associated with the picture, or an unwillingness to leave it because of the happiness associated with it. Whatever your reactions to the memory, just see if you can gently let go of your struggle with it and make room for all of those reactions. See if you can let yourself be willing to have that memory exactly as it is. That doesn't mean you'll like it, but that you are willing to have it.

If there is anything in that memory that you didn't fully process at the time, there will be a sense that the work in the memory is incomplete. For example, you may have felt angry in the memory but hid it. If so, see if you can go into that part of the memory and complete the work you didn't know to do then: feel what you felt, think what you thought, and so on. Your guide here is a "reverse compass." If you sense a part of you saying, "Don't go there," see if, in fact, it is possible to go there; if it is what it is, not what it says it is.

When you have thoroughly remembered your memory and have a sense that you are open to it, then put the memory back in the "file drawer."

Now, from your observer-self perspective, get back in touch with the target feeling you chose at the beginning of this exercise. Once again, open the file cabinet and start gently flipping through the cards of memories while you are in touch with your target. This time go farther back. How far back you go is up to you. If you pause over a memory, even if it doesn't seem to be related, stop and pull it out and look at it. Write it down below.

_____

_____

_____

Now with that memory, repeat all of the steps you did above.

- Who else was there?

- What were you feeling?

- What were you thinking?

- What were you doing?

- What did you want to do?

See if you can let go of any struggle that may be associated with the memory. Take your time. If you find resistance or pain, just gently go there and look at the resistance. Look at the pain. See if you can let yourself be willing to have that memory exactly as it is.

Once again, if there is anything in that memory you didn't fully process at the time, there will be a sense that the work in the memory is incomplete. Once again, see if you can go into that part of the memory and complete the work you didn't know to do then: feel what you felt, think what you thought, and so on.

Now put that memory aside. If you didn't get back into your early childhood, repeat this entire sequence one final time using a memory from your early childhood. Write it down:

_____

_____

_____

And then rethink it. Try to open up more and more to it and whatever was in that memory. Take a few minutes to do this.

When you are done, close the file drawer. Notice your breathing and take a few good deep breaths, with the air coming in through your nose and out of your mouth. See if you can connect with the fact that you are a whole, complete person. This "tin-can monster" is *in* you, and so it is an illusion that it is bigger than you are. Ask yourself: Am I willing to be me, with the history I have, and to go on from here carrying all these reactions forward as part of an empowered life?

What did you notice about the various connections between bodily sensations, emotions, thoughts, behavioral predispositions, and memories? You can write down any connections you see here:

_____

_____

_____

_____

How about the memories? What connections do you see between these memories and the issue you are struggling with today? Write down any connections you see here:

_____

_____

_____

_____

One danger in doing this kind of work is that sometimes we see the sources of our pain in our own history and we reason that we would have done better without this history. That is an illusion of language. It's true that your past brought you to where you are today, and your past is the source of the setting on your Discomfort dial. But how these thoughts and feelings *function* today is, in large part, dependent on what you do with them. The issue is this: What can you do to abandon the struggle with your history and behave more effectively *now*?

What stands between you and being fully willing to have these pieces of the tin-can monster be what they are, without allowing them to play a destructive role in your life? Ponder this for a moment and then write down your answer. (Hint: this is a trick question.)

_____

_____

_____

_____

If you wrote down something other than "nothing" or "just me," then look again. (As we said, it's a trick question.) If it is anything else, see whether you didn't write some bit of content. But what stands between you and being willing to have *that* content in a defused way? Who sets that Willingness dial anyway? You or your history?

EXERCISE: Acceptance in Real-Time

The last two exercises were constructed essentially to expose you to the adverse content in your imagination. You called to mind your target item and this brought up difficult bodily sensations, feelings, thoughts, memories, and so forth that we then took apart and evaluated piece by piece.

But what happens when you're faced with content you struggle with in real-time? What happens when you are out there in the world, going about your real life, and you are faced with situations that cause you pain? If you're an agoraphobic, for example, and you haven't been outside of your home for a long time, you are going to be facing some heavy-duty tin-can monsters when you step outside your front door. How should you handle instances like these?

The short answer is, the same way you've been learning to handle *all* of your difficult experiences. Open yourself to them by first putting yourself in the observer position, and then with your observer-self look at them with a defused, accepting, mindful posture. However, we would also like to help you deal with difficult experiences in a more concrete way than we've just described.

What we'd like to do is help you develop a set of experiences that you're quite sure will bring up the negative content you've been avoiding, and then develop a graded-exposure program in which you will actually go out into the world, seek out these scenarios, and experience your experience in real-time.

To accomplish this, you'll begin with the worksheet below. Fill in the space on the left with actual physical scenarios you think will bring up the willingness target you chose earlier. Note that there are ten spaces, so try to come up with ten scenarios. Choose a variety of different situations in which your target will present itself. Think of some that will cause you a lot of distress and some that won't cause quite so much discomfort. If you think of one scenario that feels really big and daunting, you might want to break it down into its component parts.

For example, if you are suffering from OCD, and dirt or germs set off your compulsion to clean, it may be too much for you to go out and roll around in the mud. Break it down. In this case, one scenario that might cause your target to show itself could be to put a small amount of dirt on a white cloth and carry the cloth with you for a day. Then, you might want to wear a soiled shirt. And so on and so on.

Once you have done this, order your scenarios from 1 to 10, where 1 is the scenario you think will cause you the least amount of contact with your target, and 10 is the scenario you think will cause you the greatest amount of contact with your target. Numbering them from 1 to 10 will give you a graded way to expose yourself to this material.

Scenario	Rank

Once you have done this, take your first scenario, the one you numbered 1, and decide a time and place you would like to expose yourself to it. You can limit the amount of time of your exposure just the way you did in the Willingness Scale Worksheet exercise, but, again, what you can't safely limit is your willingness to experience what the exposure brings up for you. Avoidance of any kind has to be off the table. If you aren't sure you can make that commitment, generate an even smaller step, or limit this step further with limits on the time and situation.

Take some notes in the space below about when, where, and how long you are willing to do this exposure to the first item:

_____

_____

_____

_____

During the actual exposure you will use the skills you've already learned. First we will describe these skills and then we will shrink them down to a bulleted list that you can carry with you to remind you of actions you can take in the situation.

You should notice what your body does. Localize where you feel sensations and emotions in your body. Notice the feeling's qualities, and where it begins and ends. Scan your body and notice other places where you are feelings things, and after you've noticed them, psychologically reach out and allow yourself to feel these feelings without defense or manipulation. Make sure your purpose is simply to be present and willing. Nothing else. This is not a secret way to make bad feelings diminish or vanish, and, even if your feelings happen to change, don't buy into any thoughts that tell you otherwise.

Look around you when you are exposing yourself and observe what else is happening in the world around you. If there are people there, notice them. If there are objects, or buildings, or plants or trees, notice them. Do not do this to diminish the thing you are struggling with. The point is to add to your experience—in addition to these feelings there is also life going on all around you.

Notice what thoughts come up for you. Notice them the way you would notice a cloud drift by. Do nothing to make them come or go. Do not argue with them. Do not disbelieve them or follow them where they go. Just notice them, as you might notice the sound of a radio in the background. Thank your mind for generating all its products for you.

Notice the pull to your past and future. But see if you can stay in the present by becoming present with thoughts about the past and future. If you find yourself checking the clock, let go of your attachment to the time.

Notice the pull to act. If you feel the pull to leave or avoid or dissociate just feel that pull—willingly and fully.

Have some fun. Do something (anything!) new in the situation. Tell a joke. Hum. Eat. Skip. Play little mental games. For example, if there are people around, who can you identify with the worst haircut? What interests you in this situation? Be careful! This is *not* distraction. *In addition* to what you are struggling with, the point is to notice that there is *also* the opportunity to do many, many other things. Broaden the range of things that you can do when you're in contact with your target.

If you feel *really* bold, find out what your mind is saying you cannot or must not do and consider doing more of it (but only if you are willing!). If you're anxious and your mind tells you that you might look foolish if you become too anxious, then do something foolish. Put your hat on upside down, or your glasses on backwards. Ask a passerby what month it is. If your mind tells you that you might faint and fall down on the ground, then purposefully lie on the ground and see what it feels like to be there as others react to your prone body.

Notice that you are there as an observing-self, through all of this, unchanged. Use that sense to be present with your experiences (do not use it to dissociate or avoid).

Above all, watch for every tiny little way your mind has been trying to "protect" you by avoidance. Undermine every form of avoidance, let go of it. And all of this has only one purpose: to practice being willing in the moment. No manipulation. This is not a new, secret way to regulate your internal processes. No more of *that*.

Got it? Okay, now go out and do it. Take all of your skills with you, and experience what you experience in real-time, fully and without defense. Set your limits beforehand.

Now, below you will see a bulleted list you can use to remind you of things to do. You can augment this list by adding any of the exercises you've done during the course of working with this book to help you either to defuse from or to accept thoughts and feelings, or to contact your observer-self. List anything that's worked for you. For example, if you suffer from agoraphobia, and you've decided to walk around the block for your first step, when your anxiety comes up, you might ask yourself: "If this feeling had a size, how big would it be? If this feeling had a shape, what shape would it be?"

If you want to watch your thoughts and feelings float away as leaves on a stream, then mentally do that exercise; if you want to put your thoughts and feelings into three mind-trains (without getting into the little cars yourself!), do that. If you know you might become wrapped up in your thoughts, you might try some of the defusion exercises you learned in chapter 6. Remember that you made up some things for yourself in that chapter. You could use those if your instinct is that they would help. Help do what? *Not to Help Regulate Your Target*. That goal only will undermine what we are doing here. The "help" we are taking about is helping you to be present, defused, and willing to stay in contact with what has been difficult or that you have avoided.

Take this list with you and glance at it while doing your actual exposure. Notice your body and its sensations. Make room for them.

- Notice what is around you. Appreciate your immediate environment.

- Do not avoid.

- Notice your thoughts, but just let them come and go. Don't follow them.

- Notice the pull to your past and future. Then notice you are here in the present.

- Don't fight.

- Notice the pull to act and to avoid. Do nothing about that pull except to notice it.

- Do something new. Perhaps even be playful.

- Use your reverse compass (but only if you are willing!).

- Notice you are noticing all these things.

- List other things you might do below:

  _____

  _____

  _____

- Stick to your commitment: Be present. No avoidance.

You can continue to repeat your exposure to scenario number one until you feel able to open yourself to the experience and accept what is given to you. This doesn't mean do it until your pain goes away.

This isn't about that. Do it until you can make more room for all the thoughts, feelings, urges, bodily sensations, and memories you have. Welcome them into the home of yourself. Inhale them all.

When you have accomplished that (it can take multiple exposures), move on to scenario number two and do the same thing. If you hit a level that seems beyond you, put the list aside and come back to it after you've done more work in the final chapters of this book.

You can continue working with this process indefinitely, using this list and many others. At some point, it may no longer be necessary to list scenarios and then pursue them in this manner. Once you've had some practice with your acceptance skills, you'll be able to integrate them into your daily life, and life itself will give you many chances to jump. It is amazing how when we begin to say yes, life seems to present us with just the right challenges: always slightly more or slightly earlier than we might have wished and yet doable—if we are willing.

Having Jumped

If you've made it this far, then you've done some really good work. You've taken your first steps toward willingness and taken your first leap into a different way of understanding your pain. Don't let you mind take any success you've had here and turn it into something absolute. No one is timing you. There is no "finish line" to this race. For now, anyway, just moving forward is enough.

In the next chapters, we'll take all of the defusion, mindfulness, and acceptance exercises you've learned up to this point and you'll start to learn how to use them in the context of pursuing a valued, engaged, and vital life.

CHAPTER 11

What Are Values?

Imagine that you've been driving a bus called "your life." Like any bus, as you move along, you pick up passengers. In this case, your passengers are your memories, bodily sensations, conditioned emotions, programmed thoughts, historically produced urges, and so on. You've picked up some passengers you like: these are like sweet little old ladies who you hope will sit up in the front, near you. You've picked up some you don't like: these are like tough, frightening gang members whom you would just as soon have take another bus.

Isn't it true that when you began this book you were focused on the passengers? They defined the nature of your struggle with your psychological pain. It's likely that you've spent a good deal of time trying to make certain passengers get off the bus, change their appearance, or make themselves less visible. If you were suffering from severe anxiety, difficult urges, or painful feelings of sadness, you probably tried stopping the bus and forcing the unwanted passengers to leave.

But notice the very first thing you had to do to achieve that. You had to stop the bus: you had to put your life on hold while the struggle was being fought. And, in all likelihood, the unwelcome passengers did not leave as a result of your struggle. These passengers have a mind of their own; furthermore, time goes only in one direction, not two. A painful memory, once on the bus, is on the bus for good. Short of a lobotomy, that passenger is not leaving.

After we learn that our passengers simply won't leave, as a last resort, we generally focus on their appearance and visibility. If we have a negative thought, we try to tidy it up a bit, by tweaking a word here or a nuance there. But we are still historical beings. When we argue with or try to change the passengers on our bus, we simply add to them. It's a bit like meeting a gang member and forcing him put on a suit and tie to make him appear less frightening. In memory, at least, the gang member still lives on, in his original form. Even if he's wearing an expensive suit and tie, you know he hasn't changed much underneath.

Once we've exhausted the other possibilities, typically, we try to bargain with the passengers on our bus. We try to get the most frightening ones to slouch down in their seats way in the back, with the hope that at least we won't have to see them so often. Perhaps we can even pretend they've disappeared entirely. We manufacture ways to avoid knowing the scary passengers are even on the bus. We avoid. We use controlled substances. We deny.

You may try many ways to hide your anxiety, depression, or low self-esteem from yourself, asking these thoughts and feelings to slump down in the back seat. But the cost of this last strategy is high: You barter away your freedom. To get these unwanted passengers to keep out of sight, you offer this sad bargain: If they slouch down and stay hidden, you will drive where they want to go.

For example, to get your social anxiety to move to the back of the bus, you may avoid people in situations that feel evaluative and frightening; when opportunities come up to be with others, you turn them down or you engage in socializing defensively and half-heartedly. All just to keep that frightening passenger, social anxiety, from rearing his ugly head.

Even if this final strategy works to a degree, it is at a huge cost. When you go where the passengers tell you to go, you've lost control of this bus called "your life." In the title of our book, we made a type of promise to you: that it's possible to get out of your mind and into your life. You can do that *now*. Without your mind being changed first.

It's taken us a while to get to that promise. We took the long way around. We focused on creating alternatives to getting your passengers to leave, making them look different, or bargaining with them to make them less visible. Instead of avoidance, you learned acceptance. Instead of belief and disbelief, you learned defusion and mindfulness. Instead of fearful expectations for the future or sad recollections of the past, you learned to be more present in the moment that is now. Instead of taking yourself to be who your mind says you are, you learned to notice that a transcendent "no-thing" self, a self beyond verbal categorization, is continuously present.

If you've been doing all of these things, you've learned more about how to be on the bus comfortably with your passengers—distinct from them and yet willing to carry them, with vitality and presence. You've learned how to keep from making secret deals with the passengers that turn control of the bus over to them. So, in this chapter and the two that follow, you are now ready to move to the final core issues.

When you get on a bus, you will notice that up in front there is usually a small sign that says where the bus is going. Passengers who get on the bus will be taken to that destination. It is not up to the moment-to-moment whims of the passengers to determine where the bus will go—it is up to the owners and drivers who set the destination and then drive there. So, now it is time to look at *where* you want this bus called your life to be headed. What exactly do you choose to have on that little sign? What is your path?

VALUES AS CHOSEN LIFE DIRECTIONS

First we need to state a warning. You are entering into some of the most difficult work in this entire book. Your mind is listening and watching and will want to claim everything we do together (as usual!). Values are not purely verbal events, but they are necessarily known (at least in part) verbally. This places values only a hair's breadth away from some destructive verbal processes. Your verbal organ, i.e., your "mind," may claim that the important work you are about to do means things that it does not mean.

For example, if you notice a feeling of heaviness in response to this work; if you begin to feel disempowered; if you start to feel insignificant; if, once again, you think or feel that you are holding on to the short end of the stick with nowhere to go, *stop*. These are sure signs that your mind is taking over. If you run into these kinds of feelings over the course of chapters 11, 12, and 13 take a step back and start over with this chapter using all of the strategies you have learned in the book up to this point. See if you can defuse from your mental hooks this second time around. Values are vitalizing, uplifting, and empowering. They are not another mental club to beat yourself with or another measurement to fail against.

The sign on the front of your life bus says *Values*. Values are *chosen life directions*. However, unpacking this simple definition requires an understanding of what a "direction" is and what a "choice" is.

Direction

Because values are much more than mere words, it may be helpful to return to the metaphor of your life as a bus to guide us. So, imagine that your bus is traveling through a large flat valley with many gravel roads. All around you are distant mountains, hills, trees, and rocks. In the more immediate area there are ponds, shrubs, pastures, rocks, and streams. Your bus is equipped with a compass.

You must choose a direction to follow and you say, "I think I'll go east." You look at the compass and turn your bus to head east. You see a road ahead; it isn't perfectly due east, but it leads you in that direction. You move the bus forward, come to the end of the road, and are presented with a couple of alternative routes. You study the alternatives and go forward once more, more or less in an easterly direction.

So when do you actually get to east? How will you know when you have arrived at east? When is the direction called "east" finished? When have you gone as far east as you can go?

If you are not trying to get to a specific place, but are just following a direction, the answer is "never." Directions are not something you "get" in the way that you "get" an object or "get" to a city.

In this same way, *values* are intentional qualities that join together a string of moments into a meaningful path. They are what moments are *about*, but they are never possessed as objects, because they are qualities of unfolding actions, not of particular things. Said another way, values are verbs and adverbs, not nouns or adjectives; they are something you *do* or a quality of something you do, not something you *have*. If they are something you do (or a quality of something you do), they never end. You are never finished.

For example, say one of your values is to be a loving person. This doesn't mean that as soon as you love someone for a few months you are done, as you can be done with building a house or done with earning a college degree. There is more loving to do—always. *Love is a direction, not an object.*

We will return to this metaphor as we explore values further, but to complete our definition we must also define "choice."

Choice

Choices and reasoned judgments are not the same thing. When you make a judgment, you apply your mind and its evaluative abilities to alternatives, and depending on what you want, you pick one of those alternatives. For example, you may decide to eat fish for dinner rather than fatty hamburger (even though you like the hamburger more and it costs less), because there is a lot of evidence that fish oils are good for your heart and you want to live longer. That is a judgment. You consider several factors: the taste of the food, the cost of the food, and living longer. You look at the pros and cons along those metrics: the fish may not taste as good, but it's okay (if it was disgusting, your decision might change); it costs a bit more but you have the money (if it cost a great deal more, you might go with the burger regardless of the health issue); you want to be healthy; and you think fish is healthier. You go with the fish.

Ninety percent of the time judgments work fine. The ability to use our logical judgments to pick between alternatives is a wonderful tool, and that ability is the reason why humans have done so well on the planet. But in some areas judgments don't work very well, and in still others they absolutely *cannot* work.

One area they absolutely cannot work is the area of values. Here's why: Judgments necessarily involve applying evaluative metrics to alternative action plans. For example, in the judgment we just described, one of the metrics was the health of your heart. As with applying a yardstick to a material object, we can try to measure fish and burgers on a "healthy heart" yardstick. This is true of any evaluative situation. Once you pick which yardstick to use, picking the best alternative is a mere intellectual judgment.

But what about the yardstick itself? How was *that* picked? If picking the yardstick is itself a judgment (and sometimes it is), that means there is yet another yardstick. This happens when one purpose is a means to another purpose. For example, you might use "healthy for your heart" as a measure, not because it is an end in itself but because a healthy heart makes it likelier that you will live a long and full life. But how was *that* yardstick picked? Was picking "living a full and healthy life" itself a judgment? It could be, but if it is, there is still some *other* yardstick that was applied to "living a full and healthy life" because judgment, by definition, involves applying an evaluative yardstick to two or more alternatives.

Note what is happening here. This could go on forever. In the end, judgments cannot tell you which yardstick to pick, because judgments require *applying* an evaluative metric. That works fine, but only after you've picked one.

Valuing, however, gives us a place to stop. Values are not judgments. Values are choices. *Choices* are selections between alternatives that may be made in the presence of reasons (if your mind gives you any, which it usually does, since minds chatter about everything), but this selection is not *for* those reasons in the sense that it is not explained by, justified by, or linked to them. A choice is not linked to an evaluative verbal yardstick. Said another way, choice is a defused selection among alternatives. It is different than judgment, which is a verbally guided selection among alternatives.

Have you noticed that the word "evaluation" actually contains the word "value"? That's because evaluations are a matter of applying our values and *then* making judgments based on those values. If values were judgments, it would mean that we'd have to evaluate our values, but against which values would we evaluate them?

Usually, we don't think about this much, and for a good reason: minds don't like choices. Minds know how to apply evaluative yardsticks; in fact, it is the very essence of what these relational abilities evolved to do. But minds cannot pick the ultimate directions that make all of this decision making meaningful.

With nonverbal organisms, all selections between alternatives are choices, because nonverbal organisms do not have the verbal tools to make literal judgments. Scientists studying these kinds of things in the laboratory generate and test the reasons for choices, but the animal is not guided by the "reasons" the scientists come up with in a literal sense. The animal simply chooses. In a similar fashion, if we were sitting on Mt. Olympus and knew every detail of our own lives, and how to interpret all of these influences, we might be able to reason why we made certain choices at certain points in our lives. But we are not sitting on Mt. Olympus; from the inside out we simply choose.

It is essential that human beings learn to do what all the other creatures on the planet do with ease, even though our chatterbox minds keep going on and on about everything we do. It is essential because without choice, valuing becomes impossible.

Making a Choice

In order to practice choosing, let's start with something trivial. There are two letters below. Choose one.

A   **Z**

Now for the tricky part. Watch what your mind does as this question is asked: "Why did you choose the one you chose?"

For most of you, your mind will now generate a "reason." But bring all of your defusion skills into this moment. Would it be possible to notice that thought and still pick the other? Remember the exercises we did in chapter 2 when we read a verbal rule and deliberately did something else? Let's do that again.

This time, we'll give you lots of "reasons" to be aware of. There are two letters below. Read the sentences below and then choose one. (Not as a judgment! Just notice all of the reasons in a defused, accepting, mindful, open way and pick one or the other *for* no reason at all and *with* all of the reasons you may have).

Here are all of the reasons to be aware of: Pick the one on the left. No, pick the one on the right. No, pick the one on the left. No, pick the one on the right. No, pick the one on the left. No, pick the one on the right. No, pick the one on the left. No, pick the one on the right. No, pick the one on the left. No, pick the one on the right.

Here are two letters. Choose one.

A   **Z**

Were you able to do it? Repeat this process until you can simply pick a letter without regard to all the chatter—undefended, naked, and in the wind, *without* compliance with the chatter *or* resistance to the chatter.

If you pass this test with the simple commands in mind of "pick the one on the right" and "pick the one on the left," why can't you do the same with the reasons your mind gives you about more important choices? If you apply your defusion skills, it is the same situation, despite the fact that one may be said to be "important" and one may be said to be "not important."

Let's try it and see. Try to come up with "reasons" to pick one of the letters. Of course, this is a trivial choice, so, normally, there would be no reason to do such a thing. But for the purposes of the exercise, make your word machine come up with some reasons (for example, "I like the letter A better because it is in my name," or "Z reminds me of Zorro and I remember liking those reruns on the Disney channel when I was a kid," or "I like right better than left because I'm right-handed," or "Left in Latin is 'sinister' and I don't want to pick something sinister," and so on). Now, write down some reasons to pick one of the two choices below:

Reasons to pick A on the left   **Reasons to pick Z on the right**

_____   _____

_____   _____

_____   _____

_____   _____

_____   _____

_____   _____

Now, you will make this silly little choice again. Read the list of reasons you generated and think about them all again. If your mind gives you any other reasons, deliberately think about those too. Notice them all as thoughts. Do not resist them. Do not comply with them. Simply notice them. Now, pick one of the two letters again.

A   **Z**

Repeat this process until you are clear that you can pick either letter _no matter what your mind is saying_. That doesn't mean disobeying your mind, like a child who puts beans in her nose as soon as she's told not to. In that case, your mind is still in control; it's just the form that has changed (this is why we say that neither rebelliousness nor compliance are, at their core, forms of independence). It means noticing all of these mental events _and_ simply picking one of the letters, _with_ these reasons, but neither for nor against these reasons.

Minds hate this exercise! Minds can't understand it because minds _generate_ and _apply_ verbal reasons to all alternatives. But _humans_ can do this. That's because humans are more than their verbal repertoire.

This small exercise was done with a meaningless choice. Values, however, are anything but meaningless. So the chatter will be louder, and the reasons will be stronger. But the action will be the same. We can be about anything we want to be about. Who can stop us?

WHAT VALUES ARE AND ARE NOT

In the next two chapters you will explore your values in some detail, and you will learn how to become clearer on what you want them to be. In this chapter, we are simply describing what values are and what they are not. This relatively wordy task is worth doing because the process of valuing is hard for minds to understand. Values go beyond words, but minds try to claim them, and if we are not careful, they can become distorted to fit with the ordinary evaluative and predictive relations that our verbal word machine knows how to use.

Values Are Not Goals

Goals are the things you can obtain while walking a valued path. *Goals* are concrete achievable events, situations, or objects. They can be completed, possessed, or finished. Goals are not the same as directions. If goals are confused with directions, once they have been achieved, progress must necessarily stop.

This actually happens all the time, which is one reason why depression sometimes follows getting a degree, getting married, or getting a promotion at work. If, say, getting a degree is an end in itself, there is likely to be an enormous loss of life direction immediately after graduation. Someone who gets a degree as an end in itself, or as a way to reach still other goals (for example, feeling better about herself) may only be mocked by her achievement.

Goals are wonderful and empowering once the distinction between goals and values is clear. It sometimes helps (after a direction is chosen) to focus on goals as a way of keeping on track. If you are standing in a valley surrounded by mountains, hills, trees, and rock formations with only a compass, it may help to sight along your chosen direction to a prominent landmark and then head for that. There is a competitive sport called "orienteering" that relies heavily on this process: participants find their way from point to point on a map, usually using a compass and natural or manmade objects to provide an anchor for that direction.

Similarly, a person who values, say, helping others, might get a degree to be in a better position to help others. Immediately after getting the degree there will be lots of interesting and vital things to do that are not about the degree but about the value, that of helping others.

If you are using goals in that way, it helps to have goals close enough to be seen and achievable, but far enough away to be useful. A goal that is an inch in front of your foot will help you get started, but as you learn to move, it won't be very effective in helping you "orienteer" in your life. Conversely, a goal somewhere on the other side of a mountain range won't help you maintain your direction. In the same way, it usually makes sense to set concrete, short-term goals to get going, but then, as you learn to move, to set more medium-range goals for yourself.

Values Are Not Feelings

Presumably, all of our experiences inform our values, in the sense that a whole person makes the choices. Sometimes that means there are feelings that accompany valued choices. Over time, you will learn the degree to which feelings can help you know when you are living in accord with your values. For example, many people feel a sense of vitality when their actions line up with their chosen values. That doesn't mean that values are feelings. Most especially, it doesn't mean that values are doing what feels good, particularly in the short-term.

A person with a drug addiction feels good when using drugs. That doesn't mean that being high is a valued outcome. Suppose the person really values being close to others, but when he takes steps in that direction, he feels frightened and vulnerable. He hates that feeling, so he uses drugs or alcohol again. If this person stops using and begins to walk in a valued direction, he won't "feel good" anytime soon. He will feel frightened and vulnerable. Thus, walking in a valued direction may not feel good for this person, but it will "work good" or "live good."

There is another problem with thinking of feelings as values, or with valuing feelings per se, and we will explore that problem in chapters 12 and 13. Feelings are things you can have. By definition, values are not anything you can possess the way you can possess an object. Moreover, feelings are not something you can control, while choosing a direction is something you can control. For those reasons, statements like "I value feeling good about myself" are based on a misunderstanding of values.

Pain and Values

Feeling can be related to values in a different, and less obvious, way than the linkage between good feelings and values. Suppose someone who is a social phobic shudders at the thought of going to a party. Why? Very likely, this is a person who values connections with others. If connecting with others was not of any importance, the person would not be socially phobic. One reason we began this book with an emphasis on acceptance is that, in our pain, we are given some guidance toward our values. The reverse is also true: in our values, we find our pain. You cannot value anything without being woundable, indeed, your values are the most intimate part of you.

An ACT client once said in a therapy session something like "I don't really value family, or intimate relationships, or children. I just don't think that life is for me." A week or two later that person came in and said, "I'm such a liar, even to myself." Then he reported the following incident: He had been sitting in a Burger King having a hamburger when a family came in and sat down at the next table: Mom, Dad, and two small children. He looked up from his burger at the family and began to cry. At that moment, he realized he wanted a family and children of his own more than anything else. His parents had treated him badly and his history of betrayals had led him to deny his strongest desire, because when he admitted it, he felt such pain and vulnerability. As a result of this admission, he was enabled to go on and have a family, using his acceptance skills to deal with his fear and vulnerability, and using his values as a guide for the direction he wanted his life to take.

Values Are Not Outcomes

Although living your life according to your values often leads to wonderful outcomes, they are not a sneaky way to "getting what you want" in the concrete world. Values are directions, not outcomes.

You can think of it as similar to the way that gravity acts on water in a bowl. Gravity specifies that down is the direction, not up. Gravity is a direction, not an outcome. If there is any way for the water to follow that direction (for example, if there is a hole in the bowl), it will. If there are no ways to move, however, you will not see the water flow. From the outside, it might appear as though there is no "direction" at all, but it is there all along, and it will be revealed given any opportunity.

Values are like gravity. Suppose you value having a loving relationship with your father, but your father wants nothing at all to do with you. Your letters are ignored; your calls and visits are refused. Like water contained in a bowl, the value may rarely be manifested in a way that others can see beyond the small "leaks" in the form of birthday cards you send (whether or not they are read), or comments you make to others about your father. Like water held in a bowl, this value can be continuously present, waiting for better opportunities to manifest itself. If the opening comes, if one day Dad calls and says he wants to meet with you, the value will be visible in a more obvious way.

Values Do Not Mean Our Paths Are Always Straight

If you were on a bus trying to go east in a maze of dirt roads in a large valley, you might not be able to tell your direction from moment to moment. If someone took a series of snapshots, sometimes the bus might be facing north, or south, or even west, even though all the while this is a journey to the east.

Paths are not straight because obstacles sometimes prevent movement in the desired direction. A person who values creating a loving family may nevertheless have to go through a divorce. In that situation, the intention to be loving may be revealed only in limited ways, such as not establishing oppositions between yourself and your spouse that will negatively affect your children, or treating a soon-to-be ex-spouse fairly in the division of assets. Only over time will the underlying value become evident, like tracks left in the snow that show, even though the path is not straight, it *is* headed east.

Paths are also not straight because we are human. We may intend to go east, but our attention may wander, and we may find ourselves heading north. Someone in recovery from a drug addiction who values sobriety and helping others may still relapse. That person's mind may be screaming, "See, you can't go east! You are a liar and a failure! You can't be trusted!" as if to say, "Because you are heading north, as usual, you cannot value heading east." In such an instance, that person's task will be to thank his or her mind, feel the sadness and pain that comes from relapse, and then turn and head east once again.

Values Are Not in the Future

Let's go back to our valley. Notice that from the very instant you chose to go east, every action you took was a part of that decision. You looked at your compass. That was part of going east. You noticed the direction you were heading toward, and that was part of going east. Perhaps you noticed you were veering north; if so, noticing that was also part of going east. You began to turn to your right until you were actually heading east, and that turn was part of going east. Then you took a step, which was part of going east. Then another step was taken, which was more of going east. All of this was *about going east.*

Suppose you were asked, "Which of all of these moments, including the choice to go east, is part of going east"? The only sensible answer seems to be *All of them—no one more than any other.* One of the useful implications of this answer is this: the very instant you choose your values, you are taking a valued path. Another useful implication: you have the benefit of values being lived *now.* They are seemingly "about" the future but, in fact, they are really about the present.

We have another way of saying this: We say, "The outcome is the process through which process becomes the outcome." Your values are themselves the "outcome" you are looking for and you get to have that "outcome" *now* because those values empower the process of living *now.* Every step you take in the direction of those values is a part of that process. Once you have chosen your values, the process you take to head in that direction is all values-laden. Having a direction allows a coherent trip to be taken; and it is the trip that is actually worthwhile. Your life becomes empowered by your values. It is like a journey down a never-ending path. This is a trip that has no finish line; it is not literally about an outcome. It is about the journey you take on your way there.

Suppose you value being a loving person. This is a trip that never ends. No matter how many loving things you do, there are always more loving things to do. The benefits of this path are not in the future; you get to have a life that is about loving relationships now. And now. And now. But you never strike your hands together because you are done. This is a direction that will not end.

Values and Failing

Values entail responsibility: that is, acknowledging that you always have the ability to respond. The response you can *always* engage in is valuing, even when there is little you can currently do in a specific situation to make your values manifest (like the water in that bowl). Most of the time, however, there are things we can do and our values allow us to see when we've failed to live up to the directions we've chosen. Like a bright beam on a roadway, our values bring us back to our path even when road signs tempt us to take wrong turns crowd the roadway, or even when we have mindlessly driven down yet another embankment. The pain of failure supports us in starting anew.

No one always lives according to his or her values. But that is different than *being* a failure. If we use our values to beat ourselves up, we are buying into the thought that we can't be about the values we actually have, merely because sometimes we wander. Ask yourself this question when you think you've failed: What is buying *that* thought in the service of? What value does it comport with? Being right? Never failing? Never being vulnerable? Is *that* what you want your life to be about? If not, take responsibility even for your mind chattering on about what a failure you are. Feel the pain. Learn from it. Then move on.

When you feel guilt or shame at your limitations, it is time to use your defusion and mindfulness skills to acknowledge the chatter that comes in at those moments. It is time to use your acceptance skills to acknowledge the pain that comes in at those moments. And it is time to use your capacity for choice to reconnect with your chosen direction so that you can once again begin moving in the direction you choose to move, as the situation allows.

Values Are Always Perfect

One of the joyous facts about values is that ultimate values are perfect for the individual valuing them. We do not mean "perfect" in the sense of "evaluated as good." We mean it in its original sense: thoroughly made or whole (from the Latin "per" meaning "thoroughly" and "fect" meaning "made," the same Latin root found in "factory"). If you view your values as being broken or wanting, it must mean that you actually already have some *other* values that allow you to see that.

Suppose a businesswoman bemoans her frequent absences from her home because she "values work too much." Clearly, this means that in addition to her work she also values being with her family. What she needs to work on is finding a way to balance and integrate these two different sets of values. Her values are perfect—it is her behavior that needs work.

This means that if you are willing to value, you immediately win. Since the joy is in the journey, not the outcome, and your values are perfect so far as you know (which doesn't mean they can't change, it means they can't be evaluated), nothing is missing. It is just a matter of living, moment by moment, day by day, staying true to your values as an act of self-fidelity.

The usual mental game is that you "win" when you get positive outcomes. But minds always demand more and more. Even if you "win," your mind will suggest worries about "winning" the next time. A recent newspaper story about a world-class athlete is revealing in this regard. She was number one in the world in her event and had won two consecutive *world* championships. Only a few handfuls of human beings on the planet ever reach that level of athletic achievement. Yet, upon winning her second championship, she said her primary emotion was neither elation nor satisfaction, but fear. The reason? She was afraid she wouldn't win next year.

Minds are like that. They will never change. They are evaluative, predictive, comparative, worrying "organs." But in the case of values, it is different. Once you choose them, you are in fact choosing them. You've won. Then they allow you to follow your path and to measure your progress on that path.

Choosing to Value

If it didn't matter where you were going, it wouldn't matter where your internal struggles took you. The very fact that you are reading this book demonstrates that where you are going does matter to you. Examine yourself and see if it isn't true that the largest pain in your life isn't your anxiety, depression, urges, memories, trauma, anger, sadness, and so forth, but that your life is not being thoroughly and whole-heartedly *lived*. Your life was put on hold while that war we discussed in the introduction was being fought. So each tick of the clock mocks you: it is one more second passing of a life not fully lived.

The key problem here is not that you have problems, it is that you've put the choices that are here to be made on hold. Vitality and engagement in your life does not require you to eliminate your pain first. It requires quite the opposite: opening up to the joy (and pain!) that comes from having your life be about what you really, really want it to be about.

So, here's a question to ask the person you see in the mirror. What do you want your life to be about? Really?

CHAPTER 12

Choosing *Your* Values

Defining what matters to you and actively choosing to pursue that direction is what this book is ultimately all about. Although the defusion, mindfulness, and acceptance exercises you've explored up to this point are useful in themselves, this information is an empty shell if it isn't used in the service of living a meaningful life.

Chapter 11 should have helped you understand what we mean by "values." Choosing what you value and pursuing that path can make your life rich and meaningful, even in the face of great adversity. This chapter is about doing just that.

THE MASTERS YOU SERVE

To live a valued life is to act in the service of what you value. It was Bob Dylan who wrote, "You've got to serve somebody." The question is: Who (or what) will you serve? Your experience, this book, and your current psychological dilemmas have probably shown you that living in the service of pain reduction is no way to live at all. If your agoraphobia tells you that going outside isn't an option, when everything else in you knows that going out is the vital thing to do, serving your agoraphobia probably won't lead you down the path you want to follow.

Understanding this can be a scary place to be in some ways. If you decide that basing your decisions on what your mind gives you isn't an option, then on what can you base your actions? If you can really be about whatever you choose, how do you know what you want to do? What should your compass point be in this seemingly endless sea of options?

We believe that right now at this very moment, you have all the tools you need to make meaningful and inspiring life choices for yourself. You not only have the opportunity, but the actual ability to live in the service of what you value. That doesn't mean that circumstances will necessarily allow you to achieve all of your goals; this is not a guarantee about outcome. And it doesn't mean you have all the skills you need to accomplish your stated goals. But it does mean you have what you need to choose a direction.

The word "values" comes from a Latin root that means "worthy and strong." It carries an implication of action, which is why that same root leads to the word "wield." It connotes actually using what is important and strong. Values define not only what you want to pursue from day to day but what you want your life to be about. In some sense, what's at stake here is a matter of life and death, or at least the difference between a vital life and a deadened life.

EXERCISE: Attending Your Own Funeral

When people die, what is left behind is what they stood for. Think of someone who is no longer alive but whose life you look up to and admire. Think of your heroes. Now see if it isn't true that *what they stood for* is now, after their passing, most important. What's important is neither their material possessions nor their inner doubts. The values reflected in their lives are what's important.

You have only so much time on this earth, and you don't know how much. The question "Are you going to live, knowing you will die?" is not fundamentally different than these questions: "Are you going to love, knowing you will be hurt?" Or, "Are you going to commit to living a valued life knowing you will sometimes not meet your commitments?" Or, "Will you reach for success knowing you will sometimes fail?" The potential for pain and the sense of vitality you gain from these experiences go together. If your life is truly going to be about something, it helps to look at it from the perspective of what you would want the path your life leaves behind to mean.

One of the foundations for avoidance is our verbal awareness that life on this planet is finite. We recognize that it might seem macabre to go to the end of your life in imagination and look back. It is not meant to be morbid but to be grounded. If you could live your life so that it is actually *about* what you would choose to have it be about from here until it is over, what would be evident? That is, what would be clear about the kind of life you led?

This is not a prediction, or guess, or description. The question is not about what you've done or expect to do. We ask this question in the form of what you would hope those close to you will see. But this is not a question about social approval; rather, if your values mean something, they will be evident. We are asking only this: What would be evident if you could freely choose what your life stood for?

You may only whisper this question to yourself, but since this is a choice, we are asking you open yourself up to your own yearning to be *about* something. If your life could be about anything; if it were just between you and your heart; if no one would laugh or say it is impossible; if you were *bold* about your innermost aspirations, what would you want to be about? And to be that—so powerfully—that it was evident to those around you?

Now, find a place and time in which you can quietly concentrate. Make sure there aren't too many distractions, and give yourself plenty of time to completely visualize the following scenario, then answer the questions below.

Keep in mind that if you take the time to do this exercise, it can be a powerful and emotional experience. It is not our intention to have this be about "facing your death"; it is about facing your life. Nevertheless, part of what often prevents people from embracing a valued life is that any value carries with it knowledge of how finite our lives are. Avoiding that knowledge means you can't really, fully be about anything, and see if that's not too high a price to pay. If you find yourself becoming wrapped up in your emotions and unable to "carry on," remember the techniques you've used throughout this book, implement one or two of them, and know that you are doing this exercise in the service of something potentially very powerful.

Now close your eyes and take a few deep breaths. Once you've calmed your mind, imagine that you've died, but by some miraculous circumstance you are able to witness your own funeral in spirit form. Think about where it would be and what it would be like. Take a few moments to visualize a clear picture of your future funeral services.

In the space below, imagine that a family member or friend is there who has been asked to stand up and say a few words about what you stood for in your life; about what you cared about; about the path you took. You will write this eulogy in two ways.

First write down what you are afraid might be said if the struggle you are currently engaged in continues to dominate in your life, or even grows. Suppose you back off from what you really want to stand for, and instead you follow a path of avoidance, mental entanglement, emotional control, and self-righteousness. Picture your family member or friend. What might he or she say? Write it down, word for word:

_____

_____

_____

_____

_____

_____

_____

_____

_____

_____

_____

_____

_____

_____

_____

Now suppose you could see inside this person's head in that moment. If no censoring was going on, no playacting, and this person's thoughts were visible to you, what else would be said (this time just privately to himself or herself) that might not have been said publicly. Write it down, word for word:

_____

_____

_____

_____

_____

_____

_____

_____

_____

_____

_____

_____

_____

That eulogy was a description of what you fear, and perhaps a description of where your past path has been leading you. If you didn't like writing what you wrote, channel that pain into the next process.

Your eulogy doesn't not have to be like that. Imagine that from here forward you'll live your life connected to that which you most value. This doesn't mean that all of your goals will be magically attained; it means the direction you are taking in your life is evident, clear, and manifest.

Now imagine who's at your funeral. Certainly your spouse, children, and closest friends would be there. Perhaps people from work, class, or church (depending on which of these you are involved with) are in attendance as well. Anybody you like can come to this funeral. There are no limits. If you have old friends or have lost contact with people whom you would like to see there, don't worry about it. They can all make it to this imagined service. Think of all the important people in your life and place them in that space. Look at them. See their faces. Watch them watching your funeral.

Now imagine that someone (you can pick which one) gives a eulogy about *you* that reflects what all of these people might see if your life had been true to your innermost values. Imagine what you would most want to have manifest in your life. This is not a test. You won't be judged on this and no one else need ever know what you are thinking.

While you get a clear idea about this, take a few minutes and write out, word for word, what you would want to hear in your eulogy about how you lived your life. Be bold! This is not a prediction. This is not self-praise. Let these words reflect the meaning you would most like to create, the purposes you would most like to reveal about the time you spent on this planet. Picture your family member or friend preparing to speak about you. What might he or she say? Write it down, word for word:

_____

_____

_____

_____

_____

_____

_____

_____

_____

_____

_____

_____

_____

_____

What was doing this exercise like for you? Besides the strangeness of watching your own funeral, what else came up for you in this exercise?

Now, go back and read what you wrote. If you said anything that seems incomplete, or off the mark, you can rewrite it. Hey, it's your funeral.

If you really reached for it, you might see inside the words you wrote something of what is already inside you. Can you see some of that which you want to manifest in your life?

The way you would want to be remembered once your life is over should give you a very good idea about what you value now. We don't know what anyone would say at your funeral, but we do know that your actions today can make a profound difference in how your life works from here. It is not your thoughts, feelings, or bodily sensations that your loved ones will remember you by, but the choices you make and the actions you take each day of your life. Couldn't that begin today? Couldn't that begin now?

Let's see if we can use the method of looking back at your life to dig out what is most dear one more time. Let's try to distill all of this down to a shorter version.

When people are buried, an epitaph is often written. They say things like "Here lies Sue. She loved her family with all her heart." If the headstone below was yours, what inscription would you like to see on it? How would you most like your life to be characterized? Again, this is neither a description nor a prediction; it is a hope; an aspiration; a wish. It is between you and the person in the mirror. What would you like your life to stand for?

Think about it for a moment, and see if you can distill your innermost values into a short epitaph and write it out on the illustration of the tombstone below.

Here Lies

Figure 12.1: Your epitaph.

TAKING IT A STEP FURTHER: TEN VALUED DOMAINS

The short exercises you've just completed provide a broad beginning. Hopefully, they've stirred up something in you that will allow you to become bolder and clearer about what it is you really want to be about. You are alive, not dead. How to you want to *live*?

To give this question some structure, consider the following ten domains that might be of some importance to you:

1. Marriage/couple/intimate relationship

2. Parenting

3. Family relations (other than intimate relations and parenting)

4. Friendship/social relations

5. Career/employment

6. Education/training/personal growth and development

7. Recreation/leisure

8. Spirituality

9. Citizenship

10. Health/physical well-being

What follows is a brief description of each of these domains as well as space for you to describe your own values in that domain. Keep in mind, as you go through this, that values are not specific goals, but general life directions. We'll get to concrete goals later. If you find yourself writing down material things that can be obtained such as an object, stop and rethink what it is we are asking for; that is, directions that can always be made to manifest but that can never be fully obtained or finished.

Take what you've learned about values up to this point in this book and apply that to the following exercise. Remember the eulogy and the epitaph you just wrote, and see whether elements from them apply to one or more of these domains.

As you work through this exercise, you may discover that certain domains are very important to you and others are not. Some domains may be areas in which you are currently doing little. That's to be expected. It's not as though you need to value each of these different areas of life to the same degree. Different people have different values. A little later, we'll help you rate these values for yourself. For the moment, try to find a value that you hold in each domain. If there is an area for which you really can't think of anything, it's okay to skip it.

It may also be difficult to distinguish sharp boundary lines in certain areas. For example, some people have a hard time distinguishing between intimate relationships and family relations. Others may find it difficult to mark the difference between leisure and social relations. Read the description of each domain and try to keep the boundaries as clear as you can. If certain entries overlap, or you repeat a value in more than one domain, that's okay, but we encourage you not to overdo it.

This isn't a test. You need not show this to anyone if you don't want to. So be honest and open and give yourself the opportunity to explore what *you* value. Don't base this exercise on what you think your friends', family's, or society's expectations are. Write about what *you* value. There are no right or wrong answers.

Marriage/Couple/Intimate Relationship

For most people, intimate relationships are very important. This is the relationship you have with your "significant other": your spouse, lover, or partner. If you are not in such a relationship right now, you can still answer these questions in terms of what you aspire to find in such a relationship.

What kind of person would you most like to be in the context of an intimate relationship? It might help to think about specific actions you would like to take, and then use those to dig down to the underlying motives for such actions. What are those underlying motives? How do they reflect what you value in your relationship? Do not put down goals (like "getting married"); there will be an opportunity for those later.

_____

_____

_____

_____

Parenting

Think about what it means to you to be a mother or father. What would you like to be about in this role? If you don't have children, you can still answer this question. What do you want to be about in supporting this role in others?

_____

_____

_____

_____

Family Relations (Other Than Intimate Relations and Parenting)

This domain is about family, not about your husband or wife or children, but about other areas of family life. Think about what it means to be a son, daughter, aunt, uncle, cousin, grandparent, or in-law. What would you like to be about in your family relationships? You may think about this broadly or only in terms of your nuclear family. What values would you like to see manifest in your life in this area?

_____

_____

_____

_____

Friendship/Social Relations

Friendships are another area of personal relations that most people value. What kind of friend would you like to be? Think about your closest friends and see if you can connect with what you would like to have manifest in your life regarding your friends.

_____

_____

_____

_____

Career/Employment

Work and careers are important for most people because that area is where a great deal of your life is spent. Whether your work is humble or grand, the question of values in work pertains. What kind of an employee do you most want to be? What do you want to stand for in your work? What kind of a difference do you want to make through your job?

_____

_____

_____

_____

Education/Training/Personal Growth and Development

This area can cover all kinds of learning and personal development. School-based education is one. But this area includes all the things you do to learn, as well. Working through this book could be an example. What type of learner do you want to be? How would you like to engage with that area of your life?

_____

_____

_____

_____

Recreation/Leisure

Recreation, leisure, and relaxation are important to most of us. It is in those areas that we recharge our batteries; the activities in this area are often where we connect with family and friends. Think about what is meaningful to you about your hobbies, sports, avocations, play, vacations, and other forms of recreation. In these areas, what would you like to have manifest in your life?

_____

_____

_____

_____

Spirituality

By spirituality, we don't necessarily mean organized religion, although that could certainly be included in this section. Spirituality includes everything that helps you feel connected to something larger than yourself, to a sense of wonder and transcendence in life. It includes your faith, spiritual and religious practices, and your connection with others in this domain. What do you most want to be about in this area of your life?

_____

_____

_____

_____

Citizenship

How would you like to contribute to society and be a member of the community? What do you really want to be about in social/political/charitable and community areas?

_____

_____

_____

_____

Health/Physical Well-Being

We are physical beings, and taking care of our bodies and our health through diet, exercise, and sound health practices is another important domain. What do you want to have revealed in your life in these areas?

_____

_____

_____

_____

Sometimes, we find that clients get confused about what values are, even at this point in the program. People often make the mistake of stating that they value something when, in fact, that chosen value has been dictated by the desire of others.

To test your values, look over the exercises above and ask yourself the following question in regard to each of the values you wrote down: "If no one knew that I was working on this, would I still do it?" If you find that you've written down statements that don't "ring true," or are more a matter of "being a good boy or girl" than stating what is truly in your heart, go back and edit what you wrote. This list is not for anyone else. It is for you.

RANKING AND TESTING YOUR VALUES

In some ways, it's not very important that certain values are more meaningful to you than others. All of the things you wrote about in the exercises above are areas of your life that you would like to pursue in order to live more completely. However, it can be useful to put a rank marker on your values in order to see in which areas of your life you might begin to take action. Chapter 13 is about committed action. But before we get there, let's figure out what you might want to commit to.

Look back over the work you just finished. Now, distill each area down to one key value (if you have several, you can pick the most important one), and write a phrase to remind you of that key value in the space below. Now rate each area in two ways. First, ask yourself how important this particular area is to you right now on a scale of 1 to 10, with 1 meaning not at all important and 10 meaning extremely important. We aren't asking if this area is important in your actual behavior; we are asking what you would want if you could have your life be as you would want it to be.

Then, rate each area according to your actual current behavior. How well have you been currently living this value on a scale of 1 to 10? With 1 meaning it is not at all manifested in my behavior to 10 meaning it is extremely well-manifested in my behavior.

Finally, subtract the score you got for your actual current behavior from the importance score above that to arrive at the total of your "life deviation" score.

Table 12.1: Ranking Your Values		Importance	Manifestation	Life Deviation
Domain	**Value**			
Marriage/Couple/ Intimate Relationships				
Parenting				
Other Family Relations				
Friendship/ Social Relations				
Career/Employment				
Education/Training/ Personal Growth				
Recreation/Leisure				
Spirituality				
Citizenship				
Health/ Physical Well-Being				

The number on the far right is probably the most important. The higher that number, the more your life needs to change in this area to bring it in line with what you really care about. High numbers under the Life Deviation column are a sign and source of suffering. You may want to highlight or circle those numbers that show the largest gap between the importance of your values and their actual presence in your life.

COMMITTED ACTION

In chapter 13, you will take the information you gathered here, and we will help you to develop a specific means by which you can pursue the values you have uncovered in this chapter. The wonderful thing about values is that you can live them. Everything you have written about in this chapter is achievable. Note that we haven't discussed "getting over" your emotional pain as a value. It isn't. We have been discussing the kind of life you want to live. That life is available to you right now. What would your life be like if you truly got out of your mind and into your life?

CHAPTER 13

Committing to Doing It

You know what you want to be about. You probably knew before you even opened this book, although you may have kept it hidden from yourself to try to avoid your own vulnerability. When we care about something, we open ourselves to the possibility of feeling pain. If you really risk loving someone, you open yourself up to rejection, betrayal, and loss. If you really care about eliminating hunger, you open yourself up to a special pain when you see children having to go without.

"If I do not care, I will not be hurt" is how human minds keep values at arm's length. Unfortunately, this move hurts even more than caring; it's not the biting, alive, occasional hurt of caring and sometimes losing, but the dull, deadening, constant hurt of not living your life in a way that is true to yourself.

In the last chapters we put values on the table in some detail. The question you are now faced with is the same one we asked you earlier in the book: Given a distinction between you as a conscious being and the private experiences you've been struggling with, are you willing to experience those private experiences now, fully and without defense, as they are, not as they say they are, and actually do what takes you in the direction of your chosen values at this time and in this situation? This question requires a yes or no answer. Answering yes involves both a commitment to a course and actually changing your behavior. Some time from now, perhaps just moments from now, life will ask it again. Then again. And then again. And each time you will get to choose how you answer.

We'll ask it in a less precise form: Are you willing to accept whatever discomfort your mind provides you AND commit to the values you explored in chapters 11 and 12 and to the behavior change they imply?

Saying yes doesn't mean that your life will suddenly get easier, but it is guaranteed to become more alive. The alternative is something you already have experience with (and we've addressed it quite a bit throughout the book). You know what the costs are of sacrificing the life you want to live in behalf of your futile attempts to regulate your emotional pain. You know what it feels like to be confined and have the meaning and vitality drained out of your days by your struggle with your thoughts, feelings, behavioral predispositions, urges, memories, and bodily sensations that cause you discomfort. You know what it feels like to be trapped in your mind at the cost of your own vitality.

This chapter is all about doing it. It's about making bold, committed steps in the direction of your values. It's about doing this, not in spite of your pain (note that "spite" is a fighting word), but *with* your pain, if there is pain.

TAKING BOLD STEPS

It's time to take some bold steps in the direction you want your life to move in. In the last chapter you explored and developed some ideas about what you value. Each of those values is a compass point by which you can chart the course of your life. The next thing to do is start walking in that direction. This is basically a four-part process that repeats itself endlessly: Contacting your values, developing goals that will move you in a valued direction, taking specific actions that will allow you to achieve those goals, and contacting and working with internal barriers to action.

Creating the Road Map: Setting Goals

Go back to the final worksheet you did in chapter 12. In it, you listed some values and assigned importance, manifestation, and life-deviation scores. It's now time to decide which of those values you want to work toward enacting in your life right now. Ultimately, you'll work on all of them, but for now let's start with one. This will give you a model to follow for the other valued directions you want to take.

The values you choose to work on first can have a high life-deviation score, or if you sense that there are barriers there you are not yet ready to confront, you can choose something lower on your list. They are all important; they simply hold different levels of relative importance and you may pick any one to start with. If you want to live a fully engaged life you will pursue each of them in its course. For now, choose one area you would like to begin with. Write down your stated value on the line below:

_____

If your value is the compass point by which you want to guide your life's journey, your goals are the road map that can lead you there. Goals, as noted in earlier chapters, are different from values in that they are practical, obtainable events that move your life in the direction of your values. Goals are the guideposts by which you can mark your life's journey, and they are important for a number of reasons. Goals give you a practical means to make your values manifest. They also offer you a metric against which you can measure your progress on your valued path. You may know what you want to be about, but without goals, it's unlikely you'll be able to live these values in the real world.

There is a danger that attaches to goals that we need to emphasize before we begin: goals can be obtained. This presents a danger because our verbal faculties are very much outcome-oriented, and the whole point of values is that they are process-oriented.

Suppose you are out skiing, and when you got off the lift, you mention to the person who rode up the lift with you that you plan to ski down to the lodge where you're going to meet up with some friends for lunch. "No problem" this person replies, and suddenly he waves to a helicopter above, that upon his signal, swoops you up and speedily deposits you at the ski lodge. You protest vigorously, but the pilot is incredulous. He says, "What's your beef, my friend? It was you who said the objective was to get from the summit down to the lodge!"

The helicopter pilot would have a point if getting to the lodge were the only issue. If it is, flying down the slope achieves exactly what skiing down achieves. Both have you start at the top and end up at the lodge. The helicopter even has notable advantages: you don't get cold, or tired, or wet, for example. There is only one problem with this. The goal of getting to the lodge was meant to structure the process of skiing. That process was the true "goal."

That's what we meant when we said in chapter 11 that "outcome is the process through which process becomes the outcome." You have to value "down" over "up" or you can't do downhill skiing. Aiming at a specific goal (the lodge) allows you to "orienteer" one way to go down the hill. But the true goal is just to ski, not reaching the goal (the lodge).

In precisely the same way, the true goal of goals is to orient you toward your values so you can live a valued life, moment by moment. A successful ACT patient put it this way toward the end of therapy: "I just want to do this because that's what I want my life to be about. It's not really about any outcome. I want to be alive until I'm dead." Goals can help you do exactly that. But be careful! Your mind will often claim that the true goal is the goal itself (after all, evaluating outcomes is what this organ evolved to do), and it will suggest that you should cut corners (like violate your integrity, or ignore other valued aspects of your life) to get there. That defeats the whole purpose, and if you succumb to cutting corners, accomplishing your goals will only mock you.

Goal Setting

To start developing your goals you'll need to consider both short-term and long-term objectives. *Short-term goals* are the points on the map that are attainable in the near future; *long-term goals* are further down the road. Having both short-term and long-term goals makes for a paced journey that leads from one guidepost to the next. This is a very efficient way to travel. Theoretically, you could just wander around until you found your destination. But, as you know, that's not very effective. Goal-oriented travel is much more practical.

Look back at the value you wrote down above. Now think of one thing you could do that would allow you to make that value manifest in a practical way. In the last several chapters, there have been various discussions on values and goals. There also have been a number of examples that may offer you some guidance. Remember to think about this in terms of a practical outcome. Don't come up with something that is obviously outlandish.

If you're a fifty-year-old salesclerk who values public service, and you decide your goal is to become the president of the United States, that isn't likely to happen. Choose a goal that is a workable step in the direction of your values. If you are that fifty-year-old salesclerk who values public service, there are hundreds of ways you might approach making a public service contribution that is both practical and obtainable. For example, you could do volunteer work in your community, perhaps serve food at a soup kitchen. Or, you might want to campaign for someone running for local office.

This isn't said to discourage you from taking bold steps. Be bold. But be real. Don't be too easy on yourself, but be realistic and decide on something you can achieve.

Once you have your goal firmly in mind, write it down in the space below:

_____

_____

_____

Now check your goal for the following items:

- Is it practical?

- Is it obtainable?

- Does it work with your current situation?

- Does this goal lead you in the direction of your stated value?

If you answered yes to these questions, then you have successfully created a goal for yourself. If you couldn't answer yes to whatever you wrote down in the space above, go back over chapters 11 and 12 and try to get clearer on what a goal is. The next step is to figure out whether this is a long-term goal or a short-term goal and whether or not you will need to complete additional goals to get there.

Next, on the following time line, plot a point where this goal would fall for you. The far left of the time line is your life, starting today. The end of the time line is your death, some reasonable amount of time in the future. Where on this line does your goal fall?

_____

Life today   **End of life**

The relative distance between where you are today and when you think you could reasonably achieve this goal will tell you whether it is a long-term or short-term goal. If you've established that your goal looks like a long-term one, you'll need to develop some additional short-term goals to get there. If it's a short-term goal, you might ask where this goal is leading you and where you'd like to go after it's completed. Either way, you can return to the process described above until you are satisfied that you've produced a good set of long-term and short-term goals for the value you chose to work on. The following exercise will help you keep track of all this information.

EXERCISE: Goals Worksheet

Value: _____

This value will be manifested in the following long-term goal:

1. _____

   _____

   _____

Which, in turn, will be manifested in these short-term goals:

1. _____

   _____

   _____

2. _____

_____

_____

3. _____

_____

_____

This value will be manifested in the following long-term goal:

2. _____

_____

_____

Which, in turn, will be manifested in these short-term goals:

1. _____

_____

_____

2. _____

_____

_____

3. _____

_____

_____

Repeat this process until you have a good working set. (It need not be comprehensive; you can always add and subtract from these at any time.)

There are no hard and fast rules about how many goals you need to have. This is about your life. Think about what you would like to accomplish, and set your goals in terms of how they will fit practically into your life. The numeration in the worksheet above is arbitrary. Perhaps starting with one long-term goal makes sense for you. Or if not, a single short-term goal may be a good place to start. You need not have a particular number of goals to be "doing the right thing." If you're getting caught in thoughts of this nature, remember your mind is talking to you again. Use the strategies you've learned throughout this book and set your compass in the direction you want to live.

Setting goals is all about workability. If you don't make your goals workable within the context of your life, it's unlikely you'll get very far down the path of your values. Choose achievable, obtainable outcomes that can realistically fit with your life. Doing this makes it much more likely you'll actually be able to live your values every day. The true goal of this process is to become better able to focus on life as a valued process. Every goal is a step leading you further down the path of your life. The path itself doesn't end (at least not until your life ends). Being vital means there will always be some new way to pursue your values. Achieving your goals isn't an end, but a new beginning; a point of closure at which you can refresh your journey by starting anew. Guideposts are important, but don't be trapped by them. Celebrate goals achieved and keep on keeping on.

Walking the Walk: Actions as Steps Toward Achieving Your Goals

You can talk the talk all you want, but if you don't walk the walk, your life won't come alive for you. What we've been exploring in this book is important, but what are you going to *do* about it? If you know where you want to go and don't go there, then the knowledge makes little difference. ACT is all about action. To make a difference in your life, you need to act.

What actions are you going to take to achieve your goals? To move in the direction set by your value compass toward your first goal, what do you need to do?

Choose a short-term goal from the lists above and write it down in the space below:

_____

EXERCISE: Making Goals Happen Through Action

Because life is a process, things happen one step at a time. Once you know what you value and what your goals are, you can choose which steps to take first. You have the compass and the road map. Now you need to focus on your steps. Minds are great at this, so this part should initially be easy, at least until the possibility of action creates barriers to action (more on this in a moment).

In the following worksheet, state one of your shorter-term goals copied from above. After writing that down, define specific actions you need to take to achieve that goal. (We've left space for five, but it could be greater or fewer). Make sure you write down what you can actually *do*.

Don't be vague (e.g., "Do better"), and don't write down things you cannot directly control by action (e.g., "Feel better"). Write down a specific situated action: this is an act that has a beginning and an end, a specified form, and a specified context. For example, "Build friendships" is not a specific action. "Call friends" is better, but it is still too vague. "Call Sally" is fine. It has a beginning and end, a specified form, and a specified context. Try to include at least one thing you can do *today*.

For example, let's say, as part of a longer-term goal of letting friends know you care about them, you've decided to contact old friends. One specific action might be to call a specific old friend ("Sally") with whom you've lost contact. But this action may require others. The first thing you have to do is find out how to get in touch with her. To do this, you might call some other friends who know her, look her up on the Internet, find her number in the white pages, or contact members of her family to see where she is. Each of these options would be a specific action that would take you one step further toward your goal of getting in contact with your old friend. Try to get enough actions and subactions written down so that if you did them all, achieving your goal would become highly likely, or even certain.

Short-term goal: _____

Actions and subactions:

1. _____
   _____
   _____

2. _____
   _____
   _____

3. _____
   _____
   _____

4. _____
   _____
   _____

5. _____
   _____
   _____

What could you do right now (today) from this list? Focus on what is possible. If you are ready to do it, great. Do it. *Right now.*

Barriers

Unfortunately, it's often not so simple. (If it was, books like this would not be needed.) Unfortunately, barriers will come up. Some will come in the form of practical problems you'll face moving down your valued path. But more importantly for the work we are doing here, barriers are going to show up in the form of the experiences you've been trying to avoid, or in the form of the thoughts you've been fused with.

That's what the first parts of this book were all about. They were about being in a new place when this moment came.

Focus in on one of the specific actions you wrote down above that you could do today, and choose one that you have some psychological resistance toward doing. Write that behavior below:

_____

_____

_____

If you were to do this right now, what would you expect to encounter psychologically that would slow you down? Look for difficult thoughts, feelings, bodily sensations, memories, or urges. If you aren't sure yet, close your eyes and picture engaging in this behavior and watch for indications of the barriers. Don't allow avoidance to get in the way of this process! If you find your mind wandering, or you think, "Damn, I don't care about this anyway," or you suddenly get hungry or have to pee, be suspicious! Avoidance comes in myriad forms. Stay with this process and in the space below write down each barrier you can detect:

1. _____

_____

_____

2. _____

_____

_____

3. _____

_____

_____

4. _____

_____

_____

5. _____

_____

_____

Now that some potential barriers to action are out there, consider the strategies you have learned in this book up to this point. If you've developed "favorite" cognitive defusion, mindfulness, and acceptance strategies, you might consider using these. Flipping back through the book could help you remember what these are. If you have no idea at all, it's time to go back to the early parts of the book and go through them again.

In an ACT approach you do not "get over" barriers or "get around" barriers. You do not even "get through" barriers. You *get with* barriers. One successful ACT patient described it this way: "I used to run away from pain. Now I inhale it."

EXERCISE: Expected Barriers

In the following chart fill in a word or two to remind you of the barriers you expect to face along your valued path, as well as strategies you might use to mindfully defuse from and accept these barriers.

Barriers	ACT Strategies

You can practice "inhaling" your barriers in your imagination, but the very best way to work on this is in the context of action. Be careful! Your mind will tell you that the strategies you selected are supposed to *get rid* of barriers. That is very unlikely, and it is a very old agenda. The purpose of these strategies should be to defuse from and make room for the psychological issues that have been stopping you from acting in your own interests.

MANY MAPS FOR DIFFERENT JOURNEYS

So far, we've been exploring how you might walk down the path that a single value generates for you. But in chapter 12 we explored ten different valued domains. In each domain you may have written down more than one value. In addition, you may come up with values that don't necessarily fit the categories we've been exploring. If you valued a single thing, life would, perhaps, be simpler. But it wouldn't be as full and dynamic as it is when you value many different things. If your list of values is full, that means you have an exciting journey ahead of you.

Different journeys require different maps. Since we aren't moving toward a destination on a physical plane, we can take many different journeys at the same time. You can and should pursue different values in different domains at the same time. Life would be stripped of its richness if we weren't given this variability.

The work you've done in this chapter could be summarized on the following form:

Values Form			
Value:			
Goals	**Actions**	**Barriers**	**Strategies**

If you wish, you can summarize the information you've collected about your values and goals earlier in this chapter on this form. What's more, you can use this form in conjunction with the questions we pose throughout this chapter as a way to generate road maps for each of your valued paths.

You may want to photocopy it several times and go back to the values you worked out in chapter 12. Start with one of those values, write it down in the space at the top of the form, and do the whole process again. In this way, you'll formulate a concrete game plan for the next steps on your life path that will span the many different areas you care about.

Sometimes, you'll find that different valued paths combine quite well. In other instances, they will not. In those cases, you may have to make a choice about what your next turn is, or where you want your life to go. There are no pat answers. We can't tell you what those choices should be. The choice is always yours to make. We don't pretend to make life any easier than it is.

BUILDING PATTERNS OF EFFECTIVE ACTION

Many of the problems we suffer with are, in essence, self-control issues. Avoidance and fusion feed patterns that serve short-term interests at the expense of long-term interests. As you begin to move in a valued direction, however, you begin building larger and larger patterns of effective action.

In animal models, it has been shown that larger patterns of behavior are more resistant to short-term impulsive choices (Rachlin 1995). You can use this basic behavioral finding to serve your best interests. In this section we will explore ways of building much larger patterns, as well as the barriers that come along with doing that.

Taking Responsibility for the Larger Patterns You Are Building

There is no "time-out" from life; no dress rehearsal. This means that every single moment you are building a behavioral pattern. It helps to build larger patterns that serve your interests by acknowledging the patterns that are being constructed as they occur.

For example, suppose you want to be more mindful of your health. You plan to lose weight, eat better, and exercise more. You've decided that you'll go to the gym for one hour twice a week, you won't eat desserts for a month (just to get used to cutting out sugar, since you noticed that most of your sugar intake is in dessert form), and you will eat no more than 1800 calories a day.

Week one all goes well … you made a commitment and you stuck to it. Now comes week two and your commitment starts to fall apart. You ate a big slice of pie; you haven't exercised yet (it's already Thursday); and you forgot to keep track of your food for two days, so you can only make a "guesstimate" as to how many calories you've consumed.

Suppose you are upset. You have the feeling of being a failure (again). You find yourself thinking about giving up.

Inside the literal language the issue is content-filled: Can you do any better? Are you capable? Are you doomed?

At another level it is simply a behavioral pattern:

■   Make commitment—break commitment

In the past, this has probably been a pattern for you, which may be part of why the breakage happened. But other patterns are looming:

■   Make commitment—break commitment—quit commitment

Or perhaps:

- Make commitment—break commitment—quit commitment—feel bad about breaking commitment

Or maybe even:

- Make commitment—break commitment—quit commitment—feel bad about breaking commitment—fear making commitments—give up on making commitments

These behavioral patterns are yet to be fully formed. It is your behavior that will, or will not, form them. Nothing else. Rationalizing them is just another part of the pattern. So is rationalizing them and then feeling bad about rationalizing them.

Step back from your own mind, and watch the pattern forming. If it is forming now, you can form it in the way you would like it to be through your behavior. If you want it to be different, then it is different behavior that must occur. If "make commitment—break commitment" has been a pattern for you in the past, when you now find that yet again you've broken a commitment, you have a golden opportunity. You have the chance to create a different pattern: make commitment—break commitment—keep commitment.

If *that* pattern builds, you can squeeze down the space given to the middle term and get just a notch closer to "make commitment—keep commitment—make commitment—keep commitment." If there are a few "break commitments" in there, you can gradually weed them out. It is unlikely that you will ever get them all out, but it is empowering to reach toward that distant goal.

The process of building behavioral patterns involves noticing the pattern and taking responsibility for building larger and larger ones that align with your best interests. If you feel guilty when you see these patterns, building effective larger behavioral patterns means taking responsibility for the role that guilt is about to play in the pattern you are creating right now. If you doubt yourself, the same principle applies. If you are afraid of making any commitments for fear you will never keep them anyway, same thing. If you feel supremely confident, same thing. If you brag to others about how well you are doing, same thing. And, if all of this just seems too much, *same thing*.

You get what you *do*. Get it?

(And if you react to the seeming arrogance of that statement on our part, you have our apologies AND ... same thing!)

Breaking Up Inflexible Patterns That Don't Serve Your Interests

The biggest problem with avoidance and fusion and the conceptualized self (and so on) is that they get so rigid because they become such large patterns. Contexts of literality, reason-giving, and emotional control are ubiquitous because the language community (the language-driven world that we are surrounded by all the time) continuously supports them, even when they are not needed. Because the contexts are ubiquitous, the behaviors become so as well. Your word machine starts to take over every inch of your life.

That's why this book probably felt confusing initially: we were breaking down an habitual language pattern. We have been challenging the implicit rules of a language game that has most humans ensnared most of the time.

For new things to happen, we must break down the old things. ACT clients sometimes call this the "reverse compass." They learn that if a habit points north, it may be time to head south. That strange little item in your actual exposure exercise in chapter 10 (remember the exercise "Acceptance in Real Time" about deliberately doing more of what your mind said you could not do) was a reverse compass item.

When large, old, inflexible patterns break down, you have an opportunity to establish new patterns where they are needed. Some of these patterns can be consistent if it works for them to be so (for example, you may find that it works to keep your commitments); others can be deliberately established as more flexible patterns if being more flexible works.

Pattern Smashing

Let's give you an example of some pattern-smashing games that you might play. Suppose you notice that you always have a drink or two when you go to parties. You don't have a drinking problem, but you suspect that some of this social drinking might be part of your pattern of getting comfortable, so that you can relate to people more easily, and that, in turn, is a part of your pattern of "try not to have feelings that I don't like." That larger pattern has costs, and you see that; so, perhaps you could get a handle on breaking out of your larger pattern by attending to this small aspect of it that you just detected.

So, how about going to the next party without consuming any liquor? Just for fun. Just to see. It might be interesting to see what it's like not to have any alcohol to grease the wheels of socialization. And instead of withdrawing, how about looking a stranger in the eye and getting a real conversation going. Instead of holding back, how about saying something slightly personal? Inside all of these smaller changes, you may discover whether you've been using crutches, and what they cost you, if anything.

Suppose you notice the pull to "look good" and "be right" when you are with other people. Superficially, your efforts cost you nothing, but you suspect they are part of a larger pattern of trying not to feel small, which, in turn, is part of a larger pattern of trying not to be seen, for fear of seeming small, and that is part of a larger pattern of accepting the idea that you are, indeed, small. If you noticed that pull, you might try doing something that would create social discomfort intentionally, for no other reason than to feel what it is like to be uncomfortable socially.

For example, wear white socks with dark clothing, but don't talk about it. Skip putting on your make-up or apply it in a silly way. Tell a lame joke deliberately, but don't explain it. Deliberately misstate a fact you know, but don't admit you are doing it deliberately. Tell an embarrassing story about yourself to friends. Pay for something using only small change. Purchase something odd (like deodorant) and then return it.

Do you see the point? The goal is not to be silly or to be a fool. Once you've broken up the pattern, new behaviors will become possible. The goal is to confront your larger patterns when you detect they have built a box for you to live in that spreads into areas you care about.

For example, if you can return deodorant, you also might be slightly more likely to knock on a stranger's door and ask for a contribution to feed hungry children (if an action like that appeared on one of the "action" lists linked to your goals and values). Or you could call someone you barely know and ask for a date (if that showed up on one of the "action" lists linked to your goals and values).

One great way to break up unhelpful larger patterns is to do truly new things regularly. Paint a painting if you've never done so; learn to dance; sing a song in a karaoke bar; join a social group; take a cooking class; fix or build something yourself; write a poem; start a journal. This can be especially useful if these "things I just don't do" are part of a larger pattern of avoiding failure.

Superficially, it seems as though it wouldn't matter if you can't give a toast because, "I'll be embarrassed if it's bad." After all, how often would you have to give a toast anyway? But what larger pattern is being fed? If it is a larger pattern of playing small, you may be building yourself a straightjacket with these tiny choices. You may be feeding a conceptualized self ("I'm just not good at doing social things" or "I'm just too anxious") that is systematically narrowing your own ability to live. (See chapter 7 for a discussion about the conceptualized self.) If so, it's time to kill off that conceptualized self by breaking the pattern. This is the sense in which ACT advises "kill yourself every day."

We've identified some of the key larger patterns that language encourages: experiential avoidance, cognitive fusion, attachment to the conceptualized self, and so on. If you do *anything* different in the presence of events that normally lead to these patterns, you are helping to create more psychological flexibility. In the grandest scheme of things, that is the ultimate goal of ACT—the ability to fit your behavior creatively into the larger patterns you wish to create. Said another way, the ultimate goal of this book is psychological liberation. How much has your life been about what your mind suggests, rather than what you want it to be about?

You many wish to return to that exposure exercise in chapter 10. If you haven't finished working with all of the items, perhaps now is a good time to do so. If you have more lists to work on, perhaps now is the time to begin.

Because You Said So

As you take responsibility for building larger patterns that serve your interests, and as you break down patterns that do not, it's important to keep your eye on the linchpin in both: Can you do what you said you would do? Building the strength of that pattern is the most important pattern of all. It's a good idea always to be working on keeping small commitments for no reason at all other than you said so. Here is why.

You cannot build larger behavioral patterns in agreement with your values unless you can do what you say you will do. But if you limit doing what you say to this one area, a vulnerability opens up: What if your mind gets you confused about what is or is not a value? It seems safer to fill that gap. That way, if you make a commitment and begin to reconsider it because you now think it is not really important, you'll have the strength to maintain the pattern for long enough to complete the commitment.

The way to fill this gap is to choose to do things for no reason other than you said so. At one time in human history this was a common practice, and was considered a kind of moral training. It still exists in our spiritual and religious institutions, but at a much weaker level than it once was. Examples might include getting up and going to bed at an early hour just because; foregoing favorite foods for a period of time, just because; fasting, just because; wearing an uncomfortable shirt, just because; writing in a journal, just because.

Such commitments should be clear and time-limited. The need for clarity is obvious, but they should be time-limited because otherwise, knowing they will eventually end, your mind will suggest that the time to end them is now.

It is best that they do not seem important (that way they also provide practice in defusion from the need for importance). The importance comes when life demonstrates that keeping your commitments is useful. This is just a way to practice and build that pattern.

None of this will work, however, unless you maintain the pattern. It is sometimes surprisingly hard to do. This is in itself revealing. If the patterns are trivial, why are they so hard to change? Usually, it's because there is a strong past pattern of *not* keeping commitments, or keeping them only when you "have to," which is all the more reason to practice.

Defusing from What You Are Not Yet Ready to Address

You cannot address all of your unhelpful behavior patterns at once. But there is a huge difference between taking things one step at a time, and creating new forms of rigidity that will later become problems. Suppose, for example, you have an anxiety problem and you use tranquilizers occasionally to try to reduce your anxiety. This is not likely to be harmful as long as you are undermining experiential avoidance patterns and you stay open to considering the role of tranquilizers when you get to them.

What is dangerous is fusing with exceptions ("Whether Valium is a form of avoidance or not, I don't care. I have to have my Valium.") as if you get to decide which patterns are workable or not, regardless of their actually workability. What if you go forward so far, and then it becomes clear to you that Valium is, in fact, part of a larger avoidance pattern (we are not saying it must be … but what if?). Fusion such as this will now create a very difficult barrier indeed. It is far better to take a flexible "wait and see" posture with whatever you are not yet ready to address.

Fused statements like, "If I ever lost my mother I would just fall apart!" or "I can't face my abuse history. I can't!" are both unhelpful and dangerous. Moving in the direction you value doesn't mean getting to have it your way. One step at a time is helpful. Choosing your values is essential. "I get to pick what works and what doesn't work" is pure fantasy. If you are not yet willing in a given area, fine. Just watch for the cost and stay open and defused.

Share

There is nothing in life that is not made more real by sharing. Intimacy is a matter of sharing your values and your vulnerabilities. If you are building new patterns and breaking up old ones, share that process. If you see a form of avoidance and you are ready to let it go, tell others of what you see. It's like shining a light down a dark hole where you hide. It becomes much less appealing to hide there because at least one person will know the game you're playing. If you have a new commitment, share that too. It will make it real. Just don't expect the other person to make that new thing happen, and don't try to deflect your responsibility by sharing.

Staying Mindful of Your Values

The best way to build larger patterns is to be mindful of them. The worksheet on the next page can be very helpful in this regard. You can fit four months of data at once on it, allowing you to look at very large patterns of progress in each of the ten domains where you have done values work (our thanks to David Chantry for allowing us to use this form, which he developed).

VALUED LIVING

Use these charts to keep a record over the next few weeks of your ratings of how important each of these life areas are to you (these ratings may not change very much), and how consistent your actions have been with each of your values. Each week, mark your ratings by putting in the appropriate box a forward stroke (/) in, say, red ink for your importance ratings, and a backward stroke (\)in, say, black ink, for your consistency ratings.

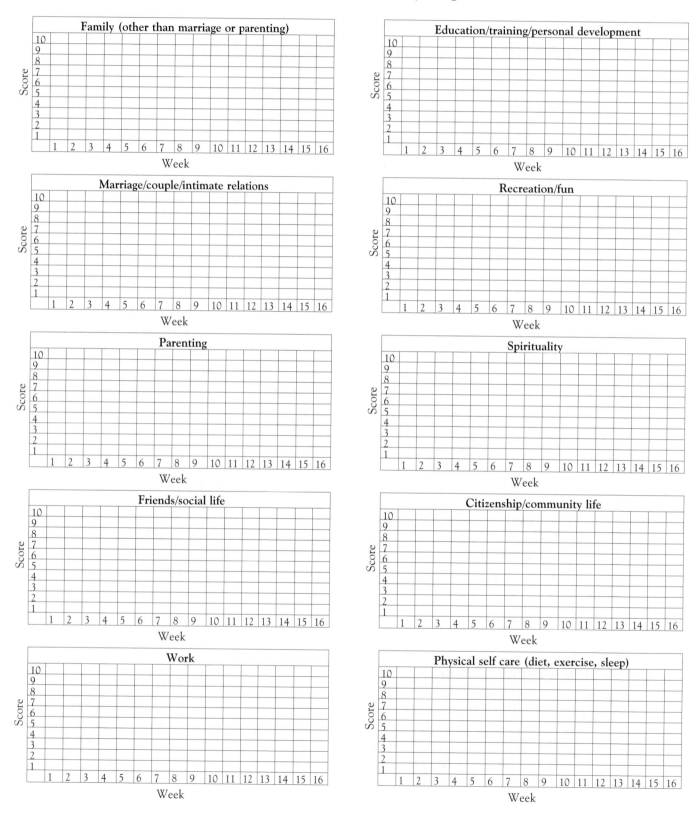

Guilt, Forgiveness, and Repair

Earlier in this book we discussed the fact that all people have an investment in keeping their "reasons" and their "stories" true, even when their bottom line is pain, or limitation. Now it's time to face another source of pain that is built into growth: that is, *guilt* over wasted time and opportunities.

Human beings don't come with owner's manuals. Most of us have to learn the hard way how normal psychological processes can become traps—by becoming trapped. ACT research demonstrates that the processes we've described in this book can be powerful sources of change. But real progress immediately confronts us with the fact that things that happened to us in our lives, which became part of very destructive patterns, did not, in hindsight, have to function that way.

Ouch.

The pull to fuse around a new form of defense is very powerful. In its most extreme form, that pull can destroy progress by using the secret function of maintaining the story "I couldn't do anything else." Usually this pattern is seen when the person realizes how much harm took place in the service of avoidance, fusion, or maintaining a conceptualized self. Marriages may have been broken needlessly. Children may have been driven away without real cause. Parents may have been blamed too harshly. Opportunities may have been spoiled forever. Sometimes it is not even possible to apologize: people have died or are no longer interested.

Ouch.

In such situations, this is precisely when the processes we've been describing are most needed. This is when you need all the kindness and compassion for yourself that you can muster. To accept these painful feelings, defuse from self-critical thoughts, and focus on what it is you really value, you must be kind to yourself. If you do that, even your pain becomes part of your new, more self-respectful, more values-consistent path. Respectfully decline your mind's invitation to beat yourself up for not knowing what was in the owner's manual you were never given. You do not need to defend that by fusing with new defensive rationalizations. You did the best you could at the time. You know more now.

Often growth processes require not just self-forgiveness of the kind we have just described, but forgiveness of others, too. Suppose, for example, early in your life, you were abused in some way and the feelings the abuse engendered became a destructive force in your life. As you learn and practice the skills of acceptance, defusion, mindfulness, and directing your life in terms of your values, you may begin to realize (1) that you've been trying to hold the abuser responsible by making sure your own life is a mess, and (2) that you have the skills to move ahead, even with your history of abuse, into a life you value.

This can be very painful. It may seem as though you are letting the abuser "off the hook" if your life prospers without that person first admitting his or her wrongdoing, or hurting the way you were hurt, or, at the very least, acknowledging your pain. In some sense this may even be true (for example, an abusive parent seeing your new progress might think, "See, I didn't really do anything so bad." Ouch).

But the "hook" went through you first … then your mind put the abuser on the hook. Letting go of keeping that person on the hook means you can now slide off too. It doesn't mean that now you think that what was done to you was right. It means moving on, and serving your own best interests.

The etymology of forgiveness is "giving what went before." Forgiveness is really a gift to yourself, not to the events or persons who created hurt in your life.

As this kind of process deepens, you will probably encounter the inverse situation. You may begin to see how avoidance and fusion led you to destructive acts toward others. You may have been self-righteous, or shown a lack of integrity. You may have been distant, or failed to be there for the people you loved. In your fear, your children may have received less than they deserved. In your addiction, your employer may have been shortchanged.

The flip side of forgiveness is responsibility. When you detect destructive patterns of behavior in yourself, taking responsibility means trying to clean up your past messes, and systematically making repairs where you can. If you skip this step and simply try to move toward what you value now, it will have a hollow ring.

WHOSE LIFE IS IT ANYWAY?

Life is hard. Life is also many other things. Ultimately your life is what you choose to make it. When the word machine dominates, life works one way. When the verbal evaluative side of you is but one source of input, life works differently. The choices themselves aren't always easy, but finding the freedom to choose is a liberating experience. It's your life. It is not the word machine's—even though (of course) it tells you otherwise.

CONCLUSION

The Choice to Live a Vital Life

When you confront a core problem within yourself, you are at a choice point much like the figure below illustrates. Off to the right lies your old path of avoidance and control. This is the path the negative passengers on the bus most want you to take. It is the logical, reasonable, sensible, verbal path. Your mind will chatter on about dangers, risk, and vulnerabilities and will present avoidance as a method of solution. You've been down this path, over and over and over again. It's not your fault; you've done what any rea-

sonable person would do. It just turns out not to be effective, vital, or empowering.

It's not your fault, but now that you know, it is your responsibility. Life can and will make you hurt. Some of that you don't get to choose: it comes regardless. An accident may confront you with physical pain; an illness may confront you with disability; a death may confront you with feelings of loss. But even then you have the ability to respond (the response-ability).

The consequences that come into your life derive from the actions you engage in, and most especially the actions we've been discussing throughout this book. No one but you can engage in acceptance or avoidance; fusion or defusion; living in your head or living in the present; taking yourself

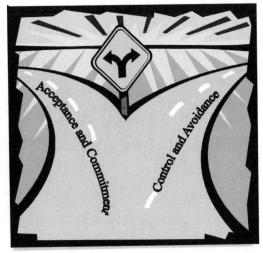

Conclusion. Figure 1: The crucial fork in the road.

to be nothing but your programming; or taking yourself to be your continuity of consciousness itself. Most of all, no one but you can choose your values.

There is a crucial fork in the road. You must choose which path to take. The less traveled path to the left is the path of acceptance, mindfulness, defusion, and valuing what you really care about. Down that road is vulnerability and risk, but it is about something.

These two roads lead to very different places. It's not that one leads to problems and one doesn't. It is not that one leads to pain and one doesn't. They both lead to problems. And they both lead to pain. To the right the problems are old and familiar; to the left they are new and even more challenging. To the right the pain is deadening and suffocating; to the left the pain is bittersweet and intensely human.

Imagine you are looking down at that fork in the road. From above you can see that this choice before you is part of a larger system of choices. Imagine that you start right in the center with your problems. You hit the fork in the road and if you go left, you go into the acceptance and commitment cycle. If you go right, you go into the control and avoidance cycle. Both of these cycles are illustrated below.

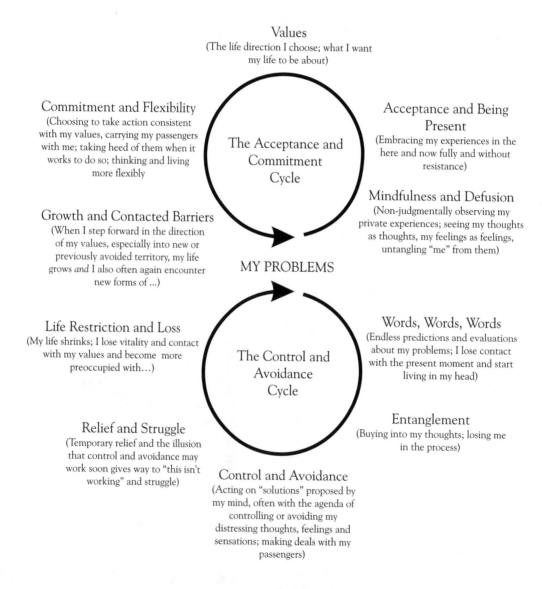

Conclusion. Figure 2: The Acceptance Cycle and the Avoidance Cycle.

In the control and avoidance cycle, life is all about what your mind tells you. You become entangled with verbal predictions and evaluations. You start trying to do what your mind says to do, even if you've tried these things before and found they didn't work. Your "life bus" is turned over to your mental passengers, and they drive right off into control and avoidance. For a little while it even feels better. At least it is predictable. You feel relieved.

You've been down this road before and at least you've always survived before. But, sooner or later, you are right back where you started, except now you are weakened. Life is a little bit smaller. More time has gone by, and somehow it's as if your life hasn't started. You not only have problems to deal with, they are the same familiar, deadening problems.

How long will this cycle go on? Think of the problems you have been struggling with. When did they start? What if the next five years are like the last five years were in this regard? The next ten years?

In the acceptance and commitment cycle, the sequence is different. You notice the chatter all right, but you don't become entangled in it. You see that there is a distinction between you, the conscious driver of the bus, and the passengers you carry. You have room on the bus for them. You accept them. You defuse from them. But then you turn your eyes back to the road and connect with that which you really value. You drive in that direction. As a result, your life grows a little, and it becomes a little more vital and flexible.

As you grow, however, you are likely to contact problems again. Often these are not quite the same old problems, they are subtly different. They are new, and perhaps even more challenging. For example, if you move in the direction of loving relationships, you now have problems of vulnerability whereas previously you may have had problems of alienation. If you move in the direction of making a contribution, you now face problems of fear of inadequacy or inability, whereas previously you faced problems of fear that you did not belong or were invalid. Sometimes, these new problems present themselves as even more fearsome than your old ones. Especially if they feel new or more intense, your mind often will scream out in fear that you've made a terrible mistake, and you are moving backwards.

And there you are. Back at the fork in the road. The whole choice gets to be repeated.

If you consistently choose to go left, life will not become any easier. It will only become

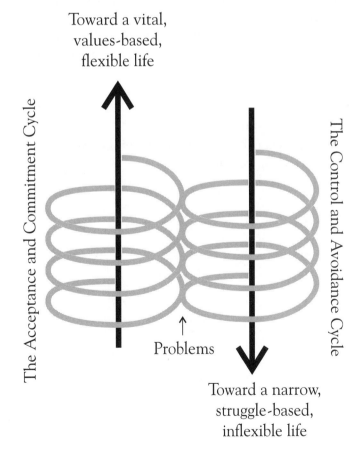

Toward a vital, values-based, flexible life

The Acceptance and Commitment Cycle

The Control and Avoidance Cycle

Problems

Toward a narrow, struggle-based, inflexible life

Conclusion. Figure 3: The spirals of vitality and inflexibility in life.

more vital. Progress is being made. It is like figure 3. As you keep taking that bus of life off into the acceptance and commitment cycle, you move up in a new direction. What looked like a circle in figure 2 is, in fact, a spiral. You still have problems, even big ones. They occur regularly. But progress is being created. You are living a more vital, flexible, and values-based life. When the other path is taken, you are also in a spiral, but very likely it is one that is spiraling down in a narrower, more struggle-based and less flexible life.

Note that the presence of problems, and perhaps even their frequency or their intensity, could be the same or even greater if you take the acceptance and commitment cycle. What is different is that on the left-hand spiral you get out of your mind and into your life. You hurt, AND you are living. On the right-hand spiral you sink into the mental war of human suffering.

You've often taken the right-hand path. Haven't you had enough? By now its results are extremely predictable. Predictability makes this choice curiously "safe" but doesn't remove its deadening qualities. Acceptance and commitment offers a path with unknown ends. Its newness makes it a more frightening path but it also makes it a more vital one. To illustrate this point, we rather like the following quote:

> Until one is committed, there is hesitancy, the chance to draw back, always ineffectiveness. Concerning all acts of initiative there is one elementary truth the ignorance of which kills countless ideas and endless plans: That the moment one definitely commits oneself then providence moves, too. All sorts of things occur to help one that would never have otherwise occurred. A whole stream of events issues from the decision, raising in one's favor all manner of unforeseen incidents and meetings and material assistance which no man could have dreamed would come his way. Whatever you can do or dream you can, begin it! Boldness has genius, power, and magic in it. (Murray, partially quoting Johann Wolfgang von Goethe, 1951.)

Life is a choice. The choice here is not about whether or not to have pain. It is whether or not to live a valued, meaningful life.

You've had enough suffering. Get out of your mind and into your life.

(We are rooting for you).

APPENDIX

The Values and Data Underlying ACT

ACT comes from behavior therapy, a branch of empirical clinical psychology. As such, the developers of ACT maintain firm commitments to (1) scientific evaluation of well-specified techniques, and (2) the development of basic principles and theory adequate to guide the development of these techniques and to explain their success. Even though this is a book meant for the general public, we wanted to include this short appendix to show how ACT developers maintain these commitments, and to guide readers and professionals to needed resources.

THEORY AND BASIC PRINCIPLES

In several places, we've mentioned that ACT is based on a comprehensive basic research program on the nature of human verbal and cognitive processes called Relational Frame Theory (RFT; Hayes, Barnes-Holmes, and Roche 2001). We've done what we can to make some of this work accessible. It is technical, extensive, and it is hard to explain in a book meant for a general audience. The research studies on RFT will soon pass one hundred papers, and the methods and concepts are often complex and frankly arcane. Furthermore, because the work is part of behavior analysis, its naturalistic and contextualistic philosophical basis is foreign to the general lay culture.

We've dealt with this problem in this book by expressing many of these findings in relatively lay language that is quite different from the language used to develop this knowledge. For example, we've frequently spoken of the "mind" or "mental processes," rather than "your repertoire of arbitrarily applicable derived relational responding" because using technically correct naturalistic terms would have no meaning and would make the book virtually impossible to read. In a scientific context we would speak differently, but because we believe that "meaning is use" we've used words that seem more likely to make a difference, even if they aren't technically correct within the scientific tradition that created and sustained ACT.

Underneath every sentence a more technical account is possible, or at least so we believe, and we stand ready to make the translation if our scientific colleagues wish. Many publications are available of that kind as well (e.g., see Hayes, Barnes-Holmes, and Roche 2001). The downside of our approach (beyond the fact that some of our behavioral colleagues will be startled) is that this book may sound at times as though its basic scientific foundations are not strong, or that it is based on a common sense understanding of how language and cognition works. We believe that those with a scientific bent who are willing to explore the area will find that is not the case. A list of RFT studies is available on the RFT Web site (www.relationalframetheory.com).

The clinical theory (the theory of psychopathology and change processes) that is based on RFT and that underlies ACT is similarly scientifically grounded. ACT researchers have studied the impact of experiential avoidance and cognitive fusion extensively. The other aspects of the theory (development of different senses of self; the importance of contact with the present moment, values, and psychological flexibility; mindfulness; and so forth) have received research attention, as well. So far, the data are supportive of the theory, and mediational analysis (that is, analyses designed to determine whether the clinical outcomes of ACT are produced by the processes the theory says are key to success) are also supportive (Hayes, et al., forthcoming). The research program is still young, so we will have to await the data before drawing firm conclusions, but in its broad outlines it now seems clear that this analysis of human problems has scientific support. A list of relevant research studies is available on the ACT Web site (www.acceptanceandcommitmenttherapy.com).

OUTCOMES

None of this would matter if it were not linked to actual positive clinical outcomes. In the few years since the ACT book (Hayes, Strosahl, and Wilson 1999) first appeared, outcome research in ACT has exploded. A review of the outcome research on ACT written just a short while ago is already completely out of date (Hayes, Masuda, et al. 2004; See Hayes, Luoma, et al. forthcoming for a more recent interview).

Clinical research scientists study the impact of technologies like ACT in a variety of ways, but some of the most important studies are randomized controlled trials and controlled time-series analyses. Right now, the number of completed studies of that kind on ACT are approaching two dozen, most of which are now in the published literature.

So far, all of the studies support the positive impact of ACT, and in all cases of which we are aware, all of the studies that were designed to look at processes of change have provided some support for the theory underlying ACT. A few of these studies have compared ACT to other well-developed and empirically supported methods.

In almost all of the published comparisons so far, ACT has done as well as or (in some cases) better than existing methods known to be effective. So far there are supportive controlled outcome studies in the areas of anxiety, stress, obsessive-compulsive and OCD spectrum disorders, depression, smoking, substance abuse, stress, stigma and prejudice, chronic pain, willingness to learn new procedures, ability to learn new procedures, coping with psychosis, diabetes management, coping with cancer, coping with epi-lepsy, and employee burnout. If you want to see more about the current state of the evidence, you can visit the ACT Web site.

The fact that these data are themselves so broad is one reason we've cast this book very broadly. If the theory underlying ACT is correct, the processes we are targeting are shared among human beings because they are based on core language processes. That is the empirical justification for not targeting specific syndromes in this volume. We felt these issues are relevant to people in general, not just to people struggling with one or another specific problem.

THIS BOOK

For a scientist committed to empirical evaluation, it is important to show that materials can be helpful out-side the context of a therapeutic relationship, so, generally speaking, we know that a book like this is likely to be helpful. Several of the specific components in this book have been tested, sometimes in a form very similar to the way you are contacting this material. For example, several studies evaluated the impact of short passages drawn nearly word for word from ACT materials (very similar to what you've read) that were recorded on audiotape, read aloud by a research assistant, or were presented to the participants to read.

Typically, these studies focused on the ability of participants to tolerate distress of various kinds, such as gas-induced panic-like symptoms, extreme cold, extreme heat, or electric shock. A few studies looked at the distress produced by difficult or intrusive cognitions, or clinically relevant anxiety. Some were done with patients, others with normal populations.

The specific ACT components that have been examined so far include defusion, acceptance, mind-fulness, and values. The techniques included exercises, metaphors, and rationales, including several that can be found in this book (e.g., word repetition, physicalizing, leaves on a stream, the quicksand metaphor, the Chinese finger trap metaphor, and so forth). Thus, it seems fair to say that it is known that at least some of what you've read can be helpful at least some of the time outside of the context of a therapeutic relationship, when presented in a form similar to the form in which you have contacted this material.

Examples of these kinds of studies can be found in Eifert and Heffner 2003; Gutiérrez et al. 2004; Hayes, Strosahl, and Wilson 1999; Levitt et al. 2004; Marcks, and Woods, forthcoming; Masuda et al. 2004; Takahashi et al. 2002 (see the list on the ACT Web site for other examples). Partial validation does not mean that this book *en toto* is validated in this form. The only way to make such a statement is to examine the applied impact of this exact book in this exact form. Such an analysis is underway, but even then, it will be impossible to validate this book for every specific problem to which it might be applied. Thus, as we noted in the introduction, readers need to examine their own experience to see if it is helpful for them.

ACT THERAPY

We are aware that some who read this book will want to seek out an ACT therapist, and indeed this book was designed in such a way that it could be used either as a stand-alone text or as part of a professional psychological intervention. Although several thousand therapists have at least some training in ACT, no comprehensive list of ACT therapists exists, and the ACT community has decided not to certify ACT therapists for fear of ossification and centralization. A short voluntary list of ACT therapists is available on the ACT Web site, but if that doesn't work we suggest the following.

In the United States, a list of behavior therapists and cognitive-behavior therapists is available at the Web site for the Association for Behavioral and Cognitive Therapies. An Internet search will lead you to it (it has recently changed its name, so the Web site address is changing as this is being written). In most major countries around the globe, similar societies maintain similar lists. These are empirically oriented therapists, which is good if you believe, as we do, that people should receive evidence-based care.

Because ACT is becoming increasingly well-known within that community, these are also people who might know something about it. Find a therapist in your area or (perhaps even better) a therapist who is also affiliated with a local university. Call that person and ask about a competent local person experienced in ACT or other "third wave" behavioral or cognitive behavioral interventions. If one exists, this method is the most likely way to find such a person. If they do not know of one, at least you will be talking to a scientifically oriented person who may be able to give you sensible advice about how to find other local treatment resources for your problem.

TRAINING IN ACT

We are also aware that some professionals will contact ACT through this book and will want training in these methods. There is controlled evidence that training in ACT seems to make clinicians generally more effective (Strosahl et al. 1998), so quite apart from self-interest, we can recommend it. Trainings take place regularly at major behavior therapy associations such as the Association for Behavioral and Cognitive Therapies, as well as through freestanding workshops. The ACT/RFT community is committed to the open development of this theory and technology, and we are committed to doing so in a way that is primarily focused on benefit to others.

On the ACT Web site, there is a growing list of trainers available to help you or your agency in addition to a growing set of other training resources. Listservs for behavioral health professionals are available in both ACT and RFT. Links are on the Web sites. ACT and RFT are growing, developing behavior analytic approaches, but they are not for the faint of heart. ACT is challenging, intellectually and personally. If you don't have a behavioral background, you will find it especially challenging, both because it will not fit preconceptions, and because the underlying theory and technology take time to master. If you are a professional wanting to learn, however, you will find an open door into a supportive, nonhierarchical, values-based, and scientifically focused community committed to the alleviation of human suffering through the development of a more adequate scientific psychology.

USING THIS BOOK AS AN ADJUNCT TO A PROFESSIONAL PSYCHOLOGICAL INTERVENTION

The chapters in this book were organized in such a way as to fit the normal phases of ACT. ACT can be done in different sequences, and despite the sequential nature of this book as a book, we've tried to write it so that you can assign chapters in different sequences without fear that your patients will be unable to follow the material. For example, if you do values work first, the three values chapters can be read immediately without much confusion. Just tell your clients to pass over the few parts they will not understand.

References

Barks, C. 1997. *The Illuminated Rumi*. New York: Broadway.

Barnes-Holmes, Y., D. Barnes-Holmes, and P. Smeets. 2004. Establishing relational responding in accordance with opposite as generalized operant behavior in young children. *International Journal of Psychology and Psychological Therapy* 4:531-558.

Barnes-Holmes, Y., S. C. Hayes, and S. Dymond. 2001. Self and self-directed rules. In *Relational Frame Theory: A Post-Skinnerian Account of Human Language and Cognition*, ed. S. C. Hayes, D. Barnes-Holmes, and B. Roche, 119-139. New York: Plenum Press.

Begotka, A. M., D. W. Woods, and C. T. Wetterneck. 2004. The relationship between experiential avoidance and the severity of trichotillomania in a nonreferred sample. *Journal of Behavior Therapy and Experimental Psychiatry* 35:17-24.

Bond, F. W., and D. Bunce. 2003. The role of acceptance and job control in mental health, job satisfaction, and work performance. *Journal of Applied Psychology* 88:1057-1067.

Brown, R. A., C. W. Lejuiz, C. W. Kahler, D. R. Strong, and M. J. Zvolensky. Forthcoming. Distress tolerance and early smoking lapse. *Clinical Psychology Review*.

Chiles, J. A., and K. D. Strosahl. 2004. *Clinical Manual for Assessment and Treatment of Suicidal Patients*. Washington, DC: American Psychiatric Association.

Cioffi, D., and J. Holloway. 1993. Delayed costs of suppressed pain. *Journal of Personality and Social Psychology* 64:274-282.

Dahl, J., K. G. Wilson, C. Luciano, and S. C. Hayes. 2005. *Acceptance and Commitment Therapy and Chronic Pain*. Reno, NV: Context Press.

Dahl, J., K. G. Wilson, and A. Nilsson. 2004. Acceptance and Commitment Therapy and the treatment of persons at risk for long-term disability resulting from stress and pain symptoms: A preliminary randomized trial. *Behavior Therapy* 35:785-802.

Deikman, A. J. 1982. *The Observing Self: Mysticism and Psychotherapy*. Boston: Beacon Press.

Donaldson, E. J., and F. W. Bond. 2004. Psychological acceptance and emotional intelligence in relation to workplace well-being. *British Journal of Guidance and Counselling* 34:187-203.

Dugdale, N., and C. F. Lowe. 2000. Testing for symmetry in the conditional discriminations of language trained chimpanzees. *Journal of the Experimental Analysis of Behavior* 73:5-22.

Eifert, G. H., and M. Heffner. 2003. The effects of acceptance versus control contexts on avoidance of panic-related symptoms. *Journal of Behavior Therapy and Experimental Psychiatry* 34:293-312.

Feldner, M. T., M. J. Zvolensky, G. H. Eifert, and A. P. Spira. 2003. Emotional avoidance: An experimental test of individual differences and response suppression during biological challenge. *Behaviour Research and Therapy* 41:403-411.

Gifford, E. V., B. S. Kohlenberg, S. C. Hayes, D. O. Antonuccio, M. M. Piasecki, M. L. Rasmussen-Hall, et al. 2004. Acceptance theory-based treatment for smoking cessation: An initial trial of Acceptance and Commitment Therapy. *Behavior Therapy* 35:689-705.

Gregg, J. 2004. Development of an acceptance-based treatment for the self-management of diabetes. Ph.D. diss., University of Nevada, Reno.

Gutiérrez, O., C. Luciano, M. Rodríguez, and B. C. Fink. 2004. Comparison between an acceptance-based and a cognitive-control-based protocol for coping with pain. *Behavior Therapy* 35:767-784.

Hayes, S. C. 1987. A contextual approach to therapeutic change. In *Psychotherapists in Clinical Practice: Cognitive and Behavioral Perspectives*, ed. N. Jacobson, 327-387. New York: Guilford Press.

Hayes, S. C. 2004. Acceptance and Commitment Therapy, Relational Frame Theory, and the third wave of behavior therapy. *Behavior Therapy* 35:639-665.

Hayes, S. C., and D. Barnes-Holmes. 2004. Relational operants: Processes and implications. A response to Palmer's review of "Relational Frame Theory." *Journal of the Experimental Analysis of Behavior* 82:213-224.

Hayes, S. C., D. Barnes-Holmes, and B. Roche, eds. 2001. *Relational Frame Theory: A Post-Skinnerian Account of Human Language and Cognition*. New York: Plenum Press.

Hayes, S. C., R. Bissett, Z. Korn, R. D. Zettle, I. Rosenfarb, L. Cooper, et al. 1999. The impact of acceptance versus control rationales on pain tolerance. *The Psychological Record* 49:33-47.

Hayes, S. C., V. M. Follette, and M. Linehan, eds. 2004. *Mindfulness and Acceptance: Expanding the Cognitive Behavioral Tradition*. New York: Guilford Press.

Hayes, S. C., J. Luoma, F. Bond, A. Masuda, and J. Lillis. Forthcoming. Acceptance and Commitment Therapy: Model, processes, and outcomes. *Behaviour Research and Therapy*.

Hayes, S. C., A. Masuda, R. Bissett, J. Luoma, and L. F. Guerrero. 2004. DBT, FAP, and ACT: How empirically oriented are the new behavior therapy technologies? *Behavior Therapy* 35:35-54.

Hayes, S. C., K. D. Strosahl, and K. G. Wilson. 1999. *Acceptance and Commitment Therapy: An Experiential Approach to Behavior Change*. New York: Guilford Press.

Hayes, S. C., K. D. Strosahl, K. G. Wilson, R. T. Bissett, J. Pistorello, and D. Toarmino. 2004. Measuring experiential avoidance: A preliminary test of a working model. *The Psychological Record* 54:553-578.

Hayes, S. C., K. G. Wilson, E. V. Gifford, V. M. Follette, and K. Strosahl. 1996. Emotional avoidance and behavioral disorders: A functional dimensional approach to diagnosis and treatment. *Journal of Consulting and Clinical Psychology* 64:1152-1168.

Karekla, M., J. P. Forsyth, and M. M. Kelly. 2004. Emotional avoidance and panicogenic responding to a biological challenge procedure. *Behavior Therapy* 35:725-746.

Kessler, R. C., K. A. McGonagle, S. Zhao, C. B. Nelson, et al. 1994. Lifetime and 12-month prevalence of DSM-III-R psychiatric disorders in the United States: Results from the National Comorbidity Study. *Archives of General Psychiatry* 51:8-19.

Kirsch, I., T. J. Moore, A. Scoboria, and S. S. Nicholls. 2002. The emperor's new drugs: An analysis of antidepressant medication data submitted to the U.S. Food and Drug Administration. *Prevention & Treatment* 5 (July 15), http://journals.apa.org/prevention/volume5/pre0050023a.html.

Krause, J. 1992. Spinal cord injury and its rehabilitation. *Current Opinion in Neurology and Neurosurgery* 5:669-672.

Kreider, R. M., and J. M. Fields. 2001. Number, timing, and duration of marriages and divorces: 1996. *Current Population Reports*. Washington, DC.: U.S. Census Bureau.

Langer, E. 1989. *Mindfulness*. Reading, MA: Addison-Wesley.

Levitt, J. T., T. A. Brown, S. M. Orsillo, and D. H. Barlow. 2004. The effects of acceptance versus suppression of emotion on subjective and psychophysiological response to carbon dioxide challenge in patients with panic disorder. *Behavior Therapy* 35:747-766.

Lipkens, G., S. C. Hayes, and L. J. Hayes. 1993. Longitudinal study of derived stimulus relations in an infant. *Journal of Experimental Child Psychology* 56:201-239.

Litman, G. K., J. Stapleton, A. N. Oppenheim, M. Peleg, and P. Jackson. 1984. The relationship between coping behaviors, their effectiveness and alcoholism relapse and survival. *British Journal of Addiction* 79:283-291.

Marcks, B. A., and D. W. Woods. 2005. A comparison of thought suppression to an acceptance-based technique in the management of personal intrusive thoughts: A controlled evaluation. *Behaviour Research and Therapy* 43:433-445.

Marx, B. P., and D. M. Sloan. Forthcoming (a). Peritraumatic dissociation and experiential avoidance as predictors of posttraumatic stress symptomatology. *Behaviour Research and Therapy*.

Marx, B. P., and D. M. Sloan. Forthcoming (b). The role of emotion in the psychological functioning of adult survivors of childhood sexual abuse. *Behavior Therapy*.

Masuda, A., S. C. Hayes, C. F. Sackett, and M. P. Twohig. 2004. Cognitive defusion and self-relevant negative thoughts: Examining the impact of a ninety year old technique. *Behaviour Research and Therapy* 42:477-485.

McCracken, L. M., K. E. Vowles, and C. Eccleston. 2004. Acceptance of chronic pain: Component analysis and a revised assessment method. *Pain* 107:159-166.

Melamed, S., Z. Grosswasser, and M. Stern. 1992. Acceptance of disability, work, involvement and subjective rehabilitation status of traumatic brain-injured (TBI) patients. *Brain Injury* 6:233-243.

Mennin, D. S., R. G. Heimberg, C. L. Turk, and D. M. Fresco. 2002. Applying an emotion regulation framework to integrative approaches to generalized anxiety disorder. *Clinical Psychology: Science and Practice* 9:85-90.

Murray, W. H. 1951. *The Scottish Himalaya Expedition*. London: J. M. Dent & Sons.

New York Times. 1993. June 17, p.1.

Previti, D., and P. R. Amato. 2004. Is infidelity a cause or a consequence of poor marital quality? *Journal of Social and Personal Relationships* 21:217-230.

Purdon, C., and D. A. Clark. 1993. Obsessive intrusive thoughts in nonclinical subjects. Part I. Content and relation with depressive, anxious and obsessional symptoms. *Behaviour Research and Therapy* 31:712-720.

Riegal, B. 1993. Contributors to cardiac invalidism after acute myocardial infarction. *Coronary Artery Diseases* 4:215-220.

Roemer, L., K. Salters, S. Raffa, and S. M. Orsillo. 2005. Fear and avoidance of internal experiences in GAD: Preliminary tests of a conceptual model. *Cognitive Therapy and Research* 29:71-88.

Schwartz, M. S., and N. M. Schwartz. 1995. Problems with relaxation and biofeedback: Assisted relaxation and guidelines for management. In *Biofeedback: A Practitioner's Guide*. 2nd ed. Edited by M. S. Schwartz. New York: Guilford Press.

Shoal, G. D., and P. R. Giancola. 2001. Cognition, negative affectivity and substance use in adolescent boys with and without a family history of a substance use disorder. *Journal of Studies on Alcohol* 62:675-686.

Sloan, D. M. 2004. Emotion regulation in action: Emotional reactivity in experiential avoidance. *Behaviour Research and Therapy* 42:1257-1270.

Streater, S. 2003. Drug found in area fish stirs concern. *Fort Worth Star-Telegram*, October 17.

Strosahl, K. 1994. Entering the new frontier of managed mental health care: Gold mines and land mines. *Cognitive and Behavioral Practice* 1:5-23.

Strosahl, K. D., S. C. Hayes, J. Bergan, and P. Romano. 1998. Does field-based training in behavior therapy improve clinical effectiveness? Evidence from the Acceptance and Commitment Therapy training project. *Behavior Therapy* 29:35-64.

Takahashi, M., T. Muto, M. Tada, and M. Sugiyama. 2002. Acceptance rationale and increasing pain tolerance: Acceptance-based and FEAR-based practice. *Japanese Journal of Behavior Therapy* 28:35-46.

Teasdale, J. D., R. G. Moore, H. Hayhurst, M. Pope, S. Williams, and Z. V. Segal. 2002. Metacognitive awareness and prevention of relapse in depression: Empirical evidence. *Journal of Consulting and Clinical Psychology* 70:275-287.

Wegner, D. M. 1994. Ironic processes of mental control. *Psychological Review* 101:34-52.

Wegner, D. M., M. Ansfield, and D. Pilloff. 1998. The putt and the pendulum: Ironic effects of the mental control of action. *Psychological Science* 9:196-199.

Wenzlaff, R. M., and D. M. Wegner. 2000. Thought suppression. *Annual Review of Psychology* 51:59-91.

Steven C. Hayes, Ph.D., is University of Nevada Foundation Professor of Psychology at the University of Nevada, Reno. He is author of more than 350 scientific articles and twenty-seven books, including *Acceptance and Commitment Therapy* and *Relational Frame Theory*—two books that significantly develop the concepts on which *Get Out of Your Mind and Into Your Life* is based. His research explores the nature of human language and cognition and their application to the understanding and alleviation of human suffering. In 1992, the Institute for Scientific Information reported Hayes among the highest-impact psychologists in the world during the years 1986–90 based on the citation impact of his writings. He is past-president of the Association for Advancement of Behavior Therapy, the American Association of Applied and Preventive Psychology, and Division Twenty-Five of the American Psychological Association. He was the first Secretary-Treasurer of the American Psychological Society. He is the recipient of the Don F. Hake Award for Exemplary Contributions to Basic Behavioral Research and Its Applications from Division 25 of the American Psychological Association. In 1999, US Health and Human Services Secretary Donna Shalala appointed him to a four-year term on the National Advisory Council on Drug Abuse.

Spencer Smith is a writer and editor based in Santa Rosa, CA. He is coauthor of *The Memory Doctor*.

Some Other
New Harbinger Titles

Freeing the Angry Mind, Item 4380 $14.95

Living Beyond Your Pain, Item 4097 $19.95

Transforming Anxiety, Item 4445 $12.95

Integrative Treatment for Borderline Personality Disorder, Item 4461 $24.95

Depressed and Anxious, Item 3635 $19.95

Is He Depressed or What?, Item 4240 $15.95

Cognitive Therapy for Obsessive-Compulsive Disorder, Item 4291 $39.95

Child and Adolescent Psychopharmacology Made Simple, Item 4356 $14.95

ACT* on Life Not on Anger, Item 4402 $14.95

Overcoming Medical Phobias, Item 3872 $14.95

Acceptance & Commitment Therapy for Anxiety Disorders, Item 4275 $58.95

The OCD Workbook, Item 4224 $19.95

Neural Path Therapy, Item 4267 $14.95

Overcoming Obsessive Thoughts, Item 3813 $14.95

The Interpersonal Solution to Depression, Item 4186 $19.95

Get Out of Your Mind & Into Your Life, Item 4259 $19.95

Dialectical Behavior Therapy in Private Practice, Item 4208 $54.95

The Anxiety & Phobia Workbook, 4th edition, Item 4135 $19.95

Loving Someone with OCD, Item 3295 $15.95

Overcoming Animal & Insect Phobias, Item 3880 $12.95

Overcoming Compulsive Washing, Item 4054 $14.95

Angry All the Time, Item 3929 $13.95

Handbook of Clinical Psychopharmacology for Therapists, 4th edition, Item 3996 $55.95

Writing For Emotional Balance, Item 3821 $14.95

Surviving Your Borderline Parent, Item 3287 $14.95

When Anger Hurts, 2nd edition, Item 3449 $16.95

Calming Your Anxious Mind, Item 3384 $12.95

Ending the Depression Cycle, Item 3333 $17.95

Your Surviving Spirit, Item 3570 $18.95

Coping with Anxiety, Item 3201 $10.95

The Agoraphobia Workbook, Item 3236 $19.95

Loving the Self-Absorbed, Item 3546 $14.95

Transforming Anger, Item 352X $12.95

Don't Let Your Emotions Run Your Life, Item 3090 $18.95

Call **toll free, 1-800-748-6273,** or log on to our online bookstore at **www.newharbinger.com** to order. Have your Visa or Mastercard number ready. Or send a check for the titles you want to New Harbinger Publications, Inc., 5674 Shattuck Ave., Oakland, CA 94609. Include $4.50 for the first book and 75¢ for each additional book, to cover shipping and handling. (California residents please include appropriate sales tax.) Allow two to five weeks for delivery.

Prices subject to change without notice.